Human Landscapes

SUNY series in American Philosophy and Cultural Thought
———
Randall E. Auxier and John R. Shook, editors

Human Landscapes

Contributions to a Pragmatist Anthropology

Roberta Dreon

Published by State University of New York Press, Albany

© 2022 State University of New York

All rights reserved

Printed in the United States of America

No part of this book may be used or reproduced in any manner whatsoever without written permission. No part of this book may be stored in a retrieval system or transmitted in any form or by any means including electronic, electrostatic, magnetic tape, mechanical, photocopying, recording, or otherwise without the prior permission in writing of the publisher.

For information, contact State University of New York Press, Albany, NY
www.sunypress.edu

Library of Congress Cataloging-in-Publication Data

Name: Dreon, Roberta, author.
Title: Human landscapes : contributions to a pragmatist anthropology / Roberta Dreon.
Description: Albany : State University of New York Press, [2022] | Series: SUNY series in American philosophy and cultural thought | Includes bibliographical references and index.
Identifiers: LCCN 2021038622 | ISBN 9781438488219 (hardcover : alk. paper) | ISBN 9781438488233 (ebook) | ISBN 9781438488226 (pbk. : alk. paper)
Subjects: LCSH: Psychology. | Philosophy. | Pragmatism.
Classification: LCC BF121 .D69 2022 | DDC 150—dc23/eng/20211106
LC record available at https://lccn.loc.gov/2021038622

10 9 8 7 6 5 4 3 2 1

*Dedico questo libro alla memoria di Mario Ruggenini:
la sua "ermeneutica della finitezza"
ne è stata la prima ispirazione*

Contents

ACKNOWLEDGMENTS ix

CHAPTER 1
Introduction: A Pragmatist Approach to Human Nature 1

CHAPTER 2
Looking at Human Sensibility through a Pragmatist Lens 31

CHAPTER 3
Pragmatist Contributions to a Theory of Emotions 71

CHAPTER 4
Humans Are Bundles of Habits 93

CHAPTER 5
Human Experience as Enlanguaged Experience 143

CHAPTER 6
Exploring the Continuity between Sensibility and Language 175

CONCLUSION
A Pragmatic/Pragmatist Balance 213

NOTES 219

REFERENCES 237

INDEX 257

Acknowledgments

Most of this volume was written during a sabbatical in 2019, and then completed in 2020. However, the plan for this book dates back to at least three years earlier, when I realized that some of the main issues attracting my interest as a researcher—sensibility and the emotions, habits, and the peculiar intertwining of language and experience within the human world—tended to converge toward a philosophical anthropology whose main background was represented by Classical Pragmatism, mainly Dewey. At a certain point, I found the theoretical background I was searching for in his idea of cultural naturalism, which allowed me to lend structure to my tendency to privilege topics that blur the boundaries between natural and cultural features. To put it in Jamesian terms, that was the theory which worked best, in my opinion, as a means to mediate between previous truths and new experiences. Furthermore, in this endorsement of a naturalistic, yet nonreductive, philosophical anthropology one could even perceive something akin to Joe Margolis's feeling of dissatisfaction with the strict division of labor among allegedly autonomous philosophical disciplines—particularly aesthetics, philosophy of mind, philosophy of language, and culture.

In writing the book, I benefited from the help, support, and contributions of many people—I am aware that I risk forgetting some, so I apologize in advance. First of all, I am grateful to Rosa Calcaterra, who warmly welcomed me into the community of Pragmatism scholars after the publication of my book on Dewey's aesthetics; her constant endorsement has been decisive for my researches in this field. I express my gratitude to Kenneth Stikkers, who generously introduced me to the "real American experience" of the Department of Philosophy and the Morris Library at Southern Illinois University during my sabbatical and supported my project in many ways. I am indebted to Giovanna

Colombetti, Pierre Steiner, Laura Candiotto, and Carlos Vara Sanchez for their accurate reading of a previous draft of the book in the summer of 2020: their valuable remarks on specific points of the text have been fundamental for improving my arguments, as well as the structure and the style of the book—although they are certainly not responsible for any of its shortcomings. These scholars pushed me to broaden my interests beyond Pragmatism and to develop a fruitful engagement with current views of the mind as embodied, embedded, and enacted. A special thanks goes to Ellen Dissanayake, who kindly read a provisional draft of the introduction, and to Joe Margolis, who did the same—I regret that he is no longer here to receive my gratitude. I thank Shaun Gallagher for his friendly support of the publication of the volume, as well as for his sincere openness in discussing the connections between Pragmatism and enactivism during his Venetian Lectures in 2019. Both Giancarlo Marchetti and Sarin Marchetti gave me helpful advice on finding a publisher, although independently. I express my gratitude to John Shook and Randall Auxier for supporting the inclusion of my volume in their book series at SUNY—as well as for giving me the chance to present a provisional part of the book at the American Institute for Philosophical and Cultural Thought in the lovely Victorian premises of the Institute in Murphysboro, Illinois. Thanks to Michael Rinella and Jenn Bennett-Genthner for their precise and prompt responses to my doubts regarding technicalities in editing the book and also to the anonymous reviewers for their vivid endorsements.

Throughout the various phases of the book's preparation I received suggestions and stimuli from many conferences, seminars, and groups of people. Luigi Perissinotto and, more recently, the Venice-based Claves Center have provided crucial scholarly and personal support to me and my work, extending far beyond the writing of the present book. The whole board of the *European Journal of Pragmatism and American Philosophy* as well as Associazione Pragma constituted important avenues for dialogue and engagement with Pragmatism and current philosophical debates. Of the several occasions when I presented certain material that later was to become part of the book, I wish to mention the conferences organized by Rosa Calcaterra in Rome, John Ryder and Emil Visnovsky in Prague, Laura Candiotto in Edinburgh, Pierre Steiner in Paris, Fausto Caruana and Italo Testa in Parma, Alessandra Fussi and Alberto Siani in Pisa, Sami Philström and Henrik Rydenfelt in Helsinki, Piergiorgio Donatelli in Rome, and Flavio Artese and Mark-Oliver Casper in Kassel.

Finally, I am sincerely grateful to Sergio Knipe, who patiently and repeatedly revised my manuscript to improve my English with uncommon readiness and care. Many thanks even to Giuseppe Ferrentino, who supported me in compiling the index and correcting the drafts of the volume.

A number of sections in the book include paragraphs and excerpts from some previously published papers of mine, although all of them have been more or less heavily reworked and reframed within a different context. I thank the journals and the publishers for permission to include this material.

In the Introductiofn, section 2 includes some excerpts from "On Joseph Margolis' Philosophy: An Introduction," in J. Margolis: *Three Paradoxes of Personhood: The Venetian Lectures*, vol. 21, edited by me, Milano-Udine, Italy: Mimesis International, 2017, 9–30.

Chapter 2, section 2 is partly based on my 2019 essay, "Framing Cognition: Dewey's Potential Contributions to Some Enactivist Issues," *Synthese*, Special Issue on Radical Views on Cognition: 1–22. Part of this same paper has also been reworked in chapter 4, section 4.

I published a previous version chapter 2, sections 4 and 5, in my 2021 essay, "More than Action and Perception: A Pragmatist View on Sensibility," *Reti, saperi, linguaggi*, 1 (19): 45–72.

Chapter 3, sections 2, 3, and 4 derive from a new adaptation of the two following papers: "Emozioni pragmatiste," in *Nuovi usi di vecchi concetti: Il metodo pragmatista oggi*, edited by Maura Striano, Stefano Oliverio, and Matteo Santarelli, 151–64, Milano-Udine: Mimesis, 2015; and "A Pragmatist View of Emotions: Tracing Its Significance for the Current Debate," in *The Value of Emotions for Knowledge*, edited by Laura Candiotto, 73–99, London: Palgrave Macmillan, 2019.

Chapter 4, section 2 is based on my 2010 essay, "John Dewey: l'abito fa il naturalismo culturale," *Bollettino filosofico*, XXVI, 169–82, and on my 2016 essay, "Understanding Rules as Habits: Developing a Pragmatist Anthropological Approach," *Paradigmi*, XXXIV, 103–17.

In chapter 5, sections 3 and 4, Italian readers may detect some arguments deriving from my 2007 book, *Il sentire e la parola. Linguaggio e sensibilità tra filosofie ed estetiche del novecento*, Milan: Mimesis. More direct connections are with my 2014 essay, "Dewey on Language: Elements for a Non-Dualistic Approach," *European Journal of Pragmatism and American Philosophy*, VI (2), 109–24. I had already published a similar version of chapter 6, section 3, in my 2020 essay, "James on the Stream of Language: with Some Remarks on His Influence on Wittgenstein," *Cognitio*, 21 (1), 68–82. Finally, I have drawn extensive parts of chapter 6, sections 4, 5, and 6, from my 2019 essay, "Gesti emotivi e gesti verbali: L'eredità di George Herbert Mead sulla genesi del linguaggio umano," *Sistemi intelligenti*, 1, 115–33.

As should be clear from the epitaph, I wish to dedicate this labor of mine to the memory of Mario Ruggenini, as a public acknowledgment that he has proven a decisive figure for me, although probably in a way he could not have foreseen—and who knows whether he would have approved it?

Chapter 1

Introduction

A Pragmatist Approach to Human Nature

1. Looking for a Pragmatist Anthropology: Issues and Methods at Stake

Pragmatism is philosophy with the people in.[1] I would sum up this philosophical posture through the words used by Tim Ingold to distinguish anthropology from ethnography and ethnology, regarded as merely descriptive and strictly comparative enterprises (2008). Hence, Pragmatism is (one of) the best candidate(s) to develop a philosophical anthropology, although only a few scholars have attempted to take some steps along this path and none of the Classical Pragmatists fashioned an organic anthropological theory out of their rich yet scattered insights.

My aim in this book is to contribute to the development of a philosophical picture of human nature as a form of life that is contingent, yet also relatively stable and marked by some basic common features that are still open to change and reshaping because of their constitutive dependence on a natural and naturally sociocultural environment. In other words, I will develop a philosophical anthropology within a cultural naturalistic framework, by relying on a series of contributions mainly taken from John Dewey, but also from George Herbert Mead and William James.[2] Methodologically, I will recover the most significant contributions from their legacy in order to develop an organic—yet not exhaustive—view of humans as naturally cultural organisms embedded in an environment they contribute to changing from the inside. By making deliberate use of these sources to create a new philosophical anthropology, I will bring the Pragmatists' arguments into relation to one another within a more coherent framework, radicalize them when needed, and compare them with other interesting positions in the current debate on the specificity of human sensibility, habitual behavior and the intertwining of experience and language. From the point of view of content, my main interest is to investigate some relatively stable features of human organic-cultural behaviors on which both rationality and normativity are based—a qualitative background that is dynamically reshaped by appropriating the results of more reflective practices. Of course, personhood (Margolis 2017), as well as autonomy and responsibility, is a crucial factor to define the characteristically human way of being and deserves to be considered an essential step for developing a "pragmatistic anthropology" (Quante 2018). Nonetheless, the distinctive contribution of the present book lies in the fact that it looks at human practices primarily as hinging on a shared human sensibility, as scaffolded by habits of conduct, thought, feeling, and belief, and as shaped through the thick and mongrel (in Margolis's sense) fabric of enlanguaged human experience. Certainly, human practices also involve giving and asking for reasons (Brandom 1994), but I am interested in inquiring into the background from which explicit reasons and established norms emerge and to which they return—describing a mixed, nonfoundational dynamic. Both James and Dewey—but probably even Peirce—were interested in bringing into focus the qualitative background of life in which both logic and norms are rooted (Dewey 2004; Dewey 1985a), because "Existentially speaking, a human individual is distinctive opacity of bias and preference conjoined with plasticity and permeability of needs and likings" (Dewey 1981, 186).

Consequently, I will focus on three main issues, with no pretense to exhaustiveness. The first issue—to be worked out in chapters 2 and 3—is a conception of sensibility broader than sensory perception that I propose we ground in organic life exposure to the environment and define as the affective capacity to discriminate between living conditions as favorable or adverse, in contrast to the standard ascription of feeling and qualitative experience to a merely subjective realm. In the chapter 2, my central aim will be to consider how this capacity to perceive the environment as dangerous or welcoming, which is already widespread within animal life as reconfigured by the highly social environment peculiar to humans, as well as by the cultural-linguistic characterization of the human niche. In the chapter 3, I will integrate this topic through a pragmatist approach to the emotions, by setting them within the broader framework of human sensibility, rather than considering them as specific entities (mental representations? psychic states? neuro-programs?). By bringing together and radicalizing James's, Dewey's, and Mead's contributions to the topic through a comprehensive outline, I will be able to suggest an account of emotions as modes of behavior, including affective, evaluative, and practical aspects, because of their contextualization within human beings' structural exposure to a natural and naturally social environment.

The second issue will be habits, assumed to be pervasive and structural features of human behavior characterizing human acting, thinking, and feeling. I will argue that habits are already pervasive in human life at a prepersonal level: individuals acquire most of their habits from an already habitualized social environment, by being entrained and attuning their acts, feelings, and thoughts to already existent ways of doing things and interacting with one another. In chapter 4, I claim that habits are a relatively flexible channeling of both organic and environmental resources, deriving from the strong social interdependence of human beings that is rooted in their natural fragility from birth. Through a comparison with Bourdieu's account of habitus, I will suggest a view of habits as contingent features of human conduct that are plural and exposed to change, rather than a hidden matrix of behavior.

In chapters 5 and 6, I will develop a conception of human experience as enlanguaged—a conception that goes beyond the artificial opposition between experience and language, and assumes that language is irreversibly part of each human's experience, but also that human experience is always embedded in linguistic contexts and practices, although this circumstance has come about contingently, because of the natural circumstances of human development. Consequently, I propose that we approach language not only from the perspective of each individual's utterances but also as a characteristic of the human environment, configured by the broadly linguistic practices of our ancestors and continuously reshaped by our own. Hence, language is pictured not as a separate domain but as an integral part of the human form of life. In light of this, I consider language to be a complex of various sorts of utterances, embedded in—and scaffolding—different practices: not just making reference to absent things and working virtually, but also establishing and maintaining social bonds, both with intimates and strangers; making things in common; and influencing other people's conduct.[3] I will also emphasize that language is fully embodied in gestures, sounds, prosody, and rhythm—all of them aspects of the material structure of language. In the last chapter, I will further focus on the various facets of my thesis of a strong continuity between sensibility and language. Within a naturalistic framework, and by contrast to quasi-transcendentalist approaches, I will suggest that we regard linguistic utterances as deriving from previously existing organic and environmental resources. I will also consider the profound reorganization of animal sensibility, action, and cognition caused by the advent of linguistic practices, as well as the deep intertwining of both qualitative-holistic and analytic features in linguistic habits and practices.

Certainly, such a proposal is limited and could be integrated by further research in other fields—from the point of view of contents, the issue of humans as tool makers and of the disrupting and reshaping effect of media and artifacts on human lives would be important; from the point of view of the sources, a pragmatist anthropology could be significantly enriched by reconsidering Peirce's semiotic investigations with a more specific focus on human nature and behaviors.

The method I follow in this volume is an updated version of the mixed method—partly theoretical and partly historical—I have derived from my "continental" philosophical education in Venice, where I have learned to make use of conceptual and argumentative resources inherited from the past in order to engage with current problems. This means considering historical reconstruction not as an end in itself but as a strategy to engage with the topics at stake, by exposing those resources to any criticism and integration provided by more recent theoretical debates. This sort of engagement can involve the adoption of a different vocabulary as well as a different set of references that could help consider old issues through alternative points of view. Such an approach might sound strange in most of the current English-speaking philosophical world, with its usual sharp division between, on the one hand, theoreticians engaging with philosophical problems that are dealt with independently of the discussions they have engendered in the past and, on the other hand, historians of philosophy reconstructing past ideas and philosophies with textual and historical accuracy, but with no pretense to solve any issue at stake or formulate it in an alternative way.

My preference for the mixed method also reflects a conscious choice to reject methodological individualism as the default approach in philosophy: I share the Pragmatists' assumption that a social group, an institution, a mother tongue, or a cultural tradition is already there when we are born, and that our self-identity gradually emerges out of the shared form of life we are embedded in from birth—namely, out of "the human family," in James's words (1975, 92). The old Cartesian assumption that one should start thinking exclusively by oneself and must do so in order to give up false prejudices seems artificial in light of the socially and culturally shared constraints of our individual experience (Ruggenini 2006). By contrast, I think that a person's own contribution and originality consists in the ways he or she filters, criticizes, integrates, reorganizes, or even distances him- or herself from the cultural heritage he or she comes from when exposed to different existential conditions and different sets of categories, including discourses. We cannot ignore the consequences—in terms of the way we do philosophy—of the assumption that knowledge has a social character, which is to say: the view that a new particular thought becomes true insofar as it corresponds to the complex web of previous beliefs, already stocked opinions, and rules of action each person has inherited from the previous generations (James 1975, 34 and ff.). This approach to the philosophical task can sometimes make it difficult to distinguish between an individual contribution and the inherited culture from which it takes shape, disappointing both philologists and analytical philosophers. However, I think it is worthwhile to run this risk, because discrimination is possible. In this specific case, I will draw most of my arguments from the Classical Pragmatists, as readers who are familiar with this field of research will easily see. However, the peculiar focus on sensibility and the proposal to identify the latter with the already meaningful perception of living conditions as favorable or harmful are mine alone, and cannot be found in any of the authors whose writings I make use of. I will also stress Dewey's investigations on habits in order to offer a provisional, working definition of habits as the relatively flexible channeling of resources coming from both the environment and the organism, against the background of a conception of behavior as the integral output of organic-environmental interactions. I will develop a theory of habit acquisition from the social, prepersonal level to the individual one, beyond the Pragmatists' explicit arguments. Finally, I will use arguments and ideas derived from Dewey, Mead, Frank Lorimer, and even James to support the thesis that language has become an integral part of the human niche. I will focus, in particular, on the disrupting feedback effects it has had—and still has—on humans' ways of interacting with their world, far beyond their explicit and sometimes ambivalent statements.

Of course, the point of departure for any specifically individual contribution is not bound to be other philosophies, as in my case: it might be biology, physics, or even a picture of the complex variety of everyday life, as is the case for phenomenologists as well as anthropologists dealing with the interpretation of ethnographic material. I tend to adopt a pluralistic attitude with reference to the body of knowledge one decides or happens to start from, but I think that there is no a priori best term of comparison—as, for example, physical reductionists believe.

In this regard, a philosophical anthropology should still look like an armchair enterprise to most current people involved in ethnographic work. However, my point is that not even armchair philosophers are closed within their own minds and shut off from the rest of the world. Rather, for the most part they engage with a restricted yet significant portion of the shared world, namely, the cultural heritage of concepts and arguments derived from a specific past and tradition. Certainly, that part of the world philosophers engage with is limited and different from everyday life in the traditional or contemporary societies studied by anthropologists, but I see no reason to disregard the portion represented by intellectual history and assume it did not contribute to the shaping of human forms of life.

Through the Pragmatists, I contend, we can identify some features in human behaviors that seem to be shared and relatively stable, given the natural history of humanity up to the present. These common features, as will become evident, clear the field and set the ground for the great variety and variability of human behaviors, rather than for a narrowing down of human conducts to some main possibilities, assumed to be instantiable in different ways. Philosophical anthropology has usually been identified with the German intellectual tradition developed by Arnold Gehlen and Helmuth Plessner, and generally based on a phenomenological background (Max Scheler and also Martin Heidegger), with further insights provided by theoretical biology (Jacob von Uexküll and Adolf Portmann). While sharing some important elements of this intellectual tradition (Fischer 2009), my proposal of a philosophical anthropology developed from pragmatist arguments and insights adopts a more coherent cultural naturalistic stance, with no emphasis on an allegedly radical break in organism-environment relations between man and other animals. World precariousness and stability are not seen as an exclusively human experience, as was the case in existentialism and in German philosophical anthropology, but rather as a basic fact of life in general. By contrast, I wish to emphasize the ways in which new organic and environmental conditions—including sociocultural aspects—have exercised feedback actions and contributed to reorganizing already existing animal interactions by reshaping previous forms of animal sensibility, habitual behavior, and modes of gestural communication.

An important part of the method adopted here is the constant exposition of the Pragmatists' arguments to different approaches and vocabularies from other naturalistic, but nonreductive, fields. The book makes broad references to the work of contemporary scholarship on the mind's radically embodied, embedded, enacted, and extended condition (Gallagher, Di Paolo, Colombetti, Nöe, and Hutto, among others), as well as to works on other topics that are crucial for both progressive trends in current cognitivism and for pragmatist anthropology. My contention is that a treatment of subjects such as perception and emotions, habits versus representations, and linguistic bodies could be provided more coherently by shifting the field of research from the philosophy of mind and cognition to an anthropological view of the above features as something characterizing the specific form of human life within a naturally sociocultural environment. Seen from a pragmatist perspective, cognition appears to be rooted in the phenomenon of living and limited to specific phases of experience, which leaves us enough room to draw distinctions between human forms of intelligence and other organic modes of intelligence. Likewise, the mind is approached as an emergent quality of specific human forms of interaction with the environment, but it is not assumed to be the only decisive feature shaping human behavior.

Furthermore, a pragmatist approach to human nature and its contingent history can represent a significant contribution to paleoanthropological research on human phylogenesis. In what follows, I will make some important references to the claims supported by Tattersall and Tomasello. A pragmatist anthropology shares their hypothesis of language as an *exaptive* phenomenon having disruptive effects on human development, as well as the idea of a mutual interdependence of the cultural and biological aspects of the environment and the assumption that human sociability is qualitatively different from other animal modes of being social. I will argue that pragmatist anthropology could provide a significant theoretical input for investigations of this kind, pushing them, on the one hand, to definitely abandon the residual computational framework (partly) characterizing their idea of language and, on the other hand, to definitely emancipate themselves from a mentalistic conception of intersubjectivity.

Pierre Bourdieu is also regarded as an important point of reference in the third chapter, where similarities as well as divergences with respect to Dewey's theory of habits prove crucial for highlighting the peculiarity of a pragmatist approach to the topic.

Furthermore, I will be making some references to developmental psychology, and particularly to Trevarthen's work on very early forms of multimodal communication between new and old members of the human species. This perspective is significant because of its consequences for the issue of human ontogenesis, but also because it carries on the Classical Pragmatists' early interest in this field of inquiry.

2. The State of the Art

As I hinted above, only a few scholars have sought to outline a philosophical anthropology through a pragmatist lens. Arguably, the most remarkable attempt has been made by Joseph Margolis, whose philosophical anthropology seems to be the ultimate outcome of his previous investigations into the philosophy of the arts, the avenue for a form of naturalism without reduction, and an opportunity for radical historicity (2016). In Margolis's first *Venetian Lecture* (2017),[4] it becomes clear that the central issue he is addressing is the problem of the human "gap" in animal continuity: this is the basic paradox characterizing human beings and Margolis's challenge is to interpret the distinctiveness of humans—including intentional, cultural, and self-reflective features—without resorting to extra-naturalistic causes or sources, as well as by avoiding any form of eliminativism or reduction of the personal and the cultural to physical entities. By acknowledging the complexity of the animal world—both in its social aspects and in its nondiscursive forms of intelligence—Margolis considers sociality to be an extremely important feature of being human, but believes that it is not enough to understand the emergence of human persons. Adopting such an approach would mean overlooking the highly refined forms of societal life characterizing many animal species—where nonetheless we cannot appreciate the level of self-reflectivity that is distinctive of human beings. On the contrary, the acquisition of a natural language remains a distinctively human characteristic: although it is grounded in the completely natural favorable changes in the human vocal apparatus and brain, it contributes to producing the processual construction of selves out of human animals. Margolis does not hesitate to speak of a metaphysical transformation of human primates into selves or persons, exactly as he did when supporting the idea that works of art emerge as new kinds of entities from other sorts of things or properties—whose reality cannot be denied by viewing physical entities as the sole or paradigmatic kind of real entity. However, he avoids all Kantian sirens and does not consider language to be a transcendental condition of possibility for humanity. Joseph Margolis conceives the genesis of language among human primates as a wholly natural and fortuitous process, which nonetheless produces actual changes in the previous configuration of the natural world. In speaking of persons as "natural artifacts," Margolis is not assuming a direct and one-sided causal link between language acquisition by early hominids and/or by human infants and their becoming self-reflective persons with narrative identities. On the contrary, the two changes are understood as the two sides of the same process. In other words, humans produce natural languages that, while founded on the peculiarities of human physiology, develop as a means to configure meanings that overtly exceed the mere physiological action of noises or sounds. The hybrid character of natural language, in turn, contributes to shaping humans as self-reflective beings, whose ways of operating within the environment are always naturally charged with meaning in the widest sense of the term. In other words, he sees the genesis and natural history of languages and of humans as a circular one: the contingent emergence of natural languages introduces something new in the world of early hominids, something which reacts on them by transforming them into human persons. However, we have no privileged external vantage point from which to examine it, we can only see it from within the loop we are part of.

For sure, Margolis's anthropological conception is convergent with Dewey's and Mead's proposals, but his strong emphasis on human distinctiveness is indebted to Marjorie Grene's philosophy and her original appropriation of some radical instances of Plessner and Gehlen's Philosophical Anthropology (Peterson 2010). Although brilliant when it comes to highlighting the role of language in shaping humans, Margolis's discourse tends to leave in the shadows other important features, such as the complex structure of human sensibility and pervasively habitual human behaviors. In this book, I deepen and integrate Margolis's insights, by exploring the conception of animal and human sensibility, its relationships with language, the role of habits in shaping human conduct, and the refusal to assume an opposition between experience and nature within the human world.

Twenty years ago, Sami Pihlström published a book on *Pragmatism and Philosophical Anthropology* (1998) that was more focused on providing reasons for developing a pragmatist anthropology, rather than in actually working it out. The two main reasons considered are both good: on the one hand, it becomes clear that a Jamesian ethics involves a lucid investigation into the structures of humanity and human behavior. The core issue concerns the view of men and women we adopt if we consider that there is no final and definitely correct answer to a moral problem and that, nonetheless, each answer will contribute to shaping our own identity. On the other hand, Pihlström is strongly interested in pointing out that epistemological and ontological issues related to realism, constructivism, and solipsism involve a conception of the place and role of humans with respect to the world, mainly when assuming, as William James did, that "the trail of the human serpent is [. . .] over everything" (James 1975, 37; Pihlström 1998, 4). Moreover, Pihlström gives his proposal a transcendental arrangement—closer to Kant's first and second *Critique*, rather than to his *Critique of Judgment* and to his *Anthropology from a Pragmatic Point of View*—that I do not share, as will become clear in the course of my analysis. His "transcendental naturalism" aims to determine the enabling, if contingent, conditions of our experiencing and representing the world—an enterprise indirectly related to "the question of what it is like to be a human being" (1998, 101).

On the anthropological side, Michael Jackson found an important ally for his existential anthropology in James's radical empiricism and in Dewey's empirical naturalism because of the Pragmatists' antiintellectualistic stance (1989; 1996). Both James and Dewey argued against the dominant trend in modern philosophy to assume that experience is equal to or eminently represented by cognition and that epistemology is the decisive philosophical issue at stake. However, further steps in Jackson's project are developed in a more phenomenological vein, gravitating as they do around a heterodox understanding of the phenomenological *epoché* as involving a "practical relativism": "the suspension of inquiry into the divine and objective truth of particular customs, beliefs, or worldviews in order to explore them as modalities or moments of experience" (1996, 10). I say "heterodox" because even though Merleau-Ponty reached the conclusion that the result of the phenomenological *epoché* is that the world cannot be suspended (2002), Husserl's original aim was to give philosophy a foundation through what was still a Cartesian strategy. I guess that Jackson's original relativistic interpretation is not alien to the pluralistic influence of Classical Pragmatism on his anthropological attitude, and I would definitely argue that Pragmatic pluralism provides a better framework than phenomenological foundationalism for developing a philosophical anthropology.

3. Why the Pragmatists?

Before proceeding any further, I should probably provide more detailed reasons in support of my preference for the tradition of Classical Pragmatism as a good framework for developing a philosophical anthropology. Let's start from some general historical remarks. My idea is that the Pragmatists, particularly Dewey and Mead, felt that they were contributing to a shared philosophical enterprise, by deepening and even redefining some widespread issues and topics. For sure, James's tension between his effort to develop a naturalistic psychology, on the one hand, and a sincerely pluralistic ethics, on the other, opened a gap that could be filled by anthropological means. As colleagues in Chicago—a key place for the development of the social sciences at the end of the nineteenth century—Dewey and Mead preferred to label their reflections on human nature and behavior as "social psychology," instead of "philosophical anthropology." This choice is connected to their challenging vision of psychology as not primarily centered on methodological individualism and mentalism, but as capable of dealing with human conduct—including cognitive and discursive behaviors—as something primarily socially shaped (Mead 2011, 9–17). A later remark by Dewey suggests that in his advanced years he began to doubt the actual capacity of scientific psychology to free itself from its Cartesian roots and expressed a preference for anthropology.[5] In any case, Dewey had a scientific interest in anthropology and personal connections with the two leading figures in cultural and social anthropology in his day, Franz Boas and Bronislaw Malinowski (Zask 2007; 2015; Dreon 2012). Mead had continuous exchanges with comparative, infant, and evolutionary psychologists, expanding his rich view about the emergence of intelligent behaviors and self-identities out of social transactions by drawing on empirical research. Moreover, all of the Classical Pragmatists were strongly influenced by Charles Darwin's investigations into the origins of humanity, mainly through the work of Chauncey Wright (Parravicini 2012). As becomes clear in Dewey's writing on Darwin's influence on philosophy (2007), these thinkers gave a strongly antisubstantialist as well as antideterministic, nonteleological reading of Darwin's teaching, which led them to consider the nature of living beings as something not fixed once and for all, but rather dynamically configured and open to change.

Mead and Dewey, but also James in his own way and a much less known figure, Frank Lorimer, constantly posed the question of the peculiar traits of humans within the continuity of animal life. Even Peirce provided some important conceptual tools for disentangling the issue, although his focus remained matters of logic for most of his philosophical career, which ended with a cosmological, rather than anthropological, turn (Hookway 1997; Maddalena 2003).[6] In any case, I would argue that this group of thinkers did not put much emphasis on "the human difference," as was instead the case in the works of German Philosophical Anthropology, which strongly reflected the heritage of Martin Heidegger's existential analytics. Certainly, the Classical Pragmatists were very attentive to the many differences characterizing humans in comparison to nonhuman animals as well as to the continuity among living beings.[7] However, Dewey and Mead never shared the idea that those differences could give rise to an ontological divide between organic life and human existence. They assumed continuity in life as a general framework and considered actual human conditions to derive from fortuitous yet irreversible trends in natural circumstances, and to be open to further changes and to the course of history.

In the same spirit, I make no pretension to display an exhaustive and definitive picture of what it means to be human—not least because of the huge limits of any theoretical enterprise, mine included. The main reason is that, following the Pragmatists, I endorse an idea of being human as the product of a natural history, which is to say as a conception that is not given once and for all, but constantly becomes what it is by unfolding within a dynamic environment of which it is part. Very briefly, human nature is not interpreted as an allegedly innate, fixed, and preconstituted endowment that is later exposed to cultural events, a social world, nurture, and empirical occurrences. Human nature is not behind or below the course of events happening to us: it is constituted by the rich complexity of organic and environmental circumstances—including material constrains, cultural conditions, and social factors—that are exposed to relative fixation, stratification, changes, and loop effects. Using Kant's brilliant formula against the prevailing reading of his philosophy, I would say that human nature is constituted by "the fertile *bathos* of experience" (1997, 125), itself without any ground supporting it from below or behind.[8] Of course, there are more stable kinds of interactions between eminently organic aspects and environmental features, relatively invariant relations, and common features, which we can and should discern among the immense variability of behaviors, practices, and actions that ethnologists are helping us to discover. However, I think we should resist the fascination of transcendental options: they push us to consider these relative invariances, constancies, and commonalities as quasi–a priori enabling conditions for empirical actions and events; on their turn, empirical events are assumed to be mere instantiations of general traits.

Before really delving into the topic of human nature, I can further illustrate my preference for a pragmatist framework for developing a philosophical anthropology by listing some of the main arguments and theses I derive from the Pragmatists and deploy in the different chapters of the book. In doing so, I will try to further distinguish my own original contribution from the pragmatist legacy I draw on.

In the second chapter, I question the conception that sensibility is primarily constituted by sensorial perception and reflects an eminently cognitive characterization of experience. The Pragmatists philosophical efforts offer a means for me to support a shift of focus from a conception of sensibility modeled on its possible foundational role in a representative view of cognition to sensibility understood primarily as a structural dimension of animal life in general and of human life, more specifically. Dewey and Mead basically provide the biosocial framework for the conception of sensibility I suggest: sensibility coincides with selective exposition to the environment and the active feeling capacity to discriminate between favorable and noxious aspects by an organism whose primary experience of the surrounding environment is social because of the organic conditions of emphasized interdependence from others characterizing the human form of life. Against this general background, I develop a conception of qualitative, aesthetic, or affective aspects of human experience as basically characterizing organic-environmental relationships, thereby going beyond their traditional ascription to a merely subjective realm. Moreover, by radicalizing Dewey's conception of the interdependence between qualitative experience and reflection, I endorse a nonfoundational approach to human sensibility, which is to say a conception of human feeling and perception as something that both shapes and is shaped by the sociocultural linguistic environment constituting the peculiar human niche—in opposition to a view of sensibility and language as hierarchically ordered. Finally, I put forward a theory of emotions resulting from James's, Dewey's, and Mead's combined efforts, in the context of the above-mentioned conception of sensibility as a basic feature characterizing human engagement with the environment.

The account of habits I will propose is grounded in the Classical Pragmatists' attribution of a crucial, positive, and pervasive role to habits in human experience, cognition, and will. Making use of Dewey's insights on habits, I radicalize his view and formulate an explicitly ecological, holistic, and transactional notion of habits, requiring cooperation from both the organism and its natural and naturally social environment. I suggest defining habits as the more or less flexible channeling of both organic energies and environmental resources—that are not only natural but also social and cultural, given the marked social interdependence of human beings. This idea is connected with a wider redefinition of the concept of behavior I derive from both Dewey and Mead, whereby behavior is taken to be the result of mutual and constitutive transactions between an organism and the environment it is embedded in, instead of being conceived as the property or the way of being originated by a single agent. Even in the case of habit, Dewey and Mead's general biosocial framework allows me to explicitly anchor human habits in the organic-environmental condition of human life, and to support my contention that habits originate mostly at a prepersonal and prereflective level, rather than through the repetition of an initially conscious individual act. Through a detailed comparison with C. Lloyd Morgan's conception of habit, I show that a naturalistic view of habits can avoid methodological individualism and associationism, which are the standard approach for interpreting habit, considered as the automatization of a primarily individual way of responding to a stimulus. Finally, by engaging with Pierre Bourdieu's conception of habitus, I endorse a Deweyan understanding of habit as favoring a more pluralistic, revisable view of human behaviors, definitely renouncing any distinction between actions and their alleged quasi–a priori matrix.

In the last parts of the book, I make broad use of the Pragmatists' scattered yet recurrent reflections on language to avoid any artificial opposition between experience and language, but also to support my thesis that human experience is fortuitously yet irreversibly reshaped by the advent of language. From the Pragmatists I derive a picture of language as a real part of our lives. Language is far more than a mere vehicle for rationality; it is a range of other things: a way to establish contacts, to maintain relations, and to act on them, as well as something that can be enjoyed or suffered. It is also a very powerful tool for sharing and making something common as well as for doing things together, in addition to being the most powerful means to think through symbols and meanings. The Pragmatists, I argue, were attentive to the rich complexity of human languages and offered some important contributions. From Dewey and, more extensively, from Frank Lorimer I draw an account of the natural genesis of the human mind out of previous forms of animal behavior and of the appearance of language. Lorimer is even seen to develop an idea of language as something that is continuous and functions holistically before it becomes subject to analytic distinctions—an idea originally foreseen by James and Dewey. In my view, Mead complements Dewey and Lorimer's account on the growth of language out of already existing forms of organic intelligence through a theory of the genesis of verbal gestures out of communication contexts based on a primarily affective-based mutual regulation of actions. Finally, I rely on Mead and Frank Lorimer to suggest an interpretation of the transition to properly referential and symbolic language, with marked cognitive powers. I suggest we consider their two approaches complementary. Lorimer provides an account of human reason from animal intelligence by means of words, focusing on signs as a device to refer to something absent toward which an action is directed. Mead explains the transition to verbal gestures and significant symbols through the social extension of the conversational context.

Nonetheless, a pragmatist objection might be that making use of arguments and ideas derived from James, Dewey, and Mead is not sufficient to characterize a philosophical proposal as pragmatic.[9] The pragmatic method has to do with the practical consequences of a specific notion, namely, with the difference it can make with respect to current existential conditions, as stated by James (1975, 28). Even if Michael Quante's proposal is not grounded in Pragmatism, I agree with his claim that, in order to be pragmatistic, a philosophical anthropology should assume that each concept or theory requires questions like: "How is this related to human action? What place does it have in the context of our actions?" (2018, 22).[10]

I honestly think that my proposal does not go so far as to provide any real answers about ways to ameliorate human problems and enrich human life. Nonetheless, the kind of conceptual distinctions I am suggesting certainly make some difference, insofar as they entail a change of habits in facing problems and acting in the present context. This means that before we attempt to draw a balance of the pragmatic value of the idea I am supporting in this book, we should wait until the end of the whole enterprise, when it will be possible to take its practical consequences into account. However, I can already suggest an example in order to give an idea of the ways in which a philosophical anthropology might function in our society.

Even aside from the evident health problems caused by the Covid-19 pandemic, the education of the young generations is a serious issue, and one that unfortunately is often underestimated by politicians and public opinion. Online lessons and classes have represented a decisive emergency solution in both schools and universities throughout the world. Through this tool, we have been able to fill a void (at least partially) in a way that would not have been possible during similar pandemic emergencies in the past—I am thinking of the spread of poliomyelitis in the twentieth century, for example. However, the consequences of this method of schooling—both teaching and learning—should be attentively evaluated. What kind of habits of conduct do they support? Certainly, they have represented a moment of crisis for both teachers and students, who have been—and still are—compelled to change or reorient their previous habits. Crises can be something positive, as Dewey pointed out, because they oblige people to explicitly consider their previous, largely prepersonal, habits of conduct. But what new habits of attention and interlocutions do on-line lessons favor? How is the pupil's and the teacher's capacity to take the role of the other affected? Obviously, it is also the case that the education of the young generations cannot be reduced to the mere transmission of contents. Among other things, it concerns the acquisition of implicit and explicit norms of social behavior, which are largely transmitted to students via their affectively oriented sensibility, by developing a sense of asymmetries and similarities, belongings and exclusions. To what extent does the isolated and very restricted context of being alone in front of a computer condition both learning and educational processes? Of course, I have no definite analysis and solutions to offer in relation to this huge issue. Yet I believe that this is a case where it makes a difference to adopt a view of humans as largely habitual beings, and to envisage normativity as grounded in affectively oriented sensibility.

4. What Human Nature?

As hinted above, a philosophical anthropology can have important practical consequences that should be taken into account. Speaking of "human nature" risks getting into a thorny issue, open to misunderstanding. The situation is particularly complex because, evidently, this is not a merely theoretical issue; rather, it has serious existential implications, both moral and political. As Dewey reminds us in his entry for the *Encyclopaedia of the Social Sciences*, dealing with human nature means singling out thorny problems related to people's personal cultural preferences and aversions, beyond their explicit positions and choices; in other words, it means dealing with people's sensibility, in the sense in which this term will be explored in the second chapter. Writing in 1932, Dewey rhetorically wondered whether social facts such as war and selfishness were rooted in human nature or whether some races were inferior by nature (1985b). Many years later, John Dupré emphasized the weight of a conception of human nature guided by the tendency to maximize one's own selfish interests in economics, as well as the influence of a reductive view of human structures in diagnosing attention deficit hyperactivity disorder and treating it through drugs (2001, 3, 14). Whether we consider human nature to be fixed or changeable can make a great difference in the real lives of people. Serious consequences come from assuming that behavior is determined by nature or depends on the social context. Dealing with a specific kind of action, either as innate and inherited or as due to environmental influences, opens up different practical scenarios.

Nonetheless, even if we wish to focus on a theoretical analysis of the concept, the idea of human nature seems to display a tangle of problems, punctuated by distinctions that could be useful when treated as functional and connected to specific contexts, but which are actually turned into dogmatic oppositions. One first form of dualism concerns the opposition between the innate and the acquired, between the allegedly innate equipment existing on the genetic or neural level and the properties and ways of behaving this is assumed to give rise to. To give but one example, based on Chomsky's influential hypothesis, the idea of a neural program for producing grammar encoded in our genes has been assumed to be an efficient (and sometimes sufficient) cause for specific linguistic practices. From this point of view, nurture, culture, and institutions seem to be something completely different from nature, since they supervene on an already fixed material substratum as an adjunct. In turn, cultural additions can be considered either something that must be reduced to some other feature, as is the case with eliminativists and reductionists, or as a distinctive human feature, producing an ontological gap within nature. Genetic determinism and cultural reductionism can be seen as the two extreme results of this kind of dualism. It is no longer necessary for this gap to be represented by the old-fashioned contrast between the material and the cultural: a more acceptable distinction has emerged between norms established as a theoretically self-standing realm and the allegedly closed physical realm of efficient causes. This distinction has become paradigmatic in the debate on naturalization, fueled by Jaegwon Kim's work.

The opposition between nature as innate and nurture as acquired evidently tends to slip into the dualism between a priori structures and their a posteriori instantiations in a given social and cultural environment. The asymmetries between two levels of features, stabilizing and changing at different speeds and in different times, are assumed to be ontologically different—as a priori, unchangeable enabling conditions, per se independent from contexts, on the one hand, and empirical variations of the same universal character, exposed to historical, geographical, and cultural variability, on the other hand. From an anthropological point of view, this kind of dichotomy is particularly pernicious, because it tends to stiffen two opposite positions: on one side, there are the supporters of the view of human nature as characterized by universal features that are expressed in different ways in different cultural environments. On the other side, there are the cultural relativists, who deny the existence of universal characteristics and assume the incommensurability of cultures. From the treatise on *The Expression of the Emotions in Man and Animals* to Paul Eckman's influential support of Darwin's position, this has been the case for most of the debate on emotions, for example. Nonetheless, the two factions share the common assumption that either human nature is something deep, unchanging, and preestablished for all human beings prior to the varieties of human behavior and practices it can give rise to, or there is no human nature at all. Taking a monolithic conception of human nature for granted and having to tackle the infinite range of human actions and conducts, cultural relativists deny the existence of such universal features and regard human behaviors as the result of cultural conditioning, and as having nothing to do with a natural endowment. This was the case, for example, with the controversy about the experience of time among the Hopi, which was sparked by Benjamin Lee Whorf in the 1940s (and challenged by Malotki in the 1980s). Famously, Whorf claimed that Hopi people's perception of time did not involve the experience of a continuum, proceeding at equal rates everywhere in the universe, because of the specific structures of verbs in the Hopi language.

Furthermore, cultural relativism tends to flow into a theory of cultural incommensurability that extends the misleading logic of methodological individualism to cultures, assuming the immediate accessibility of one's own first-person experience while doubting that it is possible to access the experience of other subjects. In other words, the idea of the insularity of one's own mind is mirrored by the assumption of the insularity of each culture. In a pragmatist vein, I would argue that pluralism and variability do not involve incommensurability as a necessary consequence. The incommensurability position disregards the common circumstance that linguistic and cultural translations work—they may be more or less precise, but they are often successful in meeting specific goals. A partial overlapping of different meanings, family resemblances between languages, and different linguistic games are frequent; consequently, common features, rather than universal properties, are actually shared. Moreover, common aspects are usually not substantive properties, but ways of being and relating to an environment that are largely indeterminate and a factor of change in themselves: consider learning as a common feature of humans, constituting a continuous source of change and reorganization of previous dynamics and energies (Dewey 1985b, 32).

Even the characterization of human nature as innate is problematic, and it is basically connected to the underestimating or neglecting of growth as a constitutive aspect of organic life. As Morgan said in his book on *Instinct and Habit*, a purely congenital organic action among many kinds of animals can be supposed to take place only at its very first occurrence because the second occurrence will be influenced by the result of previous experiences, however limited they may be (Morgan 1896, 136). In his entry for the *Encyclopaedia*, Dewey claims that isolating the allegedly native and original constitution of human nature is possible only through the assumption of a static point of view on it, for example, by privileging features at birth over traits characterizing the intrauterine past or the organism's future development and adulthood. As is widely known, Aristotle saw maturity as the stage most revealing of human nature because, according to him, it is only during this phase that individual potentialities are fully enacted. Taking this or that snapshot of a human could be a useful intellectual expedient in specific circumstances, but "[b]iologically all growth is modification and all organs have to be treated and understood as developments out of something else and as pointing forward to still something else" (Dewey 1985b, 32–33). Growth and change are constitutive parts of human nature as well as of each living being—although with crucial differences of degree. This is the reason why it might seem ambiguous, for example, to speak of habits as a second nature, thereby assuming that they grow out of a previous nature that is already established before any habits emerge. Human nature is not independent from its natural history, including growth and change as constitutive elements.

Likewise, human nature is not independent from the environment, including its natural and social structure, where nature develops and is what it is. The abandonment of the strongly influential paradigm of the modern self-standing subject who comes to know a reality existing "out there" is due to the acceptance of an obvious biological fact (Dewey 1989): living beings, differently from any alleged disembodied consciousness, cannot live in a vacuum, but only in and through the environment they are embedded in—an environment they are part of and which they contribute to changing through their dynamic interactions, constituting life itself. More specifically, the human environment reveals itself to be a strongly social one, because of the high degree of interdependence and cooperative action required in order for humans to survive—although, for the most part, this working together is not a harmonious affair at all.

Disregard for this aspect has led philosophers to a further dichotomy between the individual with her or his allegedly innate tendencies (which can be either good, according to Rousseau, or aggressive and selfish, according to Hobbes and Freud) and the social institutions that are necessary for her or his survival. The point in such cases is that human nature is considered to establish itself prior to any exposition to a social world, as if being human were something quite separate from the fact of living in a natural and naturally social environment and being reshaped through continuous interaction with the environment one belongs to, within a mutual, albeit asymmetrical, relationship. As stated above, by primarily focusing on life and the organic continuity between humans and other animals, the Pragmatists have exposed the philosophical fallacy of separating an organism from the environment where it lives and, as such, is what it is. Translated into metaphysical vocabulary, this means assuming that an *essence* can be separated and considered prior to its *existence*: *what* a human being is would be established independently of *how* he or she is (Heidegger 1962). In the case of humans, the mistake is even worse because it is based on a failure to take account of the social nature of the human environment, given that human mammals are particularly dependent on a mature social group in order to survive and develop.[11] This was a crucial point for Dewey and Mead, who emphasized the obvious biological fact of infants' huge degree of dependency at birth long before Adolf Portmann and evolutionary biologists. The extreme fragility of human mammals at birth represents a core anchoring of human sociality; premature exposure to culture within human physiology gives rise to a sociocultural niche in which even the most animal-like vital processes in young humans are embedded from the very beginning.[12] Cultural naturalism is a formula used to emphasize that our pronounced cultural development as human beings has its roots in our organic constitution, without being reducible to mere physical structures and chemical processes. In other words, social and cultural development appears to be required by the very physiological-environmental conditions characterizing humans (see also Peterson 2010). We share most of our natural history with other animals, but we have become what we are now through the specific combination of environmental conditions and the organic constitution that has befallen us, without the intervention of external forces, but only through the peculiar dynamics engendered among their components. These are the reasons why I believe it is important to continue to speak about human nature, although the concept has a complicated, often problematic history and remains open to misunderstanding.

To conclude this section, I will mention a further fallacy connected to the assumption of human nature as the real structure determining or enabling the complex variety of human behaviors and cultures in the physical and empirical world, which is to say as a cause or a prior condition instantiated in the several empirical occurrences it can have in the reality "out there."

In his paper on the influence of Darwin on philosophy, Dewey argued against the tendency to search for possible causes and principles underlying contingency and variability, as if the latter could not subsist independently.[13] As usual, he emphasized the ethical and political consequences of an approach that is still meta-physical, and which posits an ultimate, decisive cause for everything there is even in an evolutionary context. Dewey criticized the concept that the "duty of wholesale justification" providing the final cause or principle of empirical occurrences once and for all endorses the "habit of derogating from present meanings and uses" (2007, 10). It implicitly nourish the idea that concrete conditions of life are irrelevant compared to the alleged deep essence of things. In contrast, abandoning the logic of ultimate causes in order to focus on concrete problems and the chance to modify specific material and social conditions "introduces responsibility into intellectual life" (2007, 11).

More recently, in her essay *The Nurturing of Natures* (Oyama 2002), Susan Oyama puts forward an argument that is similar, in many respects, to Dewey's. Her point of departure is not the evolution of individual organisms, but developmental systems, assumed as complex, contingent, and ever-changing systems of interactants composed of organic factors as well as of environmental characteristics, including biotic, abiotic, and social aspects. Of course, there are causal relations between the different components of the system, but none of them can be considered an ultimate cause that gives rise to the processes occurring on the alleged surface. Oyama's antireductionism is based on the assumption that no one factor is more decisive than others for the development of the system, or can be taken as a deep, hidden cause manifesting its products on the mere surface. For example, the genome cannot be assumed to be the profound nature manifesting itself at phenotypic level, as if we were dealing with two different levels—reality and mere appearance. Rather, each organism should be considered the result of a complex web of factors—genomic factors as well as other organic aspects and further environmental conditions—and none of them is more decisive or deeper than the process itself. Oyama rejects the idea of nature as an allegedly deeper structure, beyond organisms' effective being. She explicitly repudiates the logic of searching for an ultimate cause belonging to a deeper level beyond concrete existence, whether it be the idea of the genome as a hidden principle behind its phenotypic manifestation or the idea of emotions as psychic events or neurological programs lying behind their alleged external display through bodily and facial expressions. Moreover, like Dewey, she emphasizes the political consequences of assuming that what happens is triggered by one ultimately decisive cause within a developmental system. She mentions the debate about the alleged correlation between IQ levels and race that could be used, for example, as a possible justification for the lack of public investments in certain schools. By contrast to this kind of logic, both Dewey and Oyama consider the nature of an organism to be constituted according to what the organism effectively is and what happens to it, denying it is something buried deep beyond a superficial veil. "Nature thus has no existence prior to or separate from the concrete living organism in its concrete, often living, surroundings: no Platonic ideals here, no underlying reality more basic than the being itself, no instruction manuals or little engineers in the cell nucleus" (Oyama 2002, 2).

However, Susan Oyama's proposal with regard to the concept of human nature is even more radical than the Pragmatists'. Instead of emphasizing the nature-nurture continuum as the most reasonable option, she suggests reconceptualizing nature and nurture as the two sides of the same process. "Nurture" would be the developmental process of organisms, the history of the complex organic and environmental interactions through which organisms become what they are. "Nature" would be the continuously changing and contingent result of the developmental process, the totality of the features characterizing an organism in its own environment, without assuming that they are the effect or manifestation of a more profound principle or reality. As for the Pragmatists, they embraced the idea of growth as something constitutive of human nature and, in so doing, strongly problematized the boundaries between the innate and the acquired, as in the case of the distinction between instinct and habit. However, they preferred to maintain a continuum between nature and culture, and I think this is still a good move if we are to ensure the possibility of drawing distinctions between organic nature and its contingent but irreversible development through culture, understood as a system of practices scaffolded by languages, songs, and meanings—that is, if we wish to argue that nurture can enfold human beings and their world in a variety of ways.

5. Cultural Naturalism, Loop-Effects, and Designless Emergentism

As has become more and more evident, the conceptual framework for my approach to human nature is represented by cultural naturalism—that is, a nonreductive form of naturalism that assumes culture to be continuous with nature, rooted in the very organic and environmental conditions of human life, and yet irreducible to the mere association of preexisting resources.

Among the biological features favoring the emergence of culture particular emphasis must be placed—de facto, which is to say without any appeal to an evolutionary design—on the marked immaturity of the human infant at birth, with its great level of dependence on a mature social medium and its precocious and extended exposure to an already highly socialized, acculturated, and linguistic environment. These circumstances were emphasized by Adolph Portmann (1941; 1945) and Arnold Gehlen (1988), as well as by Marjorie Grene (1974). Further connections have been established by different scholars and within different traditions. For example, the concept of the absence of a specialized niche, originally highlighted by Jacob von Uexküll (1926; 2010), together with the notion of the scarcity of quasi-automatic responses to environmental stimuli in humans, flow into Gehlen's idea of humans as still indeterminate animals and an instinctually deficient beings (1988). From this point of view, culture appears to be required by natural constraints affecting the specifically human relationships with the environment. Marjorie Grene pointed out that human anatomy is such as to make generalization possible through a loss of specialization. Among the anatomical factors underpinning cultural development, she focused on how—as originally pointed out by Erwin Straus in 1952, and recently emphasized by Shaun Gallagher in 2017—an upright posture freed the hands and allowed the larynx to descend, leading to the development of a phonatory apparatus with a much wider range of sounds compared to that of other animals (see also Leroi-Gourhan 1993). Other organic constraints supporting the development of culture are the opposable thumb, which enables the grasping of a vast array of objects, and the considerable encephalic development of humans, which ensured an unexpected number of new neuronal connections, compared to other already big animal brains (Deacon 1998). Nonetheless, Grene was very careful to avoid reducing the relationship between biological factors and culture to causal dependence: she preferred to speak of a widespread dependence of sociocultural life on biophysical reality and to consider the relation as an "anthropological circle" (Peterson 2010).

In a pragmatist spirit, all of these peculiarly human organic circumstances are not understood as the efficient causes of our social and cultural development. Rather, organic factors and sociocultural features of the human environment should be understood as mutually conditioning each other and as reciprocally reinforcing. In other words, when recognizing that cultural development is rooted and involved in specific organic-environmental features characterizing the human animal, we must assume a complementary feedback action by the cultural-linguistic niche on organic functions as the process through which our humanity has been shaped and still remains open to further reorganization (see Tomasello 1999 and 2008 on cultural evolution, as well as Tattersall 2016 and 2017 on language).

In any case, the sort of naturalism I derive from the Pragmatists excludes any appeal to external or further intervention beyond organic-environmental interactions to explain human development and the genesis of the cultural world (Margolis 2002; Shook 2003; Ryder 2020)[14]—such as the divine *nous* suggested by Aristotle, as well as the much more recent idea of reason as an a priori with respect to alleged merely empirical instantiations.[15]

This conception—broadly derived from Dewey and Mead—clearly allows for a broader variety of ways of being than only being a physical entity or event (Margolis 1974), as well as a wider series of ways of being a cause than only being an efficient cause (Deacon 2006). Moreover, as has become clear through an engagement with Susan Oyama's approach, no factor among the complex relations, interactions, and loop effects within the organic-environmental system can be assumed to be the decisive principle, giving rise to a further linear process. No single character can be taken to explain what is really at stake, as is the case for example when we consider mental processes to be ultimately reducible to physicochemical events within the brain. Physicalism and cultural reductionism are two sides of the same logic, which assumes a single feature to be the cause of a second one, while considering both to be ontologically different and, finally, supposing a linearly efficient causality to be the best tool for understanding their relationship. A living system, including any living cultural system, is what it is and cannot be reduced to some privileged components or causes—even if components and causes clearly matter—because in that case we simply lose the system itself.

In addition, I would argue that cultural naturalism entails the idea that what happens later within the development of an organic-environmental system can have a disruptive effect on the previous organization of the system: it can have feedback or loop effects on it, changing it irreversibly, if only in a contingent way. This is the case with the advent of language within the context of already existing forms of animal sensibility; and it is also the reason why I think it is appropriate to speak of emergentism, while rejecting any teleological reading of it.

Intelligent human practices can be understood as more complex and innovative forms of organizing or connecting already existing organic energies and environmental resources, in such a way as to bring out new properties and unexpected events that cannot be reduced to the mere association of preexisting elements.[16] New forms of life within a natural and naturally sociocultural environment are irreversible and involve a transformation of the previous conditions, both within the natural landscape and in relation to previous physiological behaviors, already existing among other mammals. The transformation of preexisting animal behaviors—such as supplying food and finding a sexual partner or shelter—into culturally significant practices, social habits, and institutions is connected to the complex forms of communication and language occurring among human groups, which allow the sharing of common activities and goals, that is, a marked form of sociality. Radicalizing Dewey's point of view that language is communication, that is, "the making of something common" (1991a: 52), I think we should assume that a highly refined kind of sociality and linguistic communication were jointly established and nourished each other, rather than consider the former factor to be a cause or enabling condition of the latter (Tomasello 1999). Moreover, I would argue that, in a pragmatist vein, we should focus on the feedback actions and loop effects that linguistic and cultural practices have on already existing animal sensibilities, preferences, and aversions, as well as on animal strategies for action. Even better, I think we should speak of their mutual conditioning and shaping from both an ontogenetic and phylogenetic perspective.

Radicalizing a pragmatist suggestion, I assume the emergence of human forms of life—through language, symbolic and intelligent behaviors, and cultural practices and institutions—as contingent and fortuitous, not ruled by a teleological principle that guides evolution, in turn envisaged as a progression from inferior levels of life to superior ones.

The traditional criticism of emergentism regards mainly two aspects: on the one hand, its focus on novelty would violate the principle *ex nihilo nihil fit*, whose counterpart in physics would be represented by the first principle of thermodynamics, stating that energy can neither be created nor destroyed (Deacon 2006, 111). On the other hand, according to Kim (1992; 1996), the notion of downward causation—for example, the idea that mental intention can produce an effect on arm and leg movements—would entail the violation of the physical causal closure (El-Hani and Pihlström 2002), assuming that only physical events and entities are real and that physical events can only have physical causes. As already noted, the Pragmatists adopted a much more inclusive conception of the reality of an entity than one predicated on its being a physical entity, as well as a much more complex conception of causes, not limited to efficient causes producing one-sided linear effects. In other words, the above-mentioned criticism of emergentism appears to be based on specific habits of thinking that assume linear efficient causality as an explanatory paradigm and the fact of being a physical entity as the ontological standard for being real. An alternative way of approaching causal relationships is already evident in Dewey's criticism of the reflex-arc concept as a paradigm for understanding behavior: a stimulus is only apparently the first efficient cause producing a specific action as a result, because the organism involved must already have been open to selecting that kind of stimulus in order for it to be affected by a specific stimulus among many potential others in a given context (Dewey 1972). An organic circuit is a much more fitting paradigm for understanding human behavior than the reflex-arc: circularity and mutual conditioning, not efficient causality, should be taken as a causal model. An outstanding evolutionary biologist such as Lynn Rothshild claims that there are many examples of emergent phenomena within biology and that in biological hierarchies: "there is both upwards and downwards causation" (2006, 156). Leaving aside the issue of whether the view of physics adopted by those critical of emergentism is up to date or not, Rothshild—like biological anthropologist Terrence Deacon—provides examples of emergent phenomena even within the physical world: from John Stuart Mill's famous case of salt to Deacon's case of thermodynamic systems and, more generally, examples of causal structures promoting self-constitution.[17] From a chemical point of view, salt is composed of one atom of sodium and one of chlorine. Nonetheless, the new property of making food more savory cannot be derived either from the tendency of sodium to catch fire on contact with water or from the irritating effects of chlorine on mucous membranes and organic tissues. It is the mutual interaction or the new kind of relatedness between sodium and chlorine that produces a new property, one that is not evident when we consider the two atoms separately. Something similar can be stated about thermostats, where a more comfortable (and not already existent) temperature is obtained through the mutual conditioning of the environmental temperatures detected by the thermostat, the way it affects them, and the feedback action of the new environmental temperature on the thermostat. However, as claimed by Terrence Deacon, this does not mean that the property of making food more savory comes from nothing, or that the new, pleasant temperature of the air comes from nothing. Rather, the property of salt comes from the mutually establishing and nourishing interactions that take place between the two chemical elements, just as a milder temperature arises from the mutual conditioning of physical circumstances and the functioning of the technological device. From a radical empiricist point of view, as famously claimed by James (1976), relations are as real as physical entities. Nonetheless, counterarguments and assumptions of this kind do not entail that the concept of emergence is unproblematic from a philosophical point of view.

Briefly, I would argue that the issue at stake is the risk that the concept of emergence be used to maintain a residual teleological reading of evolution, as well as an open door for theism. At the same time, a further danger lies in the use of emergence as yet another way to explain what exists by claiming that there is something beyond or beneath this allegedly superficial level—the evolutive design hinted at above—as if what occurs could not subsist on its own.

To clarify what I mean, it might be helpful to provide a short historical reconstruction of Mead's and Dewey's treatment of the reception of the theory of "emergent evolution," formulated by Samuel Alexander and Conwy Lloyd Morgan between 1912 and 1923.[18] As is well known, Mead adopted the term "emergence" in his 1930 lectures *The Philosophy of the Present*, posthumously edited by Arthur E. Murphy in 1932.[19] Here Mead makes explicit reference to Morgan and Alexander. I would argue that he adopted the term *emergentism* for one basic reason. Insofar as it marks a break with the mechanistic explanation of evolution, an emergentist approach puts great emphasis on the mutual determination of a living form and its environment, which is to say on the feedback action produced by the emergence of life within the inanimate world, so as to transform it into an environment (1932, ch. 2). In other words, a novelty is not merely a change within the organism but also a change in the environment, which is pushed to readapt to the new event occurring within it.[20]

Dewey uses the terms *emergence* and *emerge* in *Experience and Nature*, where he significantly speaks of "an emergent theory of mind" (1981). Nonetheless, he does not use the term consistently, as sometimes he adopts the verb *supervene* in place of *emerge*.[21] As has already been clarified, Dewey shared Mead's emphasis on the mutual conditioning of organic and environmental factors in evolution. He explicitly supported a nonreductive form of naturalism, endorsing the idea of the continuity of nature and culture, as well as that of the loop effect of the human form of life on the previous environment. However, his great emphasis on the contingency and fortuitousness of evolutionary processes prevented him from accepting Alexander's and Morgan's idea of "emergent evolution," which he perceived as a dogmatic doctrine, as becomes clear in a letter to Arthur Bentley dating back to 1945 (Dewey 1999).[22] The point is that Morgan's conception of emergence remains strictly connected with a view of evolution conceived as a comprehensive plan behind the sequel of events progressing from lower degrees of order to higher degrees (1923, 1). However, in contrast to the mechanical view of evolution, Morgan introduced the advent of novelty as an opportunity to explain the disruptive transition from lower forms of relatedness to higher ones. Furthermore, even if he was obliged to reckon that dissolution and disintegration are possible within the history of natural systems (1923, 12–13), he maintained that evolution goes from inferior levels to superior ones: he believed that human cognitive development should be interpreted as going from mere naive perception and sensory presentation to contemplative thought, according to a one-sided process unfolding from a lower level to a higher one (1923, 17–18). Finally, following Alexander, Morgan left some space for God within evolution, by suggesting that God could be seen in terms of a divine activity manifesting itself through "pyramidal events," which is to say the various ascending degrees of evolution (1923, 13).

Dewey could not share such a conception of evolution, involving a teleological reading, as is clear from the following quotation: "'Evolution'" has ceased to be the unwinding of what is already rolled up on the reel of destiny, an unfolding of the leaves of a scroll, and the rendering visible of passages inscribed at the beginning in a secret indelible ink. The introduction of the idea of mutation marks nothing less than a revolution in our entire scheme of interpretation" (1985b, 280–81).[23]

Dewey's adoption of Darwin's idea of constant and fortuitous variations in nature as the basis for change prevented him from making any "call for a prior intelligent causal force to plan and preordain" (2007, 9) those variations. As James wrote, "[. . .] Darwinism has once and for all displaced design from the minds of the 'scientific'" (James 1975, 39).[24] The "design argument" must be rejected because it implies the old metaphysical logic of searching for a permanent cause behind or beyond what happens, although this cause can now be mediated by the classic notion of species as involving a purpose and directing the development of an organism from its earlier stages to the realization of its complete perfection (Dewey 2007).[25]

To sum up, Dewey was clearly an emergentist. For example, he considered the human mind a new organization of interactions occurring in a completely fortuitous way between an organism and the social-linguistic environment it is embedded in. While contingent, the process is irreversible and has a disruptive effect on its environment. However, Dewey could not accept the dogmatic idea of an emergent evolution, assumed as a teleological principle explaining and directing the course of events. For him espousing that kind of logic would have meant losing the chance to get rid of the metaphysical aspiration to search for a hidden cause or principle beyond or behind what exists.[26] In a strongly pragmatist vein, the most important reason for renouncing this metaphysical claim is represented by the broadly social and political consequences it engenders: the notion that the essential goes beyond experience fosters the habit of disregarding actual conditions of life and the specific factors involved in current problems, and of forgoing any efforts to identify suitable means and ways of changing these factors when required (2007).

Chapter 2

Looking at Human Sensibility through a Pragmatist Lens

1. In Search of a Rounded Portrait

For many people who must commute to work, entering a crowded train coach is a very common experience—or at least was before the age of coronavirus. Although some philosophers and neuroscientists have been trained to deal with these kinds of situations from a strictly intellectual point of view, it would seem odd to characterize this experience as the mere registration of sensory data to be processed, whether on a mental or neurological level, in order to build an internal representation of an external state of things—by means of a mirror reflection or possibly through a more aseptic computational encoding process. For sure, such reconstructions of ordinary environmental experience are valuable and legitimate for specific purposes and their final outcomes, namely, scientific objects are very useful tools for orienting in the world. Nonetheless, they should not be assumed to be truer than qualitative, everyday experience, as Dewey remarked in his *Rejoinder* to Hans Reichenbach in 1939 (1991b).[1] When entering a coach, I will be looking for a seat to sit in or at least for a place where I can stand to avoid as much as possible being in physical contact with other people whom I perceive as almost obstructing my personal space. I will probably be disturbed by the noise of people speaking aloud on their phones, annoyed by a person laying her backpack on the floor and taking up the space before my legs, disgusted by the smell of fried chicken emanating from my neighbor's clothes, amused by the little kid staring at me with curiosity from the seat behind. Could all this simply be tossed out of the window of philosophical concern by confining it within the realm of the merely subjective?

This is not a plea for the alleged primacy of first-person experience—including, as is often the case, dogmatic assumptions about introspection as the only way to access the allegedly private realm of lived experience (Steiner 2011). Rather, my concern is to develop a richer picture of human experience than the misleading image of nonevaluative sense experience plus other additional layers, further subjective colorings deprived of cognitive significance. In pursuing this goal, I will carry to their extreme consequences some insights about sensibility that have been foreshadowed or partially developed by the Classical Pragmatists, although the latter did not use this word and never devoted a specific treatment to the topic. In what follows, I will present and make use of some of their arguments to support my view of sensibility as affectively oriented, which is to say as involving proto-evaluative aspects that concern life conditions from the very beginning. James's and Dewey's points of departure were points of dissatisfaction. I would say that the first cause of frustration for them was the traditional idea that primary experience basically consists in the perception of mere sensory data, of the sort found in standard Empiricism. In the above-mentioned example, this would mean that when entering the train coach, I record a mass of visual data that will inform my perception of people, seats, narrow corridors, exits, and so on and associate them with other sensations—with further audio, tactile, and proprioceptive givens. My primary experience in the train coach would be configured as a merely receptive phase of sensory perception—performed either at a mental level or at a neurological one—that would then undergo some kind of evaluation process—an emotion-based appraisal, a moral appraisal or a rational estimation—only later, in order to make action possible. Referring to the work of Gestalt psychologists, Hans-Georg Gadamer claimed that the idea of a pure sensation must be assumed as the reciprocal of a stimulus—meaning that both are ideal abstractions produced through the isolation of two different parts from the whole complex of an experience (2004, 78). In his *Logic*, Dewey did not deny the crucial role of sense data within scientific contexts but emphasized that they must be considered essential correlates of inquiring hypotheses, that is, of ideas by means of which sense data are selected and analytically isolated from an overall experiential situation for a specific purpose. Consequently, mere sensory information should more properly be understood as something that is "taken" rather than immediately "given," that is, as selected aspects that are reflectively separated from other aspects and relations that are ordinarily involved in an experiential situation—for example, by being distinguished from qualities, feelings, practical opportunities, and bodily engagement (Dewey 1991a, 127).[2]

A second cause of discontent among the Pragmatists was the usually unproblematic attribution of an exclusively or eminently cognitive function to sensory perception—whether this be assigned a foundational role with reference to the construction of knowledge, as in the case of empiricists, or its value be denied based on its instabilities and ambiguities, as in the case of rationalists. This kind of criticism finds historical parallels in authors such as Herbert Marcuse and Helmuth Plessner, who independently argued against the prevailing habit of regarding sensibility almost exclusively as sensory perception, whose eminent function is expected to be a cognitive one. By drawing on Schiller's theory of basic impulses and combining it with a Freudian reading, Marcuse points out that the German word *Sinnlichkeit* preserves a double meaning: on the one hand, it has an eminently epistemic characterization, whereby it means "cognitive sense-perceptiveness" and "representation (sensation)." On the other hand, its second meaning is "sensuality," which is strictly connected with "instinctual (especially sexual) gratification," that is with primary vital needs (Marcuse 1955, 182). Plessner claims that the notion of a pure sense-impression is a construction of the theory of perception (1980, section 2). By contrast, he endorses an anthropological approach to the senses, grounded in the idea of man as an organism or living being whose anatomic plan, functional level, and environment mutually adapt to one another (1980, section 1).

Obviously, no one could or would deny that sensory perception plays a crucial role in our knowledge of reality. Rather, my contention here is that this is only part of a more complex and multifaceted commerce with the world involving a kind of affectively based activity.

A third unsatisfactory point for the Classical Pragmatists was constituted by the shortcut use of the categories "subjective" and "objective" to treat the qualitative and affective aspects of experience. To return to my previous example, the point is that my feeling disgusted, disturbed, annoyed, or amused by other people's behaviors has to do with material constraints—for example, limited amount of space—as well as with the real actions of other people—such as talking too loud or continuously fidgeting. They are real components of a forced sharing of space and not mere imaginary projections of mine. I believe that the conceptual opposition between subjective and objective qualities is like a net with too wide a mesh, unable to catch the complexity of our interactions with the world. The problem, I would argue, is that this opposition often involves the idea that qualitative experience is a private, purely first-person experience, consequently posing problems of public access. This was the issue, I think, that James was trying to disentangle in his *Essays in Radical Empiricism* (James 1976) and that Dewey was finally able to dismantle in his *Experience and Nature* and *Art as Experience* (1981; 1989). Consequently, I will recover their diverse arguments and weave them together into a more coherent framework in order to escape the standard conflation of the qualitative with the private or merely subjective. Furthermore, James and Dewey were interested in recovering the kind of mongrel but in most cases effective functionality of ordinary sensibility apart from the typically epistemological lenses through which sensibility had traditionally been considered.[3] The qualitative thickness and complexity of common experience has frequently appeared to be ontologically and epistemologically vague from the point of view of Cartesian clarity and, consequently, unsuited to represent the stable foundations of the cognitive building. I would argue that we should avoid applying to ordinary sensibility precision standards that are taken from other fields—from epistemology, logic, and the like—and assumed as appropriate criteria for evaluating qualitative experience (Perissinotto 2019b). As a matter of fact, in most cases more or less unconsciously performed qualitative or affectively based discriminations are useful tools for orienting ourselves in our environment.

A preliminary sketch of the account of sensibility to be worked out in this chapter could be the following. Through pragmatist tools, I advance a conception of sensibility as what characterizes our way of living and interacting in the world around us, by considering its functions and peculiar configuration within the human living form. Although the Pragmatists did not speak of "sensibility," I derive from them a philosophically decisive move, namely, approaching sensibility within the context of organic life in general and of human life more specifically, rather than as something that is preeminently oriented toward ensuring knowledge of reality. This shift from a cognitive to a broadly biological focus is not simply realized by considering that sensibility is fully rooted in a bodily organism operating as a whole—a dynamic body whose actions and perceptions are mutually conditioned and shaped, as already noted by Maurice Merleau-Ponty (1983; 2012), and more recently by enactivist scholars (Noë 2004; Gallagher, 2017). It is not sufficient to characterize human perception as scaffolded through action; this picture must be further integrated, I suggest, because human sensibility is structurally embedded in a natural environment as well as in an already sociocultural niche to which the organism is constantly exposed. This basic exposure means that human organisms primarily feel their natural and social contexts as comfortable or menacing, as friendly, welcoming, annoying or troubling, as good places to live in or bad situations to escape from. Consequently, a fully embodied and embedded conception of sensibility should be regarded as the affective capacity to discriminate living conditions as favorable or adverse. This capacity could even be characterized as "aesthetic" (or "esthetic")[4] in James and Dewey's sense, which is to say as primarily rooted in organic feelings rather than in reflection or cognition.

Now, I would contend that the crucial point to be investigated is how this capacity to perceive the environment as favorable or hostile to life, which is already widespread in animal life, is reconfigured by the highly social environment peculiar to humans as well as by the cultural-linguistic characterization of the human niche. My suggestion is that human sensibility coincides with selective exposure to the environment and an active feeling capacity to discriminate between favorable and noxious aspects by organisms whose primary experience of the surrounding environment is sociocultural because of the organic conditions of emphasized interdependence from others characterizing the human form of life.[5] My claim is that the highly social and cultural-linguistic niche in which humans find themselves has a feedback action or loop effect on organic sensibility and contributes to reshaping it, by transforming it from animal to distinctively human sensibility. As a consequence, humans are able to feel a situation according to a significant variety of nuanced moods and emotions that goes beyond the binary opposition between favorable and adverse life conditions because of the culturally rich environment they have inherited from their predecessors. Thanks to the complex symbolic and linguistic resources of their interchanges with others, human beings became able to feel themselves and to focus on their own feelings and sense of themselves as distinct from their interlocutors. Humans' capacity to become self-reflective and acquire a sense of being a self cannot be assumed as a mere intellectual process, by interpreting self-consciousness chiefly as a form of metacognition directed toward the knower him- or herself. Animal sensibility primarily consists in feeling the relation between the environment and one's own life: human sensibility can focus on the feeling itself as well as on the self involved in a specific interaction thanks to the symbolic and linguistic resources characterizing our complex communicative interchanges, from turn-taking to grammar. This reconfiguration of sensibility by means of cultural-linguistic resources is even more evident in relation to the construction of a narrative self, one's own character and biography.

In a nutshell, I endorse a nonfoundational view of the relationships between sensibility—bodily affective experience—and language in the broad sense of the term, namely, the idea that the former cannot be considered an independently and previously configured faculty, which grounds language in the context of the human world. In contrast to the phenomenological tradition (Husserl 1973; Merleau-Ponty 2012; Dreyfus 2005; 2007) as well as from other scholars (Johnson 2007), I think that sensibility and language should be regarded as mutually shaping each other in the human world, rather than as opposed to and/or independent of each other, given that each organism's experience and conduct is not a simple product of its own either organic or cultural dispositions, but the result of its interchanges with the conditions of the environment its finds embedded in. In the human case, the environment is already laden with cultural, linguistic, and social practices that are active factors in the shaping of conduct when each individual is born. Hence, neither is an independently configured sensibility in human the ground for the development of language, nor is language the quasi–a priori condition of human sensibility—this, in a nutshell, is the meaning of my claim that their relationship is nonfoundational.

The next two sections of this chapter will be devoted to presenting some pragmatist resources for dealing with the qualitative aspects of experience and some philosophical problems raised by the introduction of subjective-objective dichotomies. Although important, these sections contain many historical and textual references to the Classical Pragmatists' philosophies. Hence, readers who have no strong interest in technicalities and reconstruction may wish to skip directly to the section 4, which can also be read on its own. The section 2 will focus on the Pragmatists' conception of experience as something broader and richer than cognition—because, in turn, cognition is understood as a specific phase within experience, responding to the needs and problems emerging from qualitative experience and ultimately returning to it. In this approach, perception through the senses and pure sense data are reframed within the context of inquiry, as features that are pointed out, discriminated, and isolated from a more holistic field of experience according to an idea, namely, the anticipation of the possible consequences of an action or a certain assumption. The section 3 will concentrate on arguments that can be derived from James and Dewey in order to deal with the qualitative richness of experience without running into the philosophical dead end represented by the idea of qualities as mere subjective features of experience. In light of the above-mentioned arguments which I find in the work of James and Dewey, I will propose some reasons in favor of my preference for the term "sensibility" over "primary experience." In section 4, I will thus provide a provisional definition of human sensibility based on the shift from an eminently cognitive approach to a broadly biological framework, centered on life's dependence and embeddedness in an environment. In section 5, I will contend that the notion of perception as skilled action involving movements and dynamism from its very beginning (Noë 2004) should be integrated by assuming that embodiment and affectivity are two intertwining sides of sensibility. Finally, section 6 will focus on the aforementioned issue related to the specificity of human sensibility, namely its being embedded in a deeply social and cultural-linguistic niche which has fortuitous yet irreversible feedback actions or loop effects on preverbal animal sensibility, thereby deeply reorganizing it.

2. Framing Cognition and Sensory Perception

My purpose in the current section is to present the resources provided by Classical Pragmatists in order to contextualize cognition within a richer and multifaceted conception of experience. From a pragmatist point of view, purely descriptive or nonevaluative sensory perception should be reframed as an analytic abstraction. As such, it is functional to the development of cognitive inquiries, that is, to forms of reflective experience engendered by a crisis in primarily qualitative experience and directed to finding a way out (Dewey 1991a).

The need to recognize the role of "gross experience" represented a central claim in Dewey's *Experience and Nature* (1981, 15, 24), matching James's insistence on the need to recognize the richness and vagueness of human experience (1981, 246; 1976, 21), as well as the reality of relations, whose consistency should not be neglected by taking discrete physical entities as the only standard for being real (1976, 22). For sure, this issue was part of an antiintellectualistic stance shared by the Classical Pragmatists—Peirce included—that ultimately led Dewey to favor a recovery of philosophy as a discipline focusing on the practical, moral, and political consequences that follow certain theoretical assumptions, rather than as a discipline exclusively dealing with its own (often artificial) problems (Dewey 1980).[6]

In both James's and Dewey's case, this kind of claim did not lead to a rejection of a theoretical attitude.[7] Instead, it pushed them, on the one hand, to find a more adequate—yet openly provisional—theoretical framework to deal with the qualitative, nonprimarily cognitive features of human beings' interactions with their environment (see Gavin 1992; Eames 2003) and, on the other hand, to circumscribe the role of cognition in experience.[8] In the Pragmatists' view, qualitative experience is not opposed to cognition; rather, the former is broader than the latter and they represent two different phases within the course of experience, which is to say within organic-environmental interactions. James's first attempt to outline a difference between the two, I suggest, is represented by his dynamic distinction between "knowledge by acquaintance" and "knowledge about," as well as by his constant attention to "affectional" (1976, 69) or "aesthetic" (1981, 1058) features in experience. In my opinion, Dewey's functional, that is, nonsubstantive, distinction between primary experience and knowing can be seen as a radicalization of James's scattered attempts in this direction. Probable further inspiration for Dewey's treatment of the qualitative or affective features of experience is represented by Peirce's theory of quality as well as by his hypothesis about a multifaceted conception of signs interpretants—emotive ones included (Calcaterra 2003; Innis 2011; Maddalena 2011; Innis 2014; Chevalier 2015). As frequently remarked by Rosa Calcaterra (2011, 413), the Classical Pragmatists de facto (in Peirce's case) or intentionally (in the case of James, Dewey, and Mead) conceived their philosophical work as a joint effort: James pushed some of Peirce's crucial insights in unexpected directions that, famously, were not appreciated by Peirce himself. Dewey instead freely radicalized some of their intuitions in a decisively naturalistic and antidualistic vein, often with George Mead's valuable collaboration, integrations, and corrections. In turn, I am proposing a further development of Dewey's ideas on this issue, by formulating a more explicitly nonfoundational theory of sensibility as eminently qualitative, aesthetic, or affective.

Retrospectively, then, I will derive a two-step strategy from these authors: first, a reframing of cognition within a broader conception of experience; second, a contextualization of mere sensory perception within inquiry, which is to say within cognitive interactions.

As hinted above, the first criticism of a dogmatic idea of knowing as something eminently constituted by explicit arguments and grounded in a direct grasp of reality can be traced back to James's distinction between knowledge by acquaintance and knowledge about in *The Principles* (1981, 216). The significance of James's distinction was probably misunderstood because of the apparently similar but more successful discrimination between knowledge by acquaintance and knowledge by description formulated by Bertrand Russell (1905; 1910/11; 1914). In introducing that difference, James was not guided—I argue—by the idea of finding an ultimate ground for propositional knowledge in the direct apprehension of objects, at least in the case of particulars (1910/11, 111). Rather, James was trying to recognize the legitimate place in our experience of the world of acquaintance, familiarity, and qualitative experience and feelings, as he puts it (1981, 218), beyond discursive knowledge, based on explicit conceptions and judgments. His characterization of knowledge by acquaintance is not focused on the presentation of objects as sense data or centered on the direct apprehension of categories (Russell 1910/11). In the words of *The Principles of Psychology*, acquaintance seems to be a kind of deeply embodied and affective experience.[9] Although within a still mentalistic framework, James declares that "The mental state usually distinguished as feeling are the emotions, and the sensations we get from skins, muscle, viscus, eye, ear, nose, and palate" (1981, 218). Memory is also conceived of as basically affective, as "endowed with a sort of warmth and intimacy that makes the perception of them [namely, of objects of memory] seem more like a process of sensation than like a thought" (James 1981, 218). Beyond describing knowledge by acquaintance as a sort of affective sensibility,[10] James also characterizes its relationship to knowledge about in continuistic and relative terms: despite the apparent dichotomy between feelings and thought, he claims that "[f]eelings are the germ and starting point of cognition, thoughts the developed tree" (1981, 218), as well as that they are "relative terms," if we consider how "the human mind practically exerts them" (1981, 217). In order to further clarify what continuity means for the Pragmatists, I would say that continuity between sensibility and cognition involves the assumption that the latter derives from the former and that cognition reciprocally contributes to changing sensibility. Hence, their relations are mutual or circular rather that linear and foundational. Furthermore, continuity means that feeling is always a more or less strong component of a cognitive process, be it in the form of interest and desire for something that is not present (Mead 2011, 27) or in the form of a pervasive quality directing the process of inquiry (Dewey 1988b). Finally, continuity means that although one can make a distinction between more cognitively oriented phases and mainly qualitative relations within an experience, the borders one traces are relative to a specific context and functional to pursuing a peculiar goal—they are not fixed a priori.

Dewey was inspired by this insight of James's (Dewey 1980; 2004; 1981), and I believe that he finally made the decisive leap by abandoning the mentalistic approach and recontextualizing the difference against a clearer naturalistic background—Darwin represented a key influence in this shift. Dewey's approach was based on an externalized idea of experience, conceived of as the interactions between organisms and the environment they depend on and are part of, consequently exonerating James of any suspicion of residual subjectivism.[11] Moreover, Dewey removed "knowledge" from the label "knowledge from acquaintance," by characterizing affective and embodied sensibility as primary or immediate experience and distinguishing it from reflection.

According to Dewey, from an empirical perspective it cannot be denied that humans primarily experience situations as "arresting and engrossing" (1981, 22), feel their surroundings as risky and fearful (1981, 43), and tend to be absorbed by what is happening around them, whether by suffering things and people or enjoying their presence. In Dewey and James's lexicon,[12] we tend to experience things aesthetically (Dewey 1981, 72, 74, 77), that is, not as a means to refer to something else and to prepare for further engagement but as focuses of direct enjoyment and suffering (Dewey 1981, 76). This is the difference, for Dewey, between knowing and having or feeling, that is between considering things and aspects of experience with reference to postponed purposes, on the one hand, and things as having a direct impact on our own existence, on the other hand. Probably, Dewey was also inspired by a heterodox interpretation of Peirce's conception of secondness: primary experience is not immediate—according to an understanding of "immediate" as excluding any relation. Rather, it implies a direct or dyadic relation, namely, the environment's impact on the organism's life, a relation that in Dewey's case is not simply causally efficient, but has affective significance for the favorable or adverse meaning a given circumstance can have in relation to organic life.

With an implicit criticism of the empirical tradition he has inherited from James, Dewey notes: "Empirically, the existence of objects of direct grasp, possession, use and enjoyment cannot be denied. Empirically, things are poignant, tragic, beautiful, humorous, settled, disturbed, comfortable, annoying, barren, harsh, consoling, splendid, fearful; are such immediately and in their own right and behalf. If one takes advantage of the word esthetic in a wider sense than that of application to the beautiful and the ugly, esthetic quality, immediate, final or self-enclosed, indubitably characterize natural situations as they empirically occur" (Dewey 1981, 82).

As already stated,[13] Dewey envisaged cognition as a specific phase of experience: it is a crucial part of experience, yet it is neither paradigmatic nor primary (1981, 28). In particular, as stressed in the introduction to the *Essays in Experimental Logic* (2004), cognition is an intermediate stage, arising from a crisis within primarily qualitative experience and responding to it. The results of an inquiry must also be regarded as intermediate, which is to say, as the outcomes of an inquiry rather than as the true nature of the everyday things people find themselves dealing with (see Dewey 1981, 10 ff.;1988a, 10). Human interactions with the environment become cognitive when situations become indeterminate, when it is difficult to know how to act, when one's usually responsive habits do not work and one needs to reconsider them analytically and come up with a new creative hypothesis to solve the impasse (Dewey 1991a, 109 ff.). Experience becomes reflective in the sense that one must return to a previous experience, originally perceived as a whole, and make analytic distinctions within it in order to imagine a possible new synthetic determination of a situation troubling us in one way or another. In contrast to "having" or "feeling," "knowing" for Dewey involves the establishment of triadic relations, with a provisional suspension of the immediate enjoyment or suffering of a specific situation—that is, of direct life-environment relations—in favor of further references to other things, events, and situations paving the way to interpretative chains, according to Peirce's semiotic approach.

Sense data must be set in such a context of inquiry: they are the products of reflective experience, which is to say of a return to the elements constituting a currently problematic situation, a return accomplished through the analytic selection and isolation of distinct features within a primary holistic situation that is qualitatively felt as a whole (Dewey,

1991a, 72 ff.). The facts of the case are selected according to a guiding idea, which Dewey conceives of as a solving hypothesis that involves a certain degree of imagination and risk—for both Dewey and Peirce, ideas are not primarily the simple generalization of inductions. Consequently, sense data are taken rather than given: they are actively selected through an analytic process governed by a synthetic, creative hypothesis, which anticipates the possible consequences of an action or even theory.

This does not mean that sense data should be understood as the mere construction of the inquiring subject in an idealistic vein. On the contrary, "the facts of the case" (Dewey, 1991a, 113) are the real existential material of an interaction—as real as the qualitative situation we are part of and that has an impact on us—but they are functionally correlated with an inquiring hypothesis and an inquiring activity. As such, they are not the primary givens constituting reality and our experience of it, but, rather, are the real products of our active engagement with existential conditions, ultimately guided by vital interests.[14] To return to the example of a train, my perception of the overcrowded coach as disturbing and my seeing a free seat in a hidden corner, trying to reach it, and making my way through the crowd of people are real constituents of a situation. Specific sense data as well as neural paths within the brain can and must be discriminated and isolated from a more complex experiential field according to particular heuristic hypothesis. However, they should not be taken as the first or ultimate elements of reality and as having ontological primacy over the objects and events of primarily qualitative experience. The crucial problem does not lie in an allegedly idealistic form of constructivism, but in the assumption that components and outcomes of cognitive processes representing intermediate phases of experience are more real than qualitatively felt situations, relations, and events (Dewey 1991a, 73; 1991b).

From this point of view, Dewey suggested a historical contextualization of the typically modern restriction of perception to sensory perception: the words *perception* and *perceive* usually had a broader spectrum of meaning in the past—as they still have in ordinary language today. They suffered from a restriction to the properly sensory field within modern philosophy and the birth of experimental science, where they were assigned a privileged epistemic status. However, both this restriction and this status can and must be reconsidered (Dewey, 1984d).[15]

To sum up, cognitive processes—be they resolutions of practical, everyday problems, or formulations of highly sophisticated theories—

emerge out of a preexisting web of thick relations between events, individuals, histories, natural aspects, and cultural meanings that are already given: "the intellectual element is set in a context which is noncognitive and which holds within it in suspense a vast complex of other qualities and things that in the experience itself are objects of esteem or aversion, of decision, of use, of suffering, of endeavor and revolt, not of knowledge" (Dewey 2004, 3).

Cognition springs from the difficulties encountered in these preexisting, qualitatively saturated contexts and responds to them through processes of analytical discrimination that require both synthetic gestures and the imagination to identify a solution (Maddalena 2015). The effectiveness of these processes can only be measured through a return to the nonreflective phases of experience, through the crystallization of the results of previous inquiries into habits of action and beliefs, into new gestures and words, into more or less shared practices and unwritten norms—that is, into a pervasive material culture, rather than a body of propositional contents that are first developed and stored in the alleged inner theater of the mind.

To conclude this section, the distinction between primarily qualitative experience and cognition entails the risk of indulging in a still foundational theory of sensibility, although no longer from an epistemological perspective. In my opinion, the acknowledgment that cognition is anchored in life should not lead us to endorse a hierarchical, one-way conception of the relations between sensibility and a more reflective engagement with the environment. Rather, I think that although primarily felt experience represents the source and the point of arrival of cognitive practices, we should take the peculiar form of life humans are dealing with into serious account. The point is that human forms of life are naturally social and naturally characterized by meaningful, linguistic, and normative practices, whose results are steeped and habitualized in our sensibility, which is constantly reshaped by the kind of naturally cultural and social environment human beings live in. In other words, it is a consequence of the naturally cultural and social character of the human environmental niche that should be taken into account: even the so-called prelinguistic baby is fully embedded in this kind of niche from birth, or even before birth. Hence, by adopting a coherent conception of cultural naturalism and emergence, I think we should favor a circular view of the relations between sensibility and reflective experience, rather than a linear one, assuming that they mutually shape each other—and, consequently, that human sensibility is not equal to nonhuman animals' sensibility, at least at the moment. This claim will be further explored in the following sections of the current chapter (particularly section 6), as well as in the last chapter of this volume.

3. Qualitative Experience beyond the Subjective/Objective Divide

Both James and Dewey were perfectly aware of the problems connected with their claim to be dealing philosophically with the acknowledgment that "The world in which we immediately live, that in which we strive, succeed, and are defeated is pre-eminently a qualitative world" (Dewey 1988b, 243). They both knew they had to face the long-standing problem of the allegedly merely subjective status of quality, when choosing to employ the old conceptual tool of "quality" to deal with sensibility, understood as the primarily aesthetic or affective experience of situations, things, and individuals. They had to deal once again with the empirical tradition they believed to have inherited and which they sought to radicalize. According to the standard narrative, thanks to Galileo Galilei's revolutionary approach to science, Locke had been able to draw a distinction between primary and secondary properties and had irrevocably ascribed so-called secondary qualities to the subjective realm. In a nutshell, James and Dewey thought that the allegedly merely subjective character of quality is an artificial philosophical problem or a theoretical dead end that should be disentangled and dissolved, because it hinders rather than aids our understanding of experience. James's first contribution is represented by his argument in favor of the reality of relations, while Dewey's decisive contribution, in my view, consists in his attempt to anchor the reality of qualitative experience in the radical exposure of human life to the environment, that is, in the broadly biological basis of the structural dependence of human living beings from the natural and naturally social environment they belong to and are constituted by. Condensed in a short formula, the place of the qualitative is moved from the mind of the subject to the engagement between organism and environment. A further important contribution I draw from Dewey is the adoption of an adverbial conception of qualities, which assumes that they are not a specific (and very problematic) kind of entity (located somewhere, possibly in the mind), but that, on the contrary, they are real modes of real relations taking place between organisms and their environment.

Consequently, the issue I wish to tackle now by means of a pragmatist approach is whether these primarily qualitative-affective or even aesthetic meanings (to use James and Dewey's lexicon) of our experience should be simply abandoned because of their allegedly merely subjective character. Are qualia real properties of perceived things or are they mere subjective projections of the perceiver's mind? Very roughly, this is how the issue has been traditionally framed, from the empiricist school down to Daniel Dennett (1998). But in a pragmatist vein the crucial issue becomes: is this the right question to pose? Does the long-standing philosophical crux of experiential qualities stem from an attempt to illegitimately extend some functional distinctions that are normally drawn for specific purposes and within specific contexts?

For example, it makes sense to say that the perception of water temperature is subjective when, at the seaside, two bathers have a different approach to swimming: one feels cold, hesitates to enter the sea and start swimming, while the other feel perfectly comfortable and makes fun of her friend for being afraid of taking a dip. An example of more serious subjective differences might be a verbal joke that is perceived as funny, although over the top, by one interlocutor and as offensive by another. In both cases, the distinction of one subjective feature is important but it does not mean that the feature itself is merely private and less true or real than other components of the two situations: it marks a difference both in the agent's behavior and in his partner's conduct. More significantly, it is incorrect to draw a general epistemic difference between merely qualitative and subjective factors, on the one hand, and objective and quantifiable characters, on the other hand, from specific distinctions within particular interchanges having a meaning that is functional within those particular contexts, not fixed once and for all.[16]

As hinted at a few lines above, the distinction between primary and secondary properties has its roots in the intersection between Galileo's foundation of the experimental method in physics and John Locke's project of an empirical theory of knowledge. The ground for this distinction was laid by Descartes's foundation of certainty on the unquestionability of the *ego cogito*, as well as on the opposition between *res cogitans* and *res extensa*—against the background of the more general attitude toward the *Mathematizierung* (quantification) of nature characterizing the emergence of modern science, as strongly emphasized by Edmund Husserl in *Crisis* of *European Sciences and Transcendental Phenomenology* and by Alexander Koyré in *From the Closed World to the Infinite Universe* (see Lanfredini 2018). In the twentieth century, the problem of qualia basically shares the usual binary setting which assumes so-called secondary qualities as mere subjective features that must be considered devoid of any cognitive value: they should either be translated into quantifiable properties in order to be assumed within a scientific framework or be abandoned when the strategy of "Quining qualia" cannot be realized (Dennett 1988).

Dewey was interested in dissolving the artificial setting of the problem of quality in experience, as can also be seen from his attempt to give a different reading of Locke's thesis on the historic-textual plane, as well as from his claim in favor of a qualitative and affective characterization of thought (1984f; 1988b) on a more theoretical level. In an essay dating back to 1926 (1984e), he claimed that it was misleading to interpret Locke's distinction between primary and secondary qualities as an opposition between physical and mental properties, between objective and subjective attributes (1984e, 143). Instead, Locke discriminated qualities with reference to substances, by drawing a threefold distinction, rather than a dual one. First, for him there are intrinsic or essential properties, namely, attributes that essentially inhere in a substance per se and constitute it, like solidity, extension, figure, and mobility (1984e, 144). A second class is that of relational properties, which characterize the connections between different substances, according to two different modes: some tend to produce effects like weight or acceleration in other things, while others produce "qualities like pain, griping, color, noise, taste by acting upon the senses of an organic body" (1984e, 145). Dewey suggested that the problem lies in Locke's incapacity to give up a "fixed separation between intrinsic essential properties and relational extrinsic ones" (1984e, 145), while emphasizing that science in his own time already treated so-called first qualities (for example, motion, and volume) as relational properties.

This way of reading Locke's text, in my view, clearly reflects the influence of James's approach in his *Essays in Radical Empiricism*, which nourished Dewey's interest in the qualitative dimension of experience. In those essays, James's revision of Empiricism is based on two complementary strategies: on the one hand, he strongly argues for the reality of relations ("A World of Pure Experience"); on the other hand, he excludes that the difference between subjective and objective features in experience might be an ontological one, founded on discontinuous classes of substances.

Instead, he regards the distinction itself as a functional and contextual one ("Does Consciousness Exist?"), particularly with reference to affective experiential aspects ("The Place of Affective Facts in a World of Pure Experience"). I would argue that James's radical empiricism also rests on a third pillar, namely, the shift from consciousness understood as a privileged subjective dimension (as in *The Principles*) to experience understood as a continuous flow, that is as something which disproves the alleged primacy of either the noetic pole or the noematic pole, to use phenomenological vocabulary (see Lanfredini 2017). Nonetheless, I will not deal with this last point in general but only in relation to James's suggestion to consider the distinction between subjective and objective, or mental and physical aspects, as a functional and contextual discrimination rather than as an ontological divide.

James's position on the reality of relations is well known: our experience of the world does not authorize us to infer from it that reality is exclusively composed of discreet things, "loose and separate," and having "no manner of connections," according to his reading of Hume (1976, 43).[17] This idea is an unwarranted assumption that is not coherent with the principle of empiricism requiring us to keep to what we experience and forbidding us to search for extra-experiential reasons to explain what happens in experience itself. A more faithful account of experience must include the acknowledgment that connections between things and events are experienced as being as real as the things themselves. Both disjunctions and conjunctive relations are constitutive parts of the fabric of experience. Neglecting them means substituting an oversimplified image of reality as exclusively composed of separate entities to the complex web of interactions forming life in its superabundance, that is, applying misleading criteria to a field where they are incongruous (James 1976, 21; cf. Perissinotto 2019b). The decisive step, I argue, would be accomplished by Dewey by means of his disambiguated characterization of experience in terms of life: experience is the process of interaction unfolding between an organism and the environment of which it is part and which it contributes to changing (1989, 19). The organism is not a fixed and complete entity prior to its interactions with the environment: there is no "before," no beginning of an engagement with the environment for an already determined organism at a certain time, because the organism actually configures itself throughout the course of its dynamic interchanges with the environment. On the other hand, the environment is not already completely defined once and for all, prior to and independently of the advent of organic life, but it is continually modified by the processes and events taking place in it. Consequently, relations are assumed as real components of experience, contributing to forging entities and individuals in their dynamic and mutual dependence on the environment.[18]

In his *Essays*, James too adopted a deflationary approach to the distinction between subjective and objective features in experience, as a way to avoid the ontological gap between different kinds of substances and Cartesian dilemmas about ways to overcome it. The frequent fluctuations in the way we understand the status of so-called affective facts is assumed as an argument in support of the thesis that the difference between subjective and objective features of experience is dependent on the practices and uses one makes of these words: they can change according to specific contexts of reference, instead of being attributed a priori (1976, 71). James explicitly mentions emotions as an example: folk psychology is likely to attribute emotions to the psychic realm and philosophy often tends to radicalize this kind of intuition by attributing to emotions and feelings an interior characterization, in principle closed off from others individuals. However, it would be odd to deny the strong organic components of fear and pain, for example; their organic basis can be considered the mere output of a mental state only by (1) assuming a dualistically metaphysical framework and (2) dogmatically assigning psychic features primacy over bodily changes, as James critically notes in *The Principles* (1981, 1058 ff.). The class of moral and aesthetic appreciations is also significant. My indignation at a racist epithet used by a politician is mental insofar as it characterizes my own feelings and way of thinking, but it is also objectively grounded in the real existential conditions in which it emerged. A similar case is represented by beauty, as testified by the long-standing debate in philosophy of art regarding the subjective or objective status of beauty. For sure, beauty is in the mind of the observer, considering differences in taste and culture with reference both to works of art and to the kind of people one is attracted to. However, it is problematic to support the view that the beauty of a painting or a sculpture could be separated and considered independently from the quality of the paint, marble, or bronze in which the work is embodied.[19]

In my view, those incipient Jamesian insights were definitely radicalized by Dewey, who did not hesitate to give a complete naturalistic account of experience—as already mentioned above—and characterized its qualitative-affective features as ways in which real interactions between organisms and the environment occur. Consequently, a conception of quality can be derived from this as an adverbial (i.e., not substantive) feature characterizing the occurrence of real organic-environmental relations. Quality is not a mental entity whose objective correlate would consequently be epistemically and ontologically problematic.[20] More precisely, it concerns the mode in which a relation is directly had or enjoyed, basically differing from the ways in which one knows something, according to Dewey. In both cases, relations are taking place: in the case of primarily qualitative-affective experience, which is to say sensibility, the relation happens directly between an organism and its environment—the relation consists in the direct, stronger or weaker, impact of the circumstances on the organism's own life. Dewey also speaks of primary experience as characterizing events that are immediately brought to their consummation. In the case of knowing, the more or less overwhelming impact of the environment on the organism—the consummatory final phase of an interchange—is provisionally delayed, and the direct relation of the environment to the organism is temporally suspended in order to enable the development of new chains of relations between things. As already mentioned, knowing involves triadic relations, as opposed to dual relations and different ways in which things can be meaningful (see previous section).

Moreover in this naturalized view, sensibility or feeling is already significant and laden with a proto-value connected with the life of the organism; in knowing a basically affective-qualitative significance is transformed into a meaning, decisively extending the range of possible actions and behavior of the human organism in her/his environment. Consequently, the distance from a conception of sense-perception as conveying a mere presentation of particular objects as well as of cognition as perception plus meaning is now evidently great (Dreon 2012, 32 ff.). For Dewey (as well as for Mead) a crucial contention is to deny that our ordinary experience of things is primarily constituted by a purely descriptive level, recording naked sensory data that would be ascribed an affective or qualitative meaning, or existential value, only later. Consider the case of sugar as an example: in perceiving something as sweet, I do not first register purely descriptive sensory data and then ascribe a certain quality to them, as if perception were basically made up of two different steps, the first one mirroring an (objective) state of things out there through the senses and the second one consisting in the projection of a (subjective) value onto it (Nussbaum 2001, 19 ff.). On the contrary, I immediately experience something as sweet: perception is already qualitatively laden, in the sense that what I feel in this case is pleasure, that is, a positive relation between a certain aspect of the environment and my own life. For Dewey and the Classical Pragmatists, perception is already charged with an affectively, qualitatively, or aesthetically oriented proto-evaluation that is meaningful with reference to the perceiver's own life. To return to my example of an overcrowded train coach, when my neighbor's body accidentally bumps into my own, I do not first register a neutral tactile impact primarily through the sense of touch, and only later attribute some value to the other's action on my body. On the contrary, I am immediately annoyed by or pleased with that casual contact that carries on a (more or less) primitive significance for my own life.

Moreover, characterizing qualities and affective features as modes of direct enjoyment or suffering of the organism because of specific environmental conditions allows us to overcome the problems deriving from dogmatically assumed distinctions between the allegedly subjective, mental, or psychical realm as distinct from the physical world. Sweetness is neither a property of sugar per se, nor the result of a subjective projection; rather, it is the peculiar output of a real relation occurring between an organism endowed with taste buds and environmental circumstances—including physical things such as sugar itself and dietary habits.

4. Sensibility: A Provisional Definition

In *Art as Experience*, Dewey recommended a shift from an ontology of art tailored to the works of art exhibited in museums to the field of basic biological assumptions about experience and life.[21] My suggestion is that a somewhat similar change of approach should take place with reference to human sensibility: the focus should shift from considering sensibility as the ground of cognition—assumed, in its turn, as the mental representation of an independent reality—to sensibility as a structural dimension of animal life in general and of human life, more specifically. This could be a good way to approach the issue, although Dewey shows no penchant for the word *sensibility* preferring as he does to speak of experience in general. In his 1925 book, he instead speaks of primary or immediate experience, to refer to the qualitative, affective, or aesthetic dimension of human experience and behaviors.

Let's take a look at the "biological commonplaces" that Dewey (1989, 20) invites the reader to focus on in order to understand what art is and what role it has—or could have—in our practices. He says that we should consider the essential conditions of life out of which artistic practices arise, that is, that we should take into account the fact that life always unfolds in an environment with which an organism is forced to interact in order to survive. "No creature lives merely under its skin; its subcutaneous organs are means of connection with what lies beyond its bodily frame, and to which, in order to live, it must adjust itself" (1989, 50). The environment—Dewey continues—both exposes each living being to dangers and gives it chances to find resources allowing it to live and flourish. "[T]he career and destiny of a living being," he says, "are bound up with interchanges with its environment, not externally but in the most intimate way" (1989, 19); in other words, environmental resources are constitutive contributions to the life of each organism. For this reason, life consists of successive phases, rhythmically alternating moments in which the living organism falls into step with its environment and phases in which this dynamic equilibrium is broken and the organism has to act in order to recover unison (Vara Sánchez, 2021). To this conclusion, Dewey adds an interesting remark, namely, that no new recovery allows a simple return to the previous state because the current point of arrival "is enriched by the state of disparity and resistance through which it has successfully passed" (1989, 19)—a remark showing the deep influence of Hegel's dialectic on his appropriation of Darwin's thought (Rorty 1980, 362; 1998; Margolis 2002; Saito 2005, 17 ff.).

Now, I would argue that the above-mentioned biological commonplaces also constitute the main assumptions for a pragmatist understanding of sensibility. In a few words, the shift required is from an epistemological framework, where the main relationship is between cognition and sensibility, to a—broadly speaking—biological stance, where sensibility is seen from the perspective of life and of organisms' constitutive dependence on their environment. By approaching sensibility as something rooted in life and environmental conditions, I suggest characterizing it as basically involving organisms that are selectively exposed to the environment and capable of discriminating between favorable and noxious aspects of it, between dangers and opportunities to grow, move, act, and improve life. Analytically, two strictly embroiled aspects can be distinguished: on the one hand, sensibility involves a form of exposure, vulnerability, or passivity of the organism whose very life, survival, and possibility to flourish depend on the environment entering its constitution in a variety of ways—from nourishment, oxygen, and heat to protection and companionship. The word *constitution*, occurring in the previous statement, should be interpreted in realistic terms: both food and parental care, for example, are real—albeit very different—factors contributing to the constitution of each organism, whose life would otherwise be fatally compromised and cease owing to the lack of environmental resources. On the other hand, sensibility includes a form of orientation, selectivity, and discrimination, that is a more active disposition rooted in a wide range of features and habits: from the physiology of the organism to physical proximity and affective intimacy, from bodily movement to more or less powerful tools through which movement itself can be enhanced, from material and cultural needs, and interests to habits of conduct and thought. Consequently, sensibility already involves a form of proto-evaluation of what is happening around the organism—an evaluation having a primarily affective-embodied characterization rather than a discursive one, based on explicit reasons and norms, and having the life of the organism as the issue at stake. Affective valence, I would argue, is not a value supervening on the merely descriptive recording of a state of affairs, because organic life cannot be indifferent to the environmental conditions in which and through which it occurs and develops.[22] In other words, affective valence—that is, the significance of the environmental impact on the life of the organism—is always there, even if it can be stronger or weaker, depending on the context.[23] As such, sensibility is a constant and pervasive feature of human experience and cannot be limited to some special moments, when emotions are more intense and there is a kind of special leading feeling that can be recognized as marking a distinct event in one's experience. Consequently, as I will suggest in the following chapter, a pragmatist approach to emotions should be framed within a more comprehensive notion of sensibility as a permanent feature of human experience, rather than the other way round.

However, as already stated, Dewey did not use the word *sensibility* to characterize the eminently aesthetic or affective phase of human beings' interactions with the world, and preferred to use expressions characterizing human experience as primarily qualitative. To be more precise, he reserved the word *feeling* and *sensitivity* for characterizing the capacity to discriminate according to a living organism's interests and sense of what is good and valuable among nonhuman animals whose body is capable of locomotion (1981, 197). With Mead, then, and diverging from the phenomenological tradition, he strongly emphasized the continuity between humans and other living forms. This continuistic assumption, nonetheless, did not prevent Dewey from considering the peculiarity of human experience. Hence, in the above-quoted pages of *Experience and Nature*, he claimed that in human organisms feelings become meanings through the emergence of language and reflective inquiry (1981, 198). This kind of change will be explored in detail in the last chapter of this book. For the moment, it is sufficient to note that at this point Dewey introduces the distinction between primary experience (1981, 15), which is characterized by directly enjoyed or suffered things and situations (1981, 70 ff.), and reflective experience or knowing, which consists in an analytical reconsideration of the qualitative whole of a previous experience. An experience becomes reflective when an interaction presents a problem and one does not know what to do and how to behave, because habitual modes of action do not work and the situation becomes indeterminate (1991a, 109). Complementarily, the results of a cognitive process are incorporated into primarily qualitative experience, which is continually reshaped, and either enriched or impoverished, by appropriating and sedimenting the outcomes of previous inquiries. In a nutshell and in other words, human sensibility is dynamically and continuously reconfigured by cultural practices.

Dewey preferred expressions characterizing human experience as primarily qualitative, I think, because he was opposing the so-called intellectual fallacy: the typically modern assumption that experience is an eminently cognitive affair, that things around us are objects to be known by a subject representing them in his mind (1981, 28), and that other people are probably other subjects entertaining eminently cognitive relationships with objects and other individuals.

By contrast, I propose to use the word "sensibility" in order to speak of the not primarily cognitive context of humans' interactions with their environment, holding "within it a vast complex of other qualities and things that in the experience itself are objects of esteem or aversion, of decision, of use, of suffering, of endeavour and revolt, not of knowledge" (2004, 3).

I favor this linguistic choice for a number of reasons. The first is that I assume the traditional ambivalence of the word in many languages as a positive feature.[24] *Sensibility* has been traditionally used both to refer to sensory experience and to characterize an affective engagement with the world, capable of a discrimination based on feelings, desires, longings and refusals, as frequently pointed out by James (1981, 1058 ff.; 1976, 69 ff.). Thanks to this double field of reference, *sensibility* can convey the idea that our fully embodied experience of the environment is primarily affective, qualitative, or aesthetic (cf. Johnson 2007), and that bodily perception is not something that is essentially conveyed by the senses alone, with the possible later addition of affective values. On the contrary, it is basically cross-modal and affectively or aesthetically configured from the very beginning, because life is always biased and selectively oriented: it cannot be indifferent to the conditions in which it occurs (Dewey 1981, 194 ff.). In spite of being a source of problems, the ambiguity of the word *sensibility* represents, in my eyes, a corroboration of the assumption that embodiment and affectivity are primarily embroiled in human experience and can be discriminated for specific purposes only at a later stage. Affectivity, in other words, is the other side of human organisms' radical embeddedness in a natural and naturally social environment. To be affected by something or someone—as the traditional emphasis of the verb *affizieren* in classical German philosophy suggests—does not primarily or only mean registering purely descriptive sense data that must be processed at a later stage, whether by the intellect or by a computing brain (or, more recently, through predictive coding). On the contrary, it means feeling or having something as important to one's own life, be it dangerous, annoying, disturbing, or joyful. From this perspective, radical embodiment means considering the senses and the whole body in their basic connections with life and its structural dependence on an environment, rather than as a means to collect information for the purpose of representing an allegedly merely external reality. Like other animals, humans are sensible beings and exist in continuity with them. However, they are at the same time sensible in a different way, that is, their sensibility differs both qualitatively and quantitatively because their form of life is structurally more exposed to the environment they belong to: humans are more immature and vulnerable at birth than other mammals, their modes of behavior are largely indeterminate and plastic, and they are able to attune their lives to the most varied material conditions.[25]

Humans are also sensible beings in a way that's different from other animals from a qualitative point of view—at least at the moment, owing to the contingent course their form of life has taken up until now. The reason for this is that the natural environment to which humans are constitutively exposed is socially and culturally shared before their birth, and is continuously reshaped by their doings and suffering in it. Both

Dewey (in *Human Nature and Conduct*) and Mead (2011, 73) frequently emphasize this point—what later came to be described as neoteny in evolutionary biology—probably based on their reading of Fiske and Chauncey Wright (Parravicini 2012).

Notwithstanding the different use of the word *cognition* and *experience*, a fruitful connection can be drawn between the view of "sensibility" I am currently suggesting and the notion of "constitutive dynamic coupling" (Gallagher 2017, 6–12; 2018b, 429 ff.; 2018a; Kirchhoff 2015). Gallagher introduces a diachronic perspective within the notion of structural coupling (Clark & Chalmers 1998), claiming that the dependence of the entire organism (brain and body included) on its environment—and vice versa—is both causal and constitutive. Organic-environmental relations are both causal and constitutive, which is to say that they are interdependent because all kinds of resources (neurological, organic, and environmental) interact on different diachronic levels to allow both the self-individuation of the human organism and the continuous reshaping of our natural and naturally cultural environment.[26] To put it in pragmatist terms, if we assume that neither organisms nor their environment are completely determined before and apart from their interactions, causality and constitution appear to be strictly intertwined. Interpreting Dewey, Thomas Alexander (1987, 135) has clearly stated that the distinction between an organism and its environment should be considered to take place dynamically and mutually: on the one hand, the organism's life depends on resources and energies of the environment; on the other hand, the organism is an integral factor of an already existing yet still *in fieri* environment that is continuously reshaped to a greater or lesser extent by organic actions and behavior (Skorburg 2013). Consequently, the equilibrium between the so-called operational closure of dynamic systems and precariousness (Di Paolo & Thompson 2014) would be altered from a pragmatist perspective. Traditionally, enactivists insist on the autonomy of living systems, considered as operationally closed webs of mutually conditioning and enabling processes. From this viewpoint, the human body is understood as "a number of overlapping autonomous systems, such as the nervous system and the immune system" (Di Paolo & Thompson 2014, 76). Even the precariousness of a system is strictly correlated to autonomy: it is envisaged as the characteristic whereby a system will decay and stop in the absence of one of its enabling conditions (Di Paolo &Thompson 2014, 72). By contrast, from a Deweyan perspective, the emphasis is on organic precariousness, understood as life's structural dependence on an environment, rather than on autonomy as a structural feature of organisms: Dewey's form of cultural naturalism focuses on the web of conjoint interdependence and loop effects between organic and environmental energies, even if the times and extent of this mutual dependence can vary dramatically. More specifically, the Pragmatists' emphasis on life's structural exposure to an uncertain environment reveals the roots of human sensibility. Consequently, uncertainty will be radically reinterpreted in affective, rather than mainly epistemological terms, as anchored in the natural condition of precariousness characterizing the life of each organism, which must always strive to maintain itself and flourish because there are no guarantees from the environment that it will endure forever. This is a second reason to favor the adoption of the word *sensibility*, that is, to stress that our engagement with the world occurs against the background of this feeling of precariousness and exposure rooted in our natural dependence on extra-organic resources—social and cultural factors included.

The other side of the coin is that emphasizing the anchoring of sensibility in the natural and naturally cultural conditions of human life makes it possible to reassert a form of nondogmatic realism as a peculiar feature of Classical Pragmatism (Hildebrand 2003; Pihlström 1998), which is to say a form of realism immune from the metaphysical claim that reality is out there, completely and definitely equipped before and regardless of any human intervention. Pragmatism does away with the traditional dichotomy between an independent subject and a merely external reality, completely defined, once and for all, before any human engagement with it. Instead, it supports the idea of living beings as integral parts of their environment, which they depend on to sustain their own life, while at the same time contributing to changing it to a greater or lesser degree. Assuming this mutual codetermination between organisms and the environment should not prevent us from recognizing a strong asymmetry between individual or group life and the material conditions in which this takes place and which primarily affect living organisms as menacing, resistant, or overwhelming. Far from being a merely subjective realm, sensibility manifests itself as a way to reaffirm the reality of our relations with the world and of the word itself on a level that is not primarily cognitive or epistemic, but is anchored in material life conditions as felt, suffered, or enjoyed.

By further developing this fruitful engagement with the current debate, it must be recalled that enactivism strongly favors a broad conception of cognition as sense-making, emphasizing an idea of experience as an active engagement with the world (Varela, Thompson, & Rosch 1991). Essentially rejecting a representationalist view of cognition as a kind of subjective mirroring of external reality, enactivists assume sense-making as a basic feature of organic life. Sense-making is an organism's "transformation of a world into a place of salience, meaning and value—into an environment (Umwelt) in the proper biological sense of the word" (Thompson & Stapleton 2009, 25); this interactive process is regarded as common to both bacteria and human minds. While sharing the idea of a structurally mutual dependence between living beings and their environment, the Pragmatists strongly affirm the need to circumscribe cognition within a broader conception of experience: inquiry is a kind of reflective interaction taking place when a situation is indeterminate, when a person actually does not know what to do, and there is uncertainty regarding how to engage with new circumstances challenging habitual forms of behavior. On my part, I suggest maintaining and improving the pragmatist functional and circular distinction between sensibility and cognition, which is to say between more qualitative phases of living interactions and reflective inquiring behavior. This operative and contextual distinction presents the advantage of discriminating between different modes of interaction (Dreon 2019a) that would be flattened by too pervasive a use of cognition and sense-making. It applies to both human and nonhuman animals, as well as to every kind of human active capacity to adapt to an environment and rule it out (Di Paolo & Thompson 2014, 73). Moreover, with reference to Dewey's use of the expression "primary" or "immediate" experience, recourse to the word *sensibility* might be helpful, in my view, to avoid any temptation to consider this distinction in a foundational way and to explicitly assume a circularity or a dialectical interdependence between sensibility and cognition as a characteristic of the human environment.

The conception of sensibility I derive from the Classical Pragmatists basically converges with Giovanna Colombetti's idea of primary affectivity "permeating" the mind (2014, 1)—that is, sense-making, conceived of as a way in which organisms behave in an environment, according to the meanings that the various aspects of that environment acquire for the organisms' lives (2014, 17, 18). As she puts it, primordial affectivity should not be conceived of as an intermittent phenomenon, episodically added to an allegedly purely sensory perception of the world:

"it is a broader phenomenon that permeates the mind, necessarily and not merely contingently" (2014, 1). Affective neuroscientists generally consider emotions and moods as their essential objects of study, as they episodically affect "an otherwise neutral, nonaffective mind" (2014, 20). On the contrary, her enactive approach converges with Dewey's idea that sensibility is structural for living beings, who are always biased because their own life is always at stake to a greater or lesser extent. Emotions and individual feelings can be assumed as more or less distinct events within experience, but sensibility is always there because being alive means being exposed to an environment in one way or another. Concern, interest and purpose, as Mead clearly saw (2011, 27 ff.), are primarily affective aspects of our conduct, rooted in our dependence on a natural as well as naturally social environment. Interest in the basic and positive sense of finding oneself in the middle (from Latin *"inter esse"*) of a situation, be it perilous or favorable, has naturalistic roots in life's dependence on an environment (cf. Santarelli 2019).

This naturalistic framework represents a decisive difference compared to the partially close idea of *Befindlichkeit* strongly supported by Heidegger (1962). Like the phenomenological view of *Befindlichkeit*, a pragmatist approach to sensibility assumes that affectivity is a structural component of human beings insofar as they always find themselves embedded in a world and depending on it. Heideggerian phenomenology, moreover, already emphasized that finding oneself in a specific mood, feeling, or emotion should not be considered a private feature of human experience, enclosing the individual in her or his own subjectivity (Hatzimoysis 2012, 215; Freeman 2015, 2). Rather, it contributes to weakening the idea of the human being as an independent subject, autonomously constituted before her or his encounter with the reality out there. However, I argue, the naturalistic anchorage characterizing the Pragmatists' view of sensibility—that is, the shift from a conception of sensibility tailored on its possible foundational role within a representative view of cognition to sensibility as a structural dimension of animal life and, more specifically, human life because this always develops in an environment—allows a more decisive emancipation from the opposition between subjective and objective features as mandatory categories to understand human qualitative, affective, or aesthetic experiences. Furthermore, the naturalistic framework makes it possible to avoid any emphasis on human existence as ontologically different from animal life, by considering sensibility as connected to organic dependence from an environment, that is as characterizing all living systems, although at different levels and in a variety of ways. In other words, Heidegger's *Geworfenheit* should not be understood as an existential human prerogative, characterizing an outstanding relationship with Being. Rather, it should be reframed within a broader form of contingency characterizing at least life on Earth, the fortuitousness of its natural histories.[27]

In the next section, I will continue to present the approach to sensibility I derive from the Pragmatists by viewing it in relation to Enactivism, and more specifically to its central thesis that perception involves movement and action—a thesis which basically undermines the linear conception of behavior as something which goes from perception to thought and action only at the end of the arc.

5. More Than Action and Perception

In the first chapter of his book *Action in Perception*, Alva Noë claims that perception is a kind of skillful activity, based on sensorimotor mastery: a sort of practical and mainly unconscious capacity to mutually coordinate selective sensations and movements in space. Together with Susan Hurley, Noë strongly criticizes the so-called input-output picture (Hurley 1998) of relations between perception and action—that is, the assumption that "perception is input from world to mind, action is output from mind to world, and thought is the mediating process" (Noë 2004, 3). On the contrary, Noë endorses the thesis that action, perception, and thought are not divorced in ordinary human behavior. Although brain activity plays a crucial role in perception, thinking is not a mediating process connecting a mirror-like perception with purely subsequent action, because people are already intelligently (i.e., skillfully, competently) acting, moving, and dynamically turning their eyes, arms, and legs toward parts and aspects of the environment around them when perceiving things. Furthermore, even though he assumes that mental activity at least partially consists in the production of internal representations—a rather controversial stance in the current enactivist debate (see Hutto & Myin 2013)—Noë rejects the kind of brain-centrism and brain-reductionism that is widespread in more traditional cognitive sciences. Skillful sensorimotor behavior is something displayed by the whole animal that "is present in the world" (2004, 22), and perception—in Noë's view—is not the activity of an eye assumed to merely mirror what is there (2004, 20).

Shaun Gallagher (2017, 50) points out that Dewey's essay on *The Reflex-Arc Concept in Psychology* (1972) could be regarded as a forerunner of the embodied-enactivist view of perception: Dewey interpreted perception in light of sensorimotor coordination, instead of understanding it in terms of sensory stimuli; he also developed a conception of brain activity as an integral part of the body, basically contributing to the regulation of different bodily processes and phases of behavior.

I will briefly reconstruct the argument Dewey presents in his 1896 essay, and which has been rightly acknowledged by his interpreters (Tiles 1999; Garrison, 2009) as marking a crucial moment in the development of his philosophy. I think that Gallagher and others (Chemero 2009, 19–20; Santarelli 2016; Baggio 2017) are right to emphasize the convergence between Dewey and enactivism on this point. Nonetheless, my contention in this section will be that an exclusive focus on the intertwining of perception, action, and thought might run the risk of dimming a more complex notion of sensibility that can be derived from Dewey's inquiries.

I am not saying this to downplay the importance of the 1896 essay: some decades before Merleau-Ponty's critique of the "longitudinal theory of nervous functioning" (2002, 8) and more or less a century before enactivists and theorists of radically embodied cognition, Dewey challenged the primacy of the reflex arc concept as a key tool for interpreting human behavior and cognition.

Dewey's criticism has strong epistemological implications, because it rests on the idea that the reflex arc concept is not a scientific description of human perception and action; on the contrary, it is a philosophical way out that philosophers are forced to follow, when they unjustifiably assume that human behavior is composed of distinct and independent parts, namely, of stimulus and response as *disiecta membra* (i.e., scattered fragments: 1972, 100), in need of being brought together. On the one hand, there would be sensation, allegedly connecting an autonomous subject to the reality out there; on the other hand, there would be motor action, namely, the physical response enacted by the body as the material counterpart to the mind and therefore capable of affecting the allegedly external world. If human behavior consists of the composition of "a series of jerks," mental activity is required to play a mediating role—by means of mental representations and/or computation, according to more conservative trends in cognitive science and philosophy of mind. The point is that this kind of picture derives from a double ontological dualism grounding the concept of the reflex arc as well as the "input-output" picture of human experience, namely the dualism between the perceiving subject and reality, and the dualism between psychical and physical activity.

Dewey's response takes its cue from James's example of a child burning his fingers and withdrawing his arms from the fire (James 1981, 36–37). Where does action begin? Does it begin with the child's eyes being indistinctly bombarded by perceptual stimuli? The point is that the child, being involved in the situation at hand, already has a tendency to select certain stimuli and neglect others, and this kind of selective job is done by his eyes, his face, and other bodily movements that allow him to engage with certain aspects of his environment rather than others. In all of this, the child's action is not a blind physical movement but is constantly guided by the need to avoid a painful touch. Consequently, perception and action are already constantly intertwined and mutually adjusting each other in an "organic circuit," rather than according to a linear connection, because a complex, multidirectional interaction between an organism and its environment is occurring. Coordination comes before distinctions that should be regarded as different phases of a single behavior, rather than as initial elements mutually connecting through the intervention of a mental activity, ontologically different from the physical reality from which the stimuli are supposed to come and on which physical movements are assumed to causally impinge. Almost forty years later, a similar idea can be found in Dewey's distinction between impulse and impulsion in *Art as Experience* (1989, 64–65). Here he states that usually experience does not begin with an impulse—an impulse being merely the specialized part of a more complex mechanism we can analytically isolate from an overall experience by means of an act of reflection. Rather, according to Dewey, an experience begins with an impulsion that is a propensity of the organism as a whole to engage with certain aspects of its environment.

Now, the issue I wish to tackle is this: how should this active propensity to engage with one's own environment be conceived? Can it simply be considered the dynamic inclination of a self-moving agent? In other words, does the thesis put forward by Merleau-Ponty in May 1960—"*Wahrnehmen* and *Sich-Bewegen* are synonyms" (1968, 255)—and echoed by Alva Noë's similar position (2004, 22) exhaust the whole issue? My contention is that it does not (cf. Johnson 2007, 52).

In the couple of pages quoted above, Dewey clearly connects the impulsion or propensity to perceive and act in a certain way to the field of needs, desires, and the like, owing to the fact that we are living organisms "demanding completion through what the environment—and it alone—can supply" (1972, 65).[28] In contrast to the enactivists, Dewey here emphasizes a passivity within our propensity to perceive and act in the world, based on the "dynamic acknowledgement of this dependence of the self for wholeness upon its surroundings" (1972, 65). This dependence is so acute because—and this is a strong ontological contention—an organism's boundaries are not clearly defined within the environment to which it belongs, even though in most cases the skin works well as a boundary. An organism is part of the environment, and environmental resources continuously become part of the organism; so, as already noted, the distinction between organic and environmental energies should be considered functional from this point of view, that is, as context- and purpose-specific. This rather provocative biological stance lies at the basis of Dewey's argument.

However, my main aim here is to answer the question formulated above, regarding an organism's impulsion to act. I think Dewey's point must be made more explicit and radicalized: the mutual coordination does not occur between a still eminently sense-oriented perception and movement, but between an affectively oriented perception and movement. An individual will engage with certain aspects of the world and neglect others because he or she is guided by her or his existential needs and emotively laden interests (as suggested by Mead in the very short essay titled "Emotion and Interest" [2011, 27 ff.]). People will move in a certain direction because they feel that a situation is dangerous, attractive, or comfortable, but also because in many cases (albeit probably less often than in our ancestors' days) they are overwhelmed, absorbed, or afflicted by what happens around them. In other words, my contention is that bodily perception is not a merely sense-channeled, if intrinsically dynamic, perception but rather an affectively, aesthetically, or qualitatively laden sensibility. This is not to say that action is guided by feeling, that is, that it is irrational. On the contrary, qualitative or affective thought—to quote Dewey again—is strictly intertwined with our bodily movements, which in turn contribute to selectively exposing us to certain aspects of the environment rather than others. To sum up, to acknowledge that perception and movement are intertwined in human behavior is to go only part of the way. Instead, I suggest we develop a more complex notion of sensibility in order to deal with perception "in the wild." Roughly speaking, embodiment and affectivity should be assumed as the two intertwining sides of sensibility.

As argued by Giovanna Colombetti, "Emotion is not a distinct step in a perception-action sequence or a distinct representation added at some point to the sequence; emotion is rather an inescapable pervasive dimension of brain activity on which sensory information impinges and from which action progresses" (2014, 64).

When entering the overcrowded train coach, I am not just dynamically facing a spatial problem while perceiving: after making a greater or lesser effort to reach a free seat, I do not only perceive the backpack of the person next to me when I am trying to avoid touching it with my legs; rather, I feel it as annoying because it obstructs my leg movement. Perception, feeling and action or, better, embodied affective sensibility and movement, are part of an integral experience whose different phases and aspects can be isolated only later for specific purposes; to quote one of the champions of enactivism, "nascent perception is an emotional contact of the infant with the centers of interest of its milieu much more than a cognitive and disinterested operation" (Merleau-Ponty 1963, 176–77).

In the next section, I will focus on the aforementioned issue related to the specificity of human sensibility, namely, its being embedded in a deeply social and cultural-linguistic niche.

6. A Culturally Naturalistic View of Sensibility, or the Loop of Qualitative and Reflective Experience

Constitutive dependence on an environment is a basic condition of life in general. For sure, it makes a difference for an animal's life whether it feels something as comfortable or repelling. Hence, it seems that humans share sensibility with at least most self-moving animals. However, human sensibility is not simply animal sensibility plus a (stronger) form of awareness. In the case of human beings, my claim is that it is important to take account of the fact that the human environment is not simply natural, but naturally social and naturally cultural, namely, that it is also made up of shared practices that are laden with deep-seated meanings, habits, rules, and so on. This means that human sensibility cannot be regarded as being exclusively connected to basic organic needs. On the contrary, our biological propensities to feel and select are always already modified and reconfigured by our cultural practices.

As already mentioned, there is a serious risk in assuming that meaning is rooted in our bodily, qualitative, affective, or aesthetic experience, because the relation between sensibility and language can be interpreted as foundational, one-way, and hierarchically ordered. In my opinion, this tendency is still present in some phenomenologically oriented perspectives, for example, that of Merleau-Ponty, who did not completely give up on the old Husserlian project of grounding language and new forms of expression in perception (Dreon 2016). The idea that meaning basically has its roots in prelinguistic bodily perception, and is only subsequently exposed to linguistic and normative practices, is still a prevalent paradigm that can be found in the work of scholars who are very attentive to the complexity of human perception, such as Hubert Dreyfus (2014). As became clear in his debate with McDowell (2007), Dreyfus strongly advocates in favor of the notion of embodied coping, which he regards as involving a form of skilled action that is essentially mindless, that is, foreign to conceptuality, rationality, and language. In his approach, he stresses the similarity between animals' behavior and experts' actions (for example, the baseman throwing the ball during a baseball match), while supporting the idea that human conduct is additionally characterized by the possibility of performing acts of "free distanced orientation" that are not pervasive, but limited to specific situations (Dreyfus 2007). In a Deweyan vein, I do not endorse McDowell's idea of the pervasiveness of the mental, the conceptual and the rational in human experience as a quasi–a priori condition of human experience. On the one hand, I would argue that the debate in question has tended to adopt an oversimplified idea of human mental behavior, conflating concepts, reasons, and language.[29] Instead, I think we should adopt a much more empirical view of language as consisting in a family of linguistic habits, skilled symbolic actions, and cultural practices that have always served various different functions, not reducible to exclusively epistemic purposes—establishing and maintaining bonds and social relations at different levels, doing things in common, defining one's own identity within a group of people, and so on. In this light, I would even endorse a revision of a static idea of conceptuality and meanings, which I cannot develop here. On the other hand, I believe we should consider the completely fortuitous yet irreversible circumstance that human embodied coping occurs within an already cultural environmental niche, made up of shared meanings and linguistic practices, whose values and significance are steeped in our actions.

An analogous, although not identical, foundational attitude regarding the relationship between perception and language can be found even among supporters of Enactivism, who strongly stress the difference between low-order and high-order cognitive practices (Hutto & Myin 2013). One of the main issues in this field is how to fill the alleged gap between first-order and second-order cognitive practices (Hutto & Myin 2017).[30] Some interesting efforts have been made to avoid such an impasse by scholars adopting radical embodied and enacted conceptions of the mind (Gallagher 2017; Di Paolo, Cuffari, & De Jaegher 2018). The central problem is the assumption of an epistemological discontinuity between bodily perception, on the one hand, and conceptual or linguistic cognition, which is to say modes of cognition based on representation, on the other hand.

Even Mark Johnson's work on the aesthetic in experience seems to adopt a somewhat similar attitude when considering the anchoring of conceptual and linguistic forms of meaning-making in radically embodied, qualitative and aesthetic experience. His primary target is the "conceptual-propositional theory of meaning," based on the assumption that meaning is exclusively or primarily conceptual or propositional in nature (2007, 8). Instead, he openly endorses an embodied view of meaning, looking for "the origins and structures of meaning in the organic activities of embodied creatures in interaction with their changing environments" (2007, 11). However, it is unclear whether he is fighting against a specific conception of language as mainly consisting of propositions and the conveying of concepts or whether he is referring to an allegedly merely bodily-aesthetic level of meaning, which would be precluded to language in general. This latter reading is supported by Johnson's claim that embodied meanings lie "beneath words and sentences"; for example, he considers early-childhood experience as providing "a meaningful contact with our world" that is "prior to language" (2007, 17, 32).[31]

For sure, James was drawn to the siren call of the idea of vague experience as something prior to language, even though there are different ways to interpret his approach to language (see Dreon 2020a). On the other hand, Dewey was not always completely free of hesitation with regard to this matter (Dreon 2014). Nonetheless, he explicitly considered human sensibility and qualitative meaning-making as having been structurally reorganized by the advent of language and linguistic shared practices (Dewey 1981, 197 ff.). This is evident in his choice to employ the word *mental* to distinguish human forms of interaction with the environment from the intelligent yet nonlinguistic behaviors characterizing other animals. As Mead noted, it is important to bear in mind that in human forms of life physiologically based emotive responses to the environment are called for by "symbolic stimuli" or "aesthetic stimuli" (1895).

In my opinion, some of the Classical Pragmatists' insights should be brought to a coherent conclusion by basically working on two sides, in order to avoid a foundational conception of language, while at the same time gaining a more rounded view on sensibility, as it unfolds in our ordinary lives. As already hinted at in response to Dreyfus, I endorse a more complex conception of language as primarily consisting in fully embodied and socially shared linguistic practices that have a variety of different ends in view and are largely regulated by an affectively or qualitatively oriented mutual sensibility. Propositions and expressions of allegedly predefined concepts do not exhaust the ordinary human experience of language, which is far more similar to a tangle of different practices largely operating according to a vague or "mongrel functionality" (Margolis 2017, 63 ff.)—that is, one largely based on sensibility. The final chapter of this volume will be devoted to the development of a qualitatively richer conception of human linguistic experience conceived as continuous, rather than as opposed to sensibility.

At the same time, I would also reject a linear foundation of linguistic and more generally higher forms of cognition on sensibility, by taking into serious account the linguistic structure of the human environment, envisaged as a completely contingent, albeit irreversible, feature. I have trouble with the idea that human experience results from the association of animal embodied coping plus further cognitive-linguistic capabilities. Rather, I believe that we should take into account the effects of the broadly linguistic structure of humans' environment on the reshaping of their sensibility, in comparison to other moving and sensitive, yet nonspeaking, forms of animal life. Consequently, the adoption of a generally continuistic view of sensibility should not prevent us from investigating the specificity of human sensibility in comparison to other animal sensibilities.

The weight of an already linguistically shared world of practices should also be taken into account when considering the configuration of sensibility in newborns, whose very first cries are nested in a complex web of social interactions, and linguistic and multimodal exchanges taking place mainly through mutual affective regulation (Stern 1985; Stern et al. 1985; Trevarthen 1993; 2002). Although evidently incapable of uttering words and syntactically well-formed propositions, young humans are embedded in an environment deeply saturated with linguistic practices from their very first days. Those practices—from so-called motherese to lullabies, nursery rhymes, and storytelling—are often specifically directed at eliciting responses from the baby and catching attention.[32] The baby's behaviors—shaking the arms, keeping the eyes wide open, squealing—are strongly embodied, even when they are vocal; but they are also affectively based and oriented responses to cultural-linguistic stimulations on the part of its caregivers. From this point of view, the idea of a purely preverbal perception taking place and developing in a completely mute environment appears artificial and one-sided, as it does not take into account the empirical environmental conditions in which perception unfolds and configures itself—unless one adopts a conception of human behavior as depending exclusively on internal resources (i.e., either neural programs or voluntary acts) and not on organic-environmental constitutive interactions. In Di Paolo, Cuffari, and De Jaegher's words, human beings are "linguistic bodies" (2018), meaning that their bodily constitution is not forged apart from, or prior to, the fact the they live in a broadly linguistic environment and that, consequently, they are selectively disposed to feel not just a physical world but even culturally configured things, events, and individuals as attractive, disgusting, or simply uninteresting. Humans' (more or less strong) affectively laden bodily impulses and reactions are embedded in a largely linguistic context of practices that are already unfolding before their most intimate perceptions of themselves take place. The point is to change our approach and to adopt the point of view of the shared social context in which an individual's first perceptions occur, rather than the still monological perspective of an isolated individual as the primary starting point of experience.

There is also a further reason to claim that human sensibility is not independent of cultural and linguistic ways of sharing an environment that (for the better or worse) is common, namely, a coherent conception of cultural naturalism and emergence. From a pragmatist perspective, the notion of emergence does not involve only the assumption that new forms of organization are irreducible to the single features they are composed of, even though no external force has played a role in the process. Emergence also includes the idea that new forms of interaction between already existent natural elements retroact or have a loop effect on previous modes of behavior because the rise of a new way of organizing the relationships between living organisms and their environment becomes part of the environment itself and modifies it from within. Consequently, living beings have to face a different environment, with the result that the two reshape each other—of course to different extents and at different times, yet constantly and irreversibly. The introduction of a new form of organism-environment relation in a pregiven structure can play a disruptive, if fortuitous and completely contingent, role that does not leave the previously existent order unchanged. From this perspective, it becomes clear why both Dewey and Mead considered the advent of a linguistic form of communication and meaning-making crucial to the emergence of the mind, assumed as a novel kind of interaction taking place among human animals.

As a result, the issue becomes figuring out what feedbacks or loop effects may have impinged on the peculiarly human form of sensibility, given the cultural-linguistic niche humans happened to live in and contributed to forging across different timescales.[33] By following or even radicalizing Mead, it could be argued that it is at least partly through the use of verbal communication that the sense of one's own self has been made possible—where self-reflection is considered to be a primarily affectively based form of awareness. While avoiding any hypostatization of interiority as a primary condition—which would give rise to the well-known philosophical problems of the internal/external, private/public dichotomies—we should consider why humans are often capable of having a rich interior experience. In insisting on the disruptive role of language in reshaping animal sensibility, I am not contending that self-awareness should be considered in propositional terms. On the contrary, it was the great opportunity to take on the role of the other offered by verbal, gesture-based conversations that made a decisive contribution to the emergence of our capacity to direct our sensibility toward ourselves (see Candiotto-Piredda 2019). The prosodic as well as grammatical features of human language have provided—and still provide—very powerful tools for discriminating the sense of one's own self as different from that of others within an interchange with intimates or strangers. This is a point I will further explore in a Meadian perspective in the last chapter, section 12.

Furthermore, a family of broadly linguistic practices may have contributed to shaping human sensibility, making it capable of being self-oriented. Role-playing, pretending, and fictionalizing in the sense conceptualized by Wolfgang Iser (1990) could be considered a virtual extension of the incipient capacity to direct sensibility toward one's own self within a communicative context. Being scaffolded by complex linguistic resources, all of those practices played—and still play—some part in the shaping of human beings' inner life and character. Another crucial contribution to the distinctively human capacity to direct sensibility toward one's own self is represented by the typically human practice of storytelling and narration by means of which a sense of one's own identity acquires depth and relative stability through variations.[34]

A further consequence for a sensibility embedded in a broadly linguistic environment may have been the expansion of the highly nuanced varieties of qualitative meanings characterizing human interactions with the environment: situations can be awful or joyful but they can also be boring, embarrassing, intriguing, and so on. The Pragmatists derived from Alexander Bain the idea that a living being's perception of the world is primarily configured as pleasure or pain, that is, it is already laden with the significance that specific circumstances have on the organism's own life. Human sensibility seems to be structured not simply in terms of a binary opposition—as favorable to life or noxious—but through subtle varieties of nuances. Emotional or affective valence in humans is too complex to be dichotomized into acceptance and refusal, approach and withdrawal, or praise and blame. It is relational (Colombetti 2005), multidimensional (Lambie & Marcel 2002), and dependent on "second-order descriptions" (Colombetti 2005, 118). Humans experience situations and contexts through a rich array of meanings that, while still anchored in life and its dependence from the surroundings, are deeply influenced by humans' embeddedness in a rich, strongly stratified and habitualized cultural environment. I think we should consider not only the fact that linguistic practices convey and express feelings, emotions, and moods, but also the great extent to which utterances and narratives contribute to scaffolding sensibility through a complex web of mutual symbolic relationships, while at the same time expanding the range of affective references and qualitative evaluations. Habits of language, communication, and thinking are deeply entrenched in human sensibility, which is also continually nourished by broadly artistic practices, as well as by the massive presence of media in our lives. This is a topic I cannot work out in the present book, but which should be considered from the point of view of an aesthetic going beyond the artificial divide between culturalistic and naturalistic accounts of the arts and considering the mutual shaping of sensibility and broadly symbolic and artistic practices.

Chapter 3

Pragmatist Contributions to a Theory of Emotions

1. Contextualizing Emotions within Sensibility

The issue I will be addressing in this chapter is a natural development of the one previously discussed, namely, the question of how to contextualize a conception of emotions within the framework of sensibility as a pervasive feature in human experience. I am devoting a separate chapter to the Pragmatists' treatment of the emotions only in order to make the reading less demanding, because I believe that this theory must be framed within the broader account of sensibility I have outlined in the previous chapter. This is the reason why I have postponed the conclusion to the previous chapter and why I prefer to draw an overall balance of chapters 2 and 3 at the end of the latter one.

Scholarship on emotions has expanded considerably in the last few years, but interest in the emotions is much older in philosophy, and can be traced back at least to the famous Platonic indictment of the pernicious effects they can have on young people through their manipulation by poets. The literature, therefore, is vast and deeply varied, going roughly from reductionist conceptions of emotions—interpreted as basically consisting in neural programs (Ekman 1999) to deeply constructivist-cultural approaches (Illouz 2007). In spite of the abundance of theories, I think that developing a pragmatist approach can still be fruitful, because it helps to get rid of many of the noxious dichotomies that have shaped the philosophical as well as psychological conception of emotions—mind-body dualisms, nature-culture gaps, and private-public oppositions.

To begin with, the Pragmatists' approach to emotions I am suggesting here is characterized by two methodological choices. The first one, evidently, consists in considering emotions within the broader framework of human sensibility, rather than as an independent object of study. Of course, the latter approach is legitimate in certain cases: for example, when a neuroscientist wants to study the correlation between fear and the neural activities occurring in the brain of a traumatized person in order to see if anything can be done pharmacologically to favor a rehabilitation process. From a pragmatist point of view, problems arise when separate emotions are taken as points of departure to develop a philosophical theory of emotions, by assuming more or less consciously that they are entities, episodes, or processes per se, supervening on the life of an affectively neutral mind at certain moments—a problem clearly stated by Giovanna Colombetti when dealing with "primordial affectivity" as a structural component of the mind (Colombetti 2014, 1).

A complementary problem, I should add, concerns the effects in terms of our understanding of sensibility deriving from the methodological choice to approach emotions and moods as exclusive objects of study, as is the case in most affective sciences. Sensibility runs the risk of being envisaged as the mere association of different discrete phenomena, such as emotions, feelings, and moods; as a consequence, the emphasis falls on their ontological status—are they mental entities? Are they neurological programs?—as if this status could be defined independently of the organic-environmental interactions within which they take place. By contrast, I suggest adopting Dewey's strategy of discriminating "an experience" within the flow of continuous, ongoing experience (Dewey 1989, 42 ff.)—a strategy by which, I argue, he reworked James's emphasis on both conjunctive and disjunctive relations as constituting the thick fabric of life. Experience is not a process beginning by means of an already fully determined subject who has to face the world of physical things and other subjects only at a certain moment, namely, when he or she must address the problem of the reality out there and face the unnatural doubt that other subjects may not be like him or her, but rather deceiving automata. In contrast, experience is the continuous flow of interactions occurring within organisms and their environment, because it is within the flow of interactions that organic life is actually shaped. An individual has already had experiences of many things, persons, and situations when he or she comes to raise the sceptical doubt. However, it sometimes happens that a specific portion of this flow imposes itself on us as "an experience," having a beginning and an end, as well as a story, marked by a kind of phenomenological prominence (Shusterman 1997) or qualitative salience, and often becoming an object of narration in our ordinary conversations with others, as well as a piece of our own biographical narratives. By adopting a parallel strategy, I suggest envisaging affective and embodied sensibility as a condition basically characterizing living beings, whose lives depend on the environment they are structurally exposed to from birth, or even from before birth, and intertwining both a passive element (exposure itself) with an active one, namely, the selective, discriminative, and oriented component that inheres in sensibility. Emotions are specific episodes or phases that are marked off within sensibility, as they have a beginning and an end, and impose themselves on us because of a distinctive character giving them phenomenological prominence. They are discrete foreground events set against the background of a continual coming and going of affective-embodied interchanges.

This strategy is convergent with Giovanna Colombetti's argument in favor of primordial affectivity as the framework within which we can consider emotions as "emotional episodes" (Colombetti 2014, 25), by contrast to (most) affective neuroscience, which generally works "with a narrower conception of affectivity" (Colombetti 2014, 20). The difference between her account and mine lies in the space assigned to the two topics: Colombetti provides a very detailed theory of emotions, while devoting only a few (albeit important) pages to primordial affectivity; conversely, the prevalent focus of my inquiry is on sensibility, from which I suggest deriving some insights regarding emotions. A further important difference regards my emphasis on the feedback action of cultural-linguistic practices on the dynamic configuration of human sensibility, as stated at the end of the previous chapter.

A second methodological choice more strictly concerns the pragmatist legacy in this sphere. William James's study of emotions is still mentioned among the many works by experts on the subject, because, for better or worse, James's radically embodied view of emotion still represents a milestone. By contrast, the work of Dewey and Mead, while rich in insights, is generally overlooked by nonspecialists.[1] Nonetheless, the approach I have followed (Dreon 2015; 2019b), and which I am again suggesting here, is not to consider James's proposal a complete theory that can be criticized in itself—even if this is a perfectly legitimate approach, of course. Based on the assumption that his conception was the beginning of an open inquiry that was further developed over the two following decades, my proposal will bring the Pragmatists' investigations of emotions together into a more coherent account. I will be focusing on some convergences and points of disagreement among the Classical Pragmatists with regard to this topic, but also on some mutual, and sometimes even radical, corrections. This kind of approach, I would argue, makes it possible to recover a challenging perspective on emotions that basically emphasizes the continuity between mental and bodily aspects, between emotive behaviors and cognitive practices, while highlighting the already social characterization of the environment where individual emotive responses take place.[2]

The following sections (2, 3, and 4) deal with specific aspects of a pragmatist theory of emotion derived from James, Dewey, and Mead and, respectively, connected with the embodied features of emotions, their role in directing conduct, and their social functions. In section 2, I will contend that, while still adopting a dualistic framework for defining emotions, James rejected a mentalistic account of them, and adopted a rich—and neither mechanistic nor basically private, nonshareable—conception of the body as a function of the environment contributing to the organism's orientation in its world. In particular, he envisaged the nervous system as being at least partially shaped by human experience. Furthermore, he foreshadowed some interesting insights on human emotions as primarily concerning interpersonal relations and a socially configured environment. In section 3, I support the thesis that Dewey got rid of the dualism between psychic and physical features of emotions, that is, between a mental state and its bodily expressions, by conceiving emotions as modes of behavior grounded in the condition of organic life within a natural as well as naturally social environment. He saw emotions as functional to life, which is to say, as responding to the organism's need to orient itself in the environment on various levels. Emotions often arise out of a break in habitual behavior and provide the organism with a kind of affective proto-evaluation of environmental conditions that can later become an object of reflection and judgment. In section 4, I focus on some important contributions that George Herbert Mead made to the organic account of emotions, which I suggest draw from the Pragmatists. In addition to emphasizing the continuity between physiological and cultural features in emotions, as well as between emotions and cognition, Mead strongly stressed the social nature of emotions. In his view, they are social from their very beginning and play a crucial role in mutual attunement, role taking, and shared action. Bodily changes and facial movements should not be understood as the mere outer expression of previously determined mental states, but as gestures, which is to say as dispositions to act that are significant for one's partner. As I will show in the final chapter, Mead formulated the hypothesis that they consequently could be considered the seed of properly verbal conversations. In the final section (5), I make some suggestions regarding the intersection between the topic of the current chapter and that of the next one, supporting the claim that sensibility is largely scaffolded by habits at different levels.

2. James's Contribution, or How Emotions Are Embodied

As is well known, the core of James's theory is constituted by a basic overturning of "our natural way of thinking about [. . .] standard emotions," according to which "the mental perception of some fact excites the mental affection called the emotion," so that "this latter state of mind gives rise to the bodily expression. My thesis, on the contrary, is that *the bodily changes follow directly the* PERCEPTION *of the exciting fact, and that our feeling of the same changes as they occur* IS *the emotion*" (1884, 189–90).[3] James rejected the standard picture of emotions as mental states causing their bodily expressions, by arguing that an emotion consists in the feeling of the changes happening in one's body, caused by the perception of something troubling, exciting, or joyful in the environment.

I am not going to conduct a detailed analysis of James's text. A way to deal with James's approach that is more in line with the current chapter is to consider what outstanding elements in James's theory may have inspired Dewey first and then, immediately afterward, Mead. I think that those aspects in James's account that attracted Dewey's interest are still significant elements for the present investigation on human sensibility. One of the most stimulating aspects of James's position is represented by his clear decision to avoid any mentalistic and representational accounts of emotions. James explicitly avoided any recourse to mental states, understood as the causes of emotionally laden bodily changes. This position could be summed up as the no "mind-stuff" argument, in James's words. This attitude was interesting for Dewey and Mead, and still is for me, but not for traditional behavioristic reasons—meaning, from the perspective of the methodological hypothesis that introspective analysis should be avoided because it is scientifically unreliable.[4] On the contrary, both Dewey and Mead were seeking to understand mind and consciousness no longer as entities or substances of a particular kind, but as particular forms of interaction between human organisms and their natural and naturally social environment or as peculiar phases of experience, basically continuous with the environment they belong to and which they contribute to transforming from the inside. In other words, they regarded organic life in an environment as the necessary background for interpreting the mind.

Of course, as is well known, James continued to adopt the kind of dualism that defined the traditional framework of his *Principles*, even though he radically overturned it, at least in the formulation of his theory of emotions.[5] Nevertheless, James's conception does not simply emphasize the involvement of the whole body—as opposed to just the brain—in a wide range of emotions. What I find interesting in James's conception of emotions is the specific idea of the body that he adopted. This was probably a second point of interest for Dewey and Mead, and one that was instead at least partially ignored by those who criticized James's theory as reductionist and as rejecting the idea of any intentional dimension to the emotions (Cunningham 1995). This point could be summarized by stating that the other Pragmatists may have found in James's seminal text a structurally interactive conception of the human body and of the nervous system in particular—where "interactive" is different from "intentional."[6] Indeed, in James's words, the feelings of the body are not understood as mere private and internal feelings, principally impeding or marginalizing the role of the alleged external world and of the objects "out there." "[M]y first point," James argued, "is to show that their [viz., of the emotions] bodily accompaniments are *more far reaching and complicated than we ordinarily suppose*" (1884, 191). The body is not conceived of as a kind of closed entity, with an alleged external stimulus having the mere function of giving rise to a mechanical process; on the contrary, by emphasizing its plasticity, James understands the nervous system as both an active and passive function of the environment, capable of reacting to some select aspects of it while ignoring others.[7] To put it in the language of the extended mind theory, one could say that for James the nervous system in a body constitutes a system coupled with its surroundings (Clark & Chalmers, 1998). Moreover, it should be noted that James's emphasis on the plasticity of the nervous system in

The Principle of Psychology could be seen as basically foreshadowing more recent ideas that the brain is at least partially configured after birth in relation to the experiences of the individual in a social and already cultural context, as contended by Fogel and Greenough (Fogel et al., 1992; Greenough, Black, & Wallace, 1987), as well as by Mithen (Mithen & Parsons, 2008).[8] James understood emotions as attitudes which our nervous system displays to react to certain environmental stimuli, or even as inclinations anticipating environmental factors to which a given organism is sensible. Our nervous system and our visceral apparatus are not seen as being completely absorbed in themselves, so to speak; instead, they are "a sort of sounding-board, which every change of our consciousness, however slight, may make reverberate" (1884, 191). Anticipating the *Essay on Radical Empiricism*, consciousness here is seen to be constituted by nothing more than the perception of a certain environmental aspect, which is crucial or at least important for that particular organism. In other words, during an intense emotional experience, the body does not simply feel itself as a sort of closed entity, but feels itself suffering or enjoying the surrounding world.[9]

A third aspect of interest for Dewey was represented by James's emphasis on the affective or aesthetic dimension of our experience of the world, which was originally appropriated and extended by Dewey through his conception of the primarily qualitative status of experience, already discussed in the previous sections of this chapter.

In turn, Mead may have been inspired by James's focus on the aesthetic aspects of human experience when it comes to its incipient intertwining of biological and social features within the structure of emotions. On the one hand, by linking emotions to pain and pleasure, to longings and refusals, Mead emphasized both the continuity between animal behavior and human experience, and the peculiarity of the latter, consisting in the symbolic character of the objects causing painful or enjoyable interactions (Mead 2011).[10] On the other hand, Mead may have found inspiration in James's acknowledgment of the fact that "the most important part of my environment is my fellow-man. The consciousness of his attitude toward me is the perception that normally unlocks most of my shames and indignations and fears" (2011, 195). In *The Social Character of Instinct* Mead was to state that the "primitive consciousness even of the physical world is social," or—to put it more explicitly—that our consciousness is primarily affectively oriented toward other people's reactions to our own actions. Consequently, this affective social perception of the world "becomes physical consciousness with the growing power of reflection." This idea of human emotions as basically dependent on human sociality seems consistent with the insights of developmental psychologist Colwin Trevarthen, who claimed that "the child is born with motives to find and use the motives of other persons in 'conversational' negotiation of purposes, emotions, experiences, and meaning" (1998, 16). Furthermore, Trevarthen characterized primary intersubjectivity as referring to the coordination of the self and the other, considering secondary intersubjectivity—including the reference to objects and the intercoordination between the interlocutors—as occurring only later, between nine and twelve months (Trevarthen & Hubley 1978; Beebe et al. 2003, 789).[11]

3. Dewey's Integrations and Amendments, or Emotions as Behavior-Orienting Tools

Dewey begins the first of his two papers on emotions published in 1894 and 1895 by explicitly declaring that his suggestions on this subject must be understood "as a possible outline for future filling in, not as a proved and finished account" (1971a,152).[12] James's theory of emotions, together with Darwin's one, constitutes the central focus of his analysis—respectively, in the second paper, "The Significance of Emotion," and in the first one, "Emotional Attitudes" (see also Quéré 2013). Moreover, Mead's work on emotion is also mentioned in a footnote, where Dewey expresses his hope that the whole theory, which was being formulated by his colleague and friend, might "soon appear in print" (1971a, 167). These elements support my interpretation of the Pragmatists' work on emotion (including that of James) as a kind of open laboratory for ideas and hypotheses.[13]

The common ground of the two essays lies in the attempt to establish an interaction between Darwin's theory and James's one, by correcting some of their crucial mistakes and bringing out some points of divergence, which James had not explicitly considered when formulating his ideas on emotions.

According to Dewey, the crucial problem faced by both the above-mentioned authors is the dichotomy between the psychical and the physical aspects of emotions, which unfortunately continued to be maintained even in James's conception. His statement that emotion is the feeling of the bodily changes following directly on the perception of an exciting fact causes a radical reversal of the elements at play: James ultimately assigns priority to physical factors over psychic ones. While sharing James's antimentalistic position on the emotions, Dewey emphasized that, in doing so, the former was confirming mind-body dualism—although he probably already found this assumption problematic and later openly sought to abandon it, as already noted. At the same time, Darwin's unquestioned premise is that emotions are prior to "organic peripheral action[s]" and that for this reason alone facial and superficial bodily changes can be understood as the outer expression or communication of emotions themselves. Incidentally, it should also be pointed out that the current theory of basic emotions (Ekman 1999) maintains that there must be something prior to changes in the body and causally eliciting them. Most current views of emotions take neural affect programs (i.e., an already fixed set of them corresponding to the alleged basic emotions) as constituting the mental stuff preceding bodily changes—meaning that a mind-centered stance is replaced by a brain-centered approach.

Consequently, it becomes important for Dewey to problematize the standard view of the visible face and of bodily movements as the outer expression of an alleged previous mental state, because this is where the traditional dualism between the inner and the outer, or the psychic and the physical, is stronger. According to his criticism, this interpretation is based on a psychologist's fallacy, namely, on the fact of conflating the observer's point of view with that of the facts observed. As James notes in his *Principles*, "The psychologist [. . .] stands outside of the mental state he speaks of," but he can unfortunately forget this and make fatal mistakes (1981, ch. 7). So, if a gnashing of teeth can be interpreted as a communication of anger by an observer, the man gnashing his teeth is not doing that in order to communicate his rage to other people, at least not primarily—and unlike an actor performing on stage.[14] For him his bodily changes are simply an integral part of his being angry and ready for aggression—Dewey will later observe that they are movements or acts inherent to his being angry, which is to say that they are emotional attitudes. In other words, bodily movements and tendencies to action, on the one hand, and feeling, on the other, are not separated, but integral parts of an emotion. Emotions for Dewey are modes of behavior, with cognitive, practical and affective aspects: they are neither subjective experiences nor mere products of action. At a subsequent stage, one can distinguish different aspects in an emotional behavior, but it should be clearly stated that these distinctions are functional or operative, which is to say that they respond to specific purposes within particular contexts—for example, when I suspect that my interlocutor is trying to deceive me about her or his own actions or when the actor on stage has to perform a certain kind of action. Consequently, distinctions between the inner and the outer, the mental and the bodily, within an emotive interaction should be dealt with in a deflationary way because they are derived distinctions. Problems arise when, slipping into the "philosophical fallacy," one tends to assume that they are primitive and constitute the ultimate elements of which an emotion is constituted.[15]

Dewey offers the reader a careful inquiry into Darwin's principles in order to explain emotions, starting from the first one, namely, his principle of "serviceable associated habits." According to this principle, bodily changes, which are useful for communicating one's own emotions to others, are selected and acquired across successive generations. In Dewey's opinion, Darwin's most important contribution to the understanding of emotions lies precisely in his teleological approach—meaning that emotional attitudes, gestures, or behaviors should be understood according to a functional perspective related to organic interactions in an environment. However, from Dewey's point of view, Darwin missed his target: emotional attitudes are not primarily significant with reference to an alleged preexisting psychic state, but with reference to useful movements; this means that they are functions of certain acts rather than of certain emotions understood as mental states. In other words, emotional attitudes must be interpreted as "acts originally useful not *qua* expressing emotion, but *qua* acts—as serving life" (1971a, 154). Dewey suggests the example of laughing, which according to his interpretation is not primarily functional toward communicating a pleasurable state of mind, but rather constitutes the termination of a period of effort.

On the other hand, Dewey ascribes an important role to Darwin's third principle for explaining emotions, while denying any basic significance to his second principle—that of "antithesis." The former principle deals with so-called cases of direct nervous discharge. According to Dewey's interpretation, those idiopathic cases in which no clear cause for a certain bodily movement can apparently be found must be understood as "cases of the failure of habitual teleological machinery" (1971a, 139), where previously successful habits can no longer supply good behavioral responses to a given situation. The functional approach is clearly always at work: the discharge of the nervous system is not meaningless and causeless, but is rather connected to a moment of crisis. Past movements and actions "formerly useful for a given end" (1971a, 175) or previously adjusted to a certain environmental requirement prove to be inappropriate, so that new forms of coordination and interaction have to be found. Consequently, emotions often arise as breaks in habitual behavior—from perturbations in organism-environment transactions that can be a source of awareness as well as of the problematization, discarding or renewal of habits, as will be argued in the next chapter.

To sum up Dewey's adoption and correction of Darwin's theory, his position could be condensed as follows: Dewey recognizes and further emphasizes the importance of the functional interpretative key for understanding emotions as parts of one's conduct. However, he reinterprets emotive gestures and bodily changes against the background of human (inter)actions embedded in and responding to a specific environmental context, rather than to an alleged interior state of mind of which they are mere external expressions.

In his second paper, Dewey focuses his attention on James's approach to the emotions by following his basic claim about the continuity between mind and body, the psychic and the physical. Furthermore, he offers a sharp critique of the traditional dualism between cognition and feeling, which appear to be integral parts of emotion, understood as "a concrete whole of experience" (1971a, 171), including the actions of the surrounding context upon us and our behaviors or acts as ways of interacting with it.

The problem with James is that he only focused on the feeling aspects of emotional experience while neglecting a series of other crucial elements, which are first of all experienced and perceived "as a whole carrying its distinctions of value within it" (Dewey 1971a, 173). From this point of view we might argue that Dewey's starting point is that of "our ordinary, everyday way of thinking of the emotions, and the phenomenology of emotional experience," whose unity, in Peter Goldie's opinion, is prior to any distinction between the mental and the material, but also, according to Dewey, between feeling, knowing, evaluating, and acting (Goldie 2002, 247). This intertwining of feeling and cognition represents an important point of convergence with Colombetti's conception of emotions, which also highlights recent neuroscientific accounts questioning the traditional assumption that "cognition and emotion are distinct psychological faculties implemented in separate neural areas" (2014, 98).[16]

Dewey amends James's interpretation by pointing out that the feeling of bodily changes is a structural part of an emotion, but does not exhaust the concrete emotional experience. Emotions must be considered modes of action and behavior, because within them, first of all, we can detect a "readiness to act in certain ways" (1971a, 172) in response to a certain situation or a specific object with which an organism is interacting; they are dispositions toward other men and women, modes of conduct or ways of behaving in a certain situation. This behavioral side of emotion is characterized as being "primarily ethical" by Dewey, because even if we can intellectually distinguish a feeling aspect from the action or reaction we are assuming, this same behavior carries a kind of proto-evaluation within it about what is better or worse, dangerous or enjoyable. As already stated, sensibility—emotions included—contains a primitive form of evaluation, which is not the result of a judgment but depends on how I feel or perceive the situation I am embedded in. In his *Ethics*, Dewey says that our reflective morality, which is to say our capacity to consciously reconsider our behaviors and norms, rests on a customary morality, based on habits as well as on our structural tendency to affectively accept or reject what is going on around us, because our lives are radically dependent on and exposed to an environment (see Dreon 2020b). In this sense, Dewey anticipated Richard Lazarus's claim in favor of a distinction between a primary appraisal and more reflective judgments, that is, a secondary appraisal (Lazarus 1966; see Colombetti 2014, 85 on this).

A further aspect of a full emotional experience is constituted by always being about a certain object, person, or situation—about being oriented toward something. This aspect could be qualified as the intentional structure of an emotion;[17] however, Dewey did not use the language of intentionality, and preferred to speak of "prepositional reference" as the character of each emotion. This focus on the ways people speak about emotions can still be found many years later, in *Experience and Nature*, where he suggests that, by looking at the grammar of emotions, we should reject the typically modern philosophical *topos* that emotions are essentially confined within our private consciousness and can in some lucky cases be expressed to the outer world by means of almost magic works of art. In fact, emotions are always *for* something, *toward* a certain person or event, *against* a given situation, *because of* a terrible or wonderful fact. So rather than confining each one of us to his or her own subjectivity, emotions reveal our structural exposure to the environmental and social forces surrounding us.

We could characterize this intentional (in the sense explicated above) or prepositional side of a concrete emotion as involving a cognitive aspect, by maintaining that in Dewey's account there is an overlapping of cognitive and aesthetic factors that make the emotional perception of an object something that cannot be divided into two allegedly separate phases, as argued by Martha Nussbaum through her weak cognitivistic or neo-Stoic approach (2001). As already remarked, in Dewey's perspective, we do not primarily perceive or register a matter of fact and then ascribe it some value. For example, I do not simply perceive a bear with my sense organs or as the mere descriptive content of an experience and then feel afraid because I am in the forest and not at the zoo looking at the bear in its cage. On the contrary, I perceive the bear as frightening if I am in the forest, or as amazing (or miserable) if I am at the zoo. Only later, can I intellectually abstract the qualitative or aesthetic elements, namely, the significance of the bear in my life, from the bear in general or from the alleged mere perception of the bear. According to the later Dewey, this abstraction is not mistaken per se, because the reflective returning to an immediate experience in order to analyze its different phases can be a way to find a solution to a moment of crisis and can enrich the following experiences. Conversely, it is a philosophical fallacy to assume the result of the abstraction—the allegedly merely descriptive sensitive or conceptual contents—as a first neutral element that can be evaluated and judged only later. It could even be said that in a concrete emotional experience we cannot primarily separate our feeling afraid from the frightening bear that is scaring us, while both the object and we as the subject emerge from a basically unitary experience (Dewey 1971a, 176).

4. Mead's Further Developments, or Emotions as Social Functions

Mead's contribution to this discussion about human emotions is especially notable in his papers dating from the period between 1894 and the first decade of the twentieth century.[18]
Mead's writing style is often very dense, so it is not always easy to find a detailed articulation of the different steps in his arguments. In order to clarify Mead's contribution to the subject of emotions, I am going to identify four main research trajectories within the complex web of his papers.

The first research strand, which emerges from the very beginning of Mead's interest in emotions, is his urge to develop the physiological components implied in Dewey's teleological or functional conception of emotion. Mead stresses the need to articulate a physiological theory of pleasure and pain as the biological precedents of human emotions. One point of philosophical interest in this proposal is the fact that he adopts—as he usually does—a deeply continuist approach, where distinctly human emotions are seen as emerging from animal instincts and as being connected to pleasure or pain. From a physiological point of view, the increasing or decreasing of the processes of nutrition of organic tissues is the same in humans and in other animals. However, there is a particular factor to be considered in the human case, namely, that "the vaso-motor processes that are originally called out only by the instinctive acts" are now called out by "symbolic stimuli" or "aesthetic" ones—as in the cases of war and love dances. These symbolic stimuli carry within themselves "an evaluation [by the organism] of the act before the coordination that leads to the particular reaction has been completed."[19] We could make Mead's intuition more explicit by emphasizing that a novelty here is represented by the action of cultural elements on physiological processes in the case of human emotions. Unfortunately, Mead does not tell us anything more here about what it means for a stimulus to be symbolic,[20] but we can appreciate the fact that he is trying to stress the peculiarity of human emotive behavior against the background of a basic continuity with animal life.

A second important point becomes clear in his paper *Emotion and Instinct*, where, once the basic emotional character of human interest has been recognized, the focus shifts to the differences between emotion and interest. One of the differences, according to Mead, regards their position within a given act: while in most cases emotion characterizes "the immediate grasping and enjoyment of the object sought," interest involves a deliberate attempt to overcome the obstacles that impede the reaching of an end in view. Emotion seems to be connected to the immediate appropriation of the desired object (or to the avoidance of a dangerous one), and consequently seems to be almost instinctively realized, without any awareness of this pursuit of a given end by a given means: one's consciousness is rather completely absorbed in the desired or rejected object. On the contrary, an interested act is very often a conscious one, explicitly taking into account both the means and the ends in view of the action. These suggestions are noteworthy because, although they are probably simplistic, they provide an interpretation of the connections and distinctions between emotion and cognition in a continuist perspective, where human instrumental reason seems to emerge from more instinctual modes of behavior when hindrances or inhibitions are at work. The emotional roots of cognition are not denied; on the contrary, they are regarded as basic components of intelligent behavior, which at the same time reveal themselves to be typically human forms of interaction with the environment.

Third, in the paper *The Social Character of Instinct* Mead definitely interprets the emotions from the social standpoint he had declared to be crucial in *Social Psychology as Counterpart of Physiological Psychology*. Here he states that an adequate account of human emotions must not only take account of the biological factors involved but also set out from human sociality as the element in light of which every peculiarly human phenomenon should be understood. If we look at other human behaviors, such as curiosity, pugnacity, subjection, self-assertion, and so on, we must recognize that they are basically referred to other individuals or to a structurally social environment. Mead calls these "instincts," according to William McDougall's use of this term, but they are definitely emotional behaviors.[21] Nonetheless, even if we look at human infancy, we cannot deny that the newborn's movements are already attuned to those of its mother (or caregiver).[22] In another unpublished essay, *The Relation of the Embryological Development to Education*, Mead draws attention to John Fiske's thesis of the primary social importance of infancy: no other animal seems to have such a long period of dependence on others as human newborns, whose marked immaturity at the moment of birth makes them structurally dependent on the community taking care of them from the very beginning (2011, 73).[23] For this reason, Mead concludes that our "primitive consciousness even of the physical world is social, and only becomes physical consciousness with the growing power of reflections" (Mead 2011, 3).

It could be said that Mead was developing an idea of the socially extended mind, to adopt Shaun Gallagher's formula (2013). Nonetheless, I would argue that the very concept of "extension" in connection to "mind" may have sounded strange to Mead because it seems to assume as a precondition the existence of a mind that could be further expanded into a social world. On the contrary, Mead was developing the idea that the individual mind and mindful behavior can only emerge out of an already socially shared environment. Although Gallagher's idea of a socially extended mind is much more radical than Clark's conception of the extended mind (Gallagher 2020; see also Candiotto 2016), the extension vocabulary seems to pay its dues to the mind-centered approach from which Gallagher has vigorously moved away.[24]

The point is even more interesting with reference to our topic: in these texts, Mead seems to develop an idea of emotions as dynamically configured in a shared interpersonal context, an idea supported many years later by Fogel et al.[25] Fogel denies that "[t]he emotion program is [. . .] the source of the patterns that are differentially reinforced with respect to variations in the social context" (Fogel et al. 1992, 130). In this case, the innate emotion program in the brain would constitute "the ghost in the machine," prior to the differentiation of emotive behaviors according to different social and cultural contexts. On the contrary, Fogel seems to develop an insight that had already been grasped by Mead, namely, that biological factors and the social environment develop reciprocally and dynamically, at least in the case of human organisms. Mead's intuition was probably supported by his specific attention to the interactions between human infants and their caregivers; largely anticipating the inquiries by Daniel Stern (1985) and Colwyn Trevarthen (1979), Mead focused on mutual attunement rather than on imitation to understand the dynamic development of mother-infant interactions.

Finally, this shift from the biological dimension of animal instincts to the social one allowed Mead to find an answer to a basic gap in Dewey's argumentation, regarding the so-called expression of emotions. Like James, Dewey rejected the traditional idea that a predefined inner state must be externally communicated by means of certain movements of the body and face. He even made use of James's psychological fallacy to criticize this kind of interpretation. However, while James essentially focused only on visceral changes in the body, Dewey's functional interpretation of emotional attitudes—that is, the visible changes on the surface of the body—did not fully consider their social context. In a probably too condensed way, Mead argued that it must be assumed that emotions play a social role, not just a functional or teleological one, even though this involves the rejection of the dualistic explanation of perceivable bodily changes and the idea of the alleged priority of the psychical over the physical. Mead was already aware of this problem because of his proximity to Wundt's thesis of the origin of language in gestures, understood as affective expressions, while having to avoid any recourse "to imitation and to expression of emotions" (Joas 1997,

103). Mead's solution is that these emotional attitudes are immediately understood or read by other social actors not as the outer transmission of a predefined inner state, but as gestures, that is, as dispositions to act in certain ways, to which the interlocutors adjust or attune their own behaviors. In this perspective emotions are an integral and basic part of one's social conduct, namely, of what later Mead will describe as the conversation of gestures, where the acts of one individual must be adjusted to others' movements. Emotional gestures are the first "means of co-ordinating social conduct," and they can be understood as signs signifying not a previous mental state, but a tendency to act or react to our interlocutor's movement "in unreflective social conduct [. . .]. [S]o we are continually reading from the attitude, the facial expressions, the gestures and the tones of the voices, the coming actions of those with reference to whom we must act" (Mead 2011, 5). This "reading" must not be regarded as a kind of explicit and articulated interpretation, or as a kind of subjective projection of one's own intentions, feelings, and ideas into another's mind, but rather as a somewhat emotional tuning, which need not be conscious. In a nutshell, it could be stated that emotions for Mead play a crucial role in shaping the mutual entrainment between mother and child, as well as between adults (see Krueger 2013).

From this point of view, the future key formulas for taking the role of the other seem to be rooted in a certain sensibility toward what the other can do—to us, with us, or against us, Dewey will add. As emphasized by Gary Cook, Mead was conscious that the phrase "taking the role of the other [. . .] is a little unfortunate because it suggests an actor's attitude which is actually more sophisticated than that which is involved in our own experience" (1993, 78). Although it is primarily affective or based on feelings, this does not mean that it consists in the capacity to look inside the other's mind.[26] On the contrary, Mead focuses on the human-specific capacity to feel and imagine the possible movements of one's interlocutor, his possible (helpful or impeding) contribution to a shared action. My identity and that of my interlocutors are not previously determined before interactions take place, because it is precisely through social, affective interaction that both identities develop or emerge. Besides, what situation can come before any form of social interaction? For Mead—as for Dewey—no such situation can be found in human experience, given the previous considerations about human structural embeddedness in a social environment due to humans' marked immaturity at birth. Mead ultimately argues that these signs and this kind of emotional cooperative conduct constitute the basis for properly linguistic gestures, that is, for symbols, and that "[t]hought and volition develop and interpret the situation that is first of all emotional." Hence, it could be said that in this essay Mead finds the origin of human language in an emotional conversation of gestures, which is not replaced by verbal interaction but continues to exist within it. This is a rather complicated issue, involving serious consideration of a feedback reaction between human language and culture, on the one hand, and human sensibility, on the other. The central sections of chapter 6 (sections 4–7) will explore this kind of interpretation.

5. At the Intersection between Habits, Sensibility, and Emotions: Some (Provisional) Conclusions and Beyond

In the last two chapters, I have derived from the Pragmatists a picture of human sensibility as basically rooted in the dependence of organic life on a natural environment, more specifically in the dependence of human life on a highly social and cultural-linguistic environment—an environmental niche both shaping specifically human forms of life and modeled by them in a loop whose starting point cannot be traced (Margolis 2017). I have argued that sensibility involves two strictly intertwined aspects: on the one hand, it consists in a form of exposure or vulnerability of the organism to environmental conditions—the actions of others as well as of the natural context—that are felt as dangerous, comfortable, or disturbing. Sensibility includes a form of passivity, namely, being stricken, overwhelmed, or absorbed by what a natural and naturally social environment can do directly to one's own existence and group life.

On the other hand, sensibility is proactive, including dispositions and habits of selective discrimination between contrasting salient features of a situation, as well as active habits and tendencies to move, act, and respond to situations. Briefly, I have argued that one of the most important points to be drawn from this approach is that the distinction between sensibility and reflective experience is not foundational, which is to say that their relation is not linear and one sided, as though allegedly "pure" sensibility were the independent ground of cognition.[27] The distinction between qualitative experience and reflective inquiries cannot be a founding element because humans are animals that, from the very beginning, finds themselves caught in the middle of communicative and linguistic interactions as well as inferential processes that belong to a community before they belong to any individual speaker and knower. All of this interferes with and has consequences for qualitative experience, which incorporates the results of previous inquiries and is modified by them, whether it be enriched or impoverished. There is a kind of circular process that moves from qualitatively thick experience to analysis, hypothesis, and inference each time a difficulty arises about what can or should be done in a specific context. On the other hand, the outputs of reflective experiences cannot but return to the primary experience out of which the need for them emerged and through which their strength will be tested. Consequently, sensibility is continuously reset and reshaped, in some way or another: people become more sensible to different aspects of the context in the course of their lives, depending on their narratives, namely on their history of interactions with and within a form of life and a socially shared environment. At the same time, people correct their disposition to act if a particular mode of action works better than another in a new context of action. Affectively, one checks the efficacy of the outputs of previous inquiries and appropriates them in largely unconscious ways when something unexpected and disrupting happens and requires a reassessment.

One way to further develop a nonfoundational conception of the relationships between sensibility and more reflective experience can unfold through a focus on the intersections between sensibility and habits. Through the young Dewey, it has been shown that an emotion frequently occurs when a habit of action does not work in a new context: a situation becomes troubling in the affective, practical, and precognitive sense of the term, the agent is disoriented and does not know what to do and how to behave. Such an affectively based sense of incertitude can give rise to a process of inquiry and an analytical treatment of the problematic situation in search for a way out, showing that cognitive processes are rooted in affective sensibility and respond to crisis and needs coming from qualitative experience. Dewey also emphasized that emotions, understood as breaks in habitual behavior, are chances for the raising of consciousness, understood as an affective phenomenon rooted in life exposure to a surrounding environment, rather than conceived of in primarily epistemic terms (Tugendhat 1986). Emotions, I would add, enter the process of habit revision and change: as abrupt interruptions of almost instinctive ways of prepersonal customs learned from the social milieu to which one belongs, emotions have a role in transforming customary, mere routine habits into possibly new intelligent habits, which is to say in promoting new ways of responding to a problematic situation—even if no success is guaranteed in advance.

Furthermore, it is possible to trace other crucial intersections between sensibility and habits. The point is that sensibility is also largely scaffolded by habits, as hinted at above (see Candiotto & Dreon, 2021). While being basically rooted in living beings' exposure to the surrounding environment, sensibility involves active aspects and supports, which is to say a wide range of affective habits through which both organic and environmental resources—cultural-linguistic meanings included—are channeled. Sensibility is scaffolded by habits of selection and salience, differing not only according to the physiology of the human body but also with reference to specific cultural practices that give emphasis to different environmental features. These can be sensorimotor habits related to the hands and eyes as well as more complex dynamic schemas, which, in their turn, can be strictly bodily schemas or can include a series of body-enhancing tools—from flint knives to mobile phones—conditioning or having loop effects on the ways human sensibility continues to be dynamically reshaped. Sensibility is also supported by habits of praise and blame, considered as primarily affective-embodied evaluative habits related to the life of the individual at stake. "Affective affordances"—things, people, and events one is aroused by, longs for, rejects, or is scared of—are structured by habits of shared action (either competitive or collaborative), valuation, and thought.

Finally, so-called bodily expressions of emotions can at least partially be understood in terms of habits. Visceral bodily changes, such as increased blood pressure, augmented breathing frequencies, the general enhancing of physiological rhythms or their abrupt interruption do not exhaust human emotions. Rather, they represent bodily aspects—including neurological processes—by which emotions are scaffolded, that is, effectively occur. Other facial gestures—smiling, grinding one's teeth, frowning—always have an affectively based communicative value among humans because of the high degree of mutual dependence of one's behavior on the actions of others. They can (and often do) become standardized habits that can be performed unconsciously or to condition the conduct of other people.

I would argue that it can be fruitful to regard sensibility as strictly intertwined with habits, because it can help avoid certain dualistic dichotomies and philosophical rigidities concerning the idea of sensibility and the emotions—philosophical problems such as whether they are merely subjective or socially shaped, whether they are part of an innate endowment or are culturally acquired, whether sensibility is in the head, whether it has any cognitive value or stands at the opposite pole from reason, and so on. One can step away from these doubts by adopting a Deweyan conception of habits as functions of organic-environmental interactions and by considering the specific features of the human environment entering one's conduct, as I will suggest in the following chapter.

Chapter 4

Humans Are Bundles of Habits

1. Introduction

In this chapter, I will present a conception of habits basically drawn from Dewey, which I will radicalize within an explicit ecological, cultural-naturalistic, and clearly naprioristic framework. I propose integrating Dewey's insights by providing some definitions of the issue at stake, a more coherent account of the reasons why habits are pervasive in human behavior, and a theory according to which habit acquisition proceeds from the social environment to the individual. This effort will integrate the philosophical anthropology I am developing with a conception that, I believe, in many respects grasps human conduct more effectively than other approaches, including moral and political ones. Before the emergence of some recent insights within the enactive and embodied cognitive sciences, as well as before Bourdieu's attribution of a key role to habitus in the field of social science, the Classical Pragmatists attributed a crucial, positive, and pervasive role to habits in human experience, cognition, and will. Consequently, I will also develop the Deweyan legacy with regard to habits through references and comparisons with the above-mentioned fields of research, with a specific focus on Bourdieu's account of habitus.

According to the pragmatist tradition, habits scaffold human behaviors: they support and orient human sensibility, sustain and nourish cognition, constitute the skeleton of action, and represent the prereflective background to implicit and explicit decision-making. If being a "personal *Lebensform*" is an outstanding subject for a philosophical anthropology (Quante 2018, 14), focusing on the role of habits as the largely prepersonal framework for the emergence of autonomy and responsibility, I contend, is a core issue for a philosophical anthropology because of the consequences it entails for a theory of action, including ethical and political implications. Habits deserves attention because of their significance and functions in relation to everyday choices—moving closer to another person or tending to exclude him or her from one's own space, empathizing with a political candidate or almost instinctively being scandalized at her or his statements. From the point of view, I endorse that individual actions arise from the depths of a "dark wood," scaffolded by the habits of conduct and practice—affective, sensorimotor, linguistic, and cognitive habits—that humans naturally absorb from their socially shared environment. Differently from Dante Alighieri's wood, the tangle of prereflective habits is not necessarily dark and distant from the straight path, but is constitutive, whether in a negative or positive sense, depending on the specific context. I will claim that, from a pragmatist point of view, habits are constitutive of human capacities as well as of one's own self and character because they lie at the intersection of biological and cultural resources, representing a pivotal component of a coherent form of cultural naturalism.

As hinted above, I will suggest an ecological, holistic, or transactional notion of habits, requiring cooperation from both the organism and its natural and naturally social environment, far removed from a linear conception of habit, understood as the repetition of a fixed connection between a perceptual stimulus and a motor response. My suggestion is to consider habits as more or less flexible channeling of both organic energies and environmental resources that are not only natural but also social and cultural, given human beings' marked degree of social interdependence. This idea is connected to a wider redefinition of the concept of behavior, which is not understood as the property of an individual or the way of being originating from a single agent, but rather as the result of mutual transactions—that is, constitutive interactions—between an organism and the environment it is embedded in.

This conception of habits that I derive from Dewey brings out the clear link between the naturalistic dimension of habits and their social facet. The one-sided emphasis on one factor at the expense of the other has led to a sterile opposition between supporters of a view of human nature as characterized by quasi–a priori universals, on the one hand, and cultural relativists, on the other. A central premise I focus on is that human life is marked by structural dependence on an adult social group from birth on, because of the specific immaturity and vulnerability characterizing humans in comparison with other mammals. Consequently, humans are bundles of habits to a more intensive and more extensive degree than other forms of life, because of their precocious and prolonged exposure to a social environment that is already laden with habits, customs, and shared practices they need to adopt and that are already at work in channeling our responses from the very beginning.

A further important point I suggest making explicit and integrating with Dewey's insights is the idea of habits as something that does not primarily derive from a first individual and conscious act. On the contrary, humans acquire most of their habits at a largely prepersonal level, by engaging with the practices, issues, and interlocutors they find in the already broadly habitualized social environment they belong to and interact with from birth on. Consequently, I propose characterizing habits also as ways of doing things and ways in which things are done that are already there before each individual makes her or his own choices. They are already a part of the environment humans are embedded in and have to engage with to find their way. To claim this is to deny that a voluntary action always plays a role at the beginning of the process of habit acquisition, which, however, does not mean that the conscious choices of an individual serve no function at all. On the contrary, this view attributes a crucial responsive role to the individual in the critical appraisal, redirection, and transformation of a previously established habit.

With a constant eye to the recent debate on habits in enactivism and embodied mind theory, I will briefly introduce the Classical Pragmatists' treatment of habits—as most notably exemplified by Peirce, James, Mead, and Frank Lorimer. After a succinct sketch of their view of the positive and pervasive role of habits in nature (section 2), I will focus on Dewey's treatment of habit as a privileged resource for understanding the reasons why humans are creatures of habit to a more extensive and intensive degree than other living beings (section 3). Through a comparison with the naturalistic interpretation of habit suggested by comparative psychologist Conwy Lloyd Morgan in 1896, I will distance myself from a linear conception of habit, conceived of as the repetition of a fixed connection between a perceptual stimulus and a motor response. Instead, I will suggest an ecological, holistic, or transactional notion of habit as something requiring cooperation from both the organism and its natural and naturally social environment. Such a proposal explicitly draws on the work of Di Paolo and Barandiaran in the enactivistic field. Habits will thus be characterized as more or less flexible channeling of both organic energies and environmental resources—that are not only natural but also social and cultural, given human beings' considerable degree of social interdependence (section 4). In section 5, I will draw an explicit connection between the naturalistic dimension of habits and their social facet, by explicitly connecting them to the marked dependence of each human being on an adult social group from birth onward. A further important thesis I will support is that the acquisition of habits occurs at a largely prepersonal level, by matching the practices, issues, and interlocutors we find in the already broadly habitualized social environment we belong to and interact with from birth. Habits are ways of doing things and ways by which things are done that are already there before each individual makes her or his own choices (section 6). Consequently, the contention I derive from Dewey is that the individual mind does not generally lie at the beginning of the process of habit acquisition, but plays a crucial intermediate role in rejecting, reappropriating or reshaping previous habits (section 7). With reference to current debates on an allegedly mindless coping with the world (Dreyfus), as well as on the divide between low-order and high-order cognitive processes (Hutto), the eight section claims that most human habits cannot be seen to take place at the purely bodily level, by means of dynamic motor schemas, because the shared environment of other acculturated bodies must be assumed to be an integral part of individual behavior. If one abandons the idea of two-level cognitive processes, habits can be seen to take place at the intersection of organic interactions with a naturally sociocultural environment and not within the (representative) mind or the (computing) brain of the agent.

I will develop a further extensive comparison with the strongly socially embedded and embodied conception of habitus famously introduced into sociology by Pierre Bourdieu in the 1970s (sections 9–10). This comparison, I argue, favors a stronger emphasis on a pluralistic conception of habits, involving the denial of any rigid distinction between an allegedly unique behavioral matrix and empirical actions. A Deweyan view of habits as both routine and intelligent, which is to say as open to change and revision, appears to be a nondogmatic option on the theoretical level, as well as a more viable alternative from the point of view of its practical consequences (section 11).

2. Introducing Habits with Peirce and James

When it comes to the two general lines of interpretation of habit traced by Clare Carlisle within the history of Western philosophy, the Classical Pragmatists most certainly championed the trend emphasizing the basic and positive role of habits in human life (2014, 3).[1] They made an impressive contribution to the development of a philosophy of habit that should be recovered and developed as a crucial category within a philosophical anthropology capable of engaging with other disciplines in an open-minded way—from sociology and anthropology to the cognitive sciences and evolutionary psychology. All of the Classical Pragmatists envisaged habits as affirmative and pervasive parts of life, by contrast to those scholars who considered habits "an obstacle to reflection and a threat to freedom" (2014, 3). It should be recalled that, even within the framework of the genuinely pluralistic approach of his *Anthropology from a Pragmatic Point of View*, Immanuel Kant maintained a strong anti-Aristotelian vein and considered moral duty to be essentially foreign to habit, because it "should always proceed, fresh and original, from one's mode of thought" (2006, 32). On the contrary, James (1983a) and Dewey (1988a) were strenuous supporters of the view of will as thoroughly constituted by habits, that is, by actual capacities to do something, rather than as beginning ex nihilo and capable of giving rise to action in a sort of purely rational *vacuum*—by adopting the language used by supporters of the view of the mind as enactive and embodied, I am claiming that human will and agency is thoroughly scaffolded by habits, although they cannot simply be reduced to habits.

Before James and Dewey, Peirce introduced habits at the heart of logic, by considering them to be doubly crucial in inferential processes. The end of an inference is basically the establishment of a belief that is—according to Peirce's original appropriation of Alexander Bain's idea—a habit or a disposition to behave in a certain way (1992–1998). We are very far from the idea of belief as a modal operator through which propositional content should be managed, an idea that is standard in doxastic logic. For Peirce, the goal of thinking is to find relief from a real doubt arising when it becomes difficult to act, because it is unclear what can and eventually should be done to face an indeterminate situation (Dewey 1991). Drawing a conclusion means solving an irritating doubt by fixing a new rule for acting and behaving. Furthermore, habits of thought—or "habits of mind," such as selecting, emphasizing, assuming, risking, and so on—are already involved in the working out of an inference, because they are the solid means by which an inferential process is actually enacted (Peirce, 1992–1998). From a reading of Peirce's anti-Cartesian essays, it becomes clear that there is neither a direct line from theory to practice, nor a direct line from practice to theory, but rather a sort of dynamic circle between different issues—some more dubious or problematic, others more likely to be taken for granted at a certain time.[2] Dewey was to radicalize Peirce's incipient antiintellectualist stance by moving toward a more naturalistic perspective, as well as by displacing the primary site of habit fixation from a conscious act of habit revision to the already existing relationship between a human being and her or his own social environment. However, Peirce did not limit his interest in habits to the decisive functions they are assumed to play in the logic of thought. As has been shown by his interpreters (Colapietro 2004; MacMullan 2013; Feodorov 2017; Bernardi 2017), later on Peirce extended the role of habits to the cosmological field by regarding them as the self-making laws of a completely contingent cosmos, where "chance" is the first category, "law" the second, and "habit-taking" the third (MacMullan 2013, 234). In passing from logic to cosmology, however, Peirce missed a properly anthropological focus on habits.

For sure, there is an echo of Peirce's cosmology in the opening paragraphs of William James's chapter on habit in his *Principles of Psychology* (MacMullan 2013, 235): "The laws of Nature are nothing but the immutable habits which the different elementary sorts of matter follow in their actions and reactions upon each other" (James 1981, 109). However, James immediately focuses on the peculiarities of habits in living creatures and, more specifically, in humans—peculiarities that are grounded in a basic continuity within nature. The key concept to understand James's interpretation of habits is that of plasticity, which was famously influenced by Darwin. Plasticity is not envisaged as the exclusive property of the nervous system, but as something characterizing all forms of matter, even inanimate matter—although, of course, differences of degree are extremely meaningful. The point is that plasticity is understood in essentially relational terms by James: "in the wide sense of the word [it] means the possession of a structure weak enough to yield to an influence, but strong enough not to yield all in one" (1981, 110). In other words, plasticity is clearly a function of the interdependence of a certain matter from the actions that can be carried out on it within a certain context. Hence, "*the phenomenon of habit in living beings is due to the plasticity of the organic materials of which their bodies are composed.*" From my point of view, "plasticity" is a first key notion allowing James and the Pragmatists to distance themselves from an associationist view of habit as something resulting from the repeated combination of simple elements, namely, a stimulus and a reaction, assumed to be essentially discontinuous phenomena (Barandarian & Di Paolo 2014, 5; see also Egbert & Barandiarian 2014). "Plasticity" introduces the idea of an organism's behavior as the result of the mutual and dynamic dependence between a living being and the environment it belongs to, paving the way for a holistic or ecological conception of habit. Dewey will bring this insight to its extreme consequences, as I will claim in the following sections.

In James's *Principles*, repeated actions and behaviors can draw neural paths as ways of responding to environmental influences because of the distinctly high degree of plasticity of our nervous system. This means that James considers the human nervous system to be not a fixed entity, completely equipped with all properties, but rather a system which dynamically configures itself in relation to what is happening around it. In contrast with the current trends toward forms of physical reductionism, and particularly the dogmatic idea of the causal closure of the physical realm,[3] James considered our brain a function of the environment and as having a history. The structure of the brain and cerebral dynamics were not assumed to be the preexisting physical causes governing our meaningful behaviors, but were rather seen as open to the retroaction of cultural uses and norms—foreshadowing Dewey's cultural naturalism (1991, 25).[4] The brain seems to be dynamically shaped by those actions that are selected, reinforced, and preferred to other behaviors because of their capacity to simplify an otherwise too complicated and indeterminate variety of responses humans can give to environmental events—since they have lost the majority of merely instinctual reactions in comparison to other animals.[5] Furthermore, habits ensure more space and time for selective attention, by allowing the majority of our behaviors to be implemented without conscious deliberation.

This was probably another point of interest for Dewey in James's treatment of habits, compared to Peirce's account of habit as originating in a conscious individual act. James explicitly acknowledges that habits are primarily enacted by the body, rather than being the output of mental representations and thoughtful inferences: "In action grown habitual, what instigates each new muscular contraction to take place in its appointed order is not a thought or a perception, but the *sensation occasioned by the muscular contraction just finished*. A strictly voluntary act has to be guided by idea, perception, and volition, throughout its whole course. In a habitual action, mere sensation is a sufficient guide, and the upper regions of brain and mind are set comparatively free" (1981, 120).

However, James is not clear about the first occurrence of a habitual action, which seems to be limited to the individual body facing a complex environment. The transition from the physiological to the social perspective on habits remains obscure in the *Principles*. In any case, I agree with Dewey's reading of James, according to which his treatment of habits was particularly meaningful with respect to this kind of continuistic and functionalistic biological approach.[6] A physiological understanding of habits did not lead James to become a radical materialist but, as stated by David E. Leary, "Habit [. . .] was the key to James's solution of the dilemma that he faced as he weighed the intellectual attractiveness of an entirely materialistic and causal explanation of humane existence [. . .] against the equally compellingly moral imperative to believe that he could and should live a responsible and meaningful life" (2013, 178).[7] Radicalizing this line of thought, Dewey claimed that approaching human action through the concept of habit could be a good way to avoid the common and long-standing dualism between body and mind (Dewey 1984b).

3. A Deweyan Privilege

As stated above, both Peirce and James made broad use of the notion of habit, applying it on a cosmological scale as well as to the inorganic world. Consequently, they saw habits as being widespread throughout the inorganic as well as organic world, albeit to different degrees.

Dewey devoted more energy and time to the treatment of the concept of habit than any other Classical Pragmatist. Nonetheless, I argue that there are other good reasons to ground the development of the philosophical significance of habit in his *Human Nature and Conduct*, in addition to the fact that he devoted more pages to the topic than any other Pragmatist.

First, Dewey's primary focus on habits is anthropological: it is deeply connected with an idea of human nature and the constitution of human individual selves within a naturally social environment. Dewey was convinced that only by seriously taking into account the natural (biological, physiological, habitual, and meaningful) ways in which humans are living beings, could it be possible to derive some important consequences on the moral and political levels—and this in relation to human facticity rather than a metaphysical picture of the will as intervening in experience from without. Dewey states: "any theory which attributes the origin of rule to deliberate design is false" (1988a, 5). He argues that in order to avoid fallacious misconceptions, philosophy should desist from severing morality "from the actualities of human physiology and psychology" (1988a, 6).

A strong naturalistic trend toward habit was already present at the end of the nineteenth century because of the Darwinian revolution. In his *Habit and Instinct* (1896), Conwy Lloyd Morgan considered habit to be a notion applicable throughout the world of living beings. He envisaged the strict relationships between habit and instinct as extensively permeating animal behavior and framed this account within an incipient evolutionary biological perspective. This naturalistic tendency to consider habit to be something pervasive in the living world was clearly confirmed in 1929 by Frank Lorimer, a scholar who had Dewey as his PhD supervisor.[8] In his book *The Growth of Reason*, he placed habit at the heart of living processes, by depicting organic life as characterized by a structural tension to affirm and maintain itself within the natural environment. "Habit formation" is the complementary phase of "organismic tension" (1929, 13), which is to say the dialectic dynamics characterizing organic-environmental systems. The "fundamental principle of habit formation" is "individual organismic adaptation in relation to actual conditions which tend to disturb organic equilibrium" (1929, 12). Although these authors' insights crucially contributed to revealing the natural continuum within the living world and to extending it even to the inorganic world in the case of Peirce and James, the issue at stake remains open from an anthropological point of view. How and to what extent—if at all—does habitual human behavior differ from other organisms' already habitual ways of interacting with the environment? On this point, Dewey's contribution—together with some important insights from Mead—is much more helpful and provides some tools to answer the question and further develop a pragmatist approach to human habits. Through Dewey and Mead, I contend, it is possible to find some answers to the question of why humans are bundles of habits in a more intensive and extensive way than plants and other animals. These answers interconnect biological, cultural, and social factors within a clearly cultural-naturalistic account and problematize dogmatic distinctions between innate and acquired, instinctual and habitual.

Second, Dewey definitely allows me to reach a strongly relational or ecological conception of habits by coherently developing some of the previous pragmatist insights. From the very beginning, it is clear that for Dewey habits are not primarily a property of an agent with a specific innate or acquired endowment, but functions of the mutual interdependence and the constitutive transactions taking place between organisms and their environment. As was the case with his criticism of the reflex-arc concept (1972), the idea that a habit is the iteration of a linear connection between a specific stimulus and a behavioral response stems from the process of isolating and abstracting specific phases of a more complex situation and unjustifiably considering their combination to provide a truthful description of their structure.

There is also a third reason, I would argue, for privileging a Deweyan conception of habits, which is because his approach coherently combines a physiological account of habits with a social one. Truth be told, William James himself had already combined a strongly naturalistic (but nonreductive, as I have argued above) conception of habit with a social and moral attitude toward the consequences of habit-formation in the fields of education and politics. It is widely known that his interests went in that direction not only in *Talk to Teachers*, but also in *Principles*, where he famously defined habits as "the enormous fly-wheel of society." However, the connection between the two sides of the concept remains unfocused and must be clarified in order to avoid dualistic misunderstandings. Dewey instead anchored his idea of habit in the explicit assumption of the naturally social structure of the human world, providing tools to analyze not only the continuity between nature and culture, but also that between social and individual factors in behavior. I would argue that his engagement with Mead's biosocial approach to behavior was crucial in promoting this line of thought and should be further developed also with reference to current interdisciplinary research (Baggio 2015).

To sum up, habit emerges as a key concept for developing a coherent form of cultural naturalism—which is to say, for grasping the continuity of human behavior within the natural world, while taking into account the relative discontinuity caused by the emergence of the human way of life within nature.

4. Giving Habits an Ecological Framework

I think we could profit from the philosophical move Dewey makes from the very beginning of his book, if we interpret the role of habit within the human form of life in light of his reframing of the usual treatment of habit. Habits should be examined within the organic-environmental setting where life takes place rather than in relation to the individual agent who first consciously performs an act and then repeats it until it becomes an almost automatic part of his conduct. This is the main significance of the comparison with physiological functions by which Dewey introduces his idea of habit: habits requires a constitutive "cooperation of organism and the environment" (1988a, 15). Just as breathing requires both the lungs and oxygen in the air; digestion both food and the tissues of the stomach; walking both legs and a more or less stable ground; and speech phonatory organs, air as a medium, and human companionship, similarly habits are "functions of the surroundings as truly as of a person" (1988a, 15). This involves explicitly giving up any methodological individualism as a privileged approach to habits by claiming that "a belief of exclusive ownership" (1988a, 15) on the part of the subject is misleading and reflects a clearly transactional (Quéré 2016, 6–7; Sullivan 2013, 258), organicist (Barandarian & Di Paolo 2014, 5), or ecological (Quéré 2016, 12) definition of habits as functions: as "ways of using and incorporating the environment in which the latter has its say as sure as the former" (Dewey 1988a, 15).

Although Dewey did not provide a definition of habit, I propose to derive from his work a conception of habit as a more or less flexible channeling of both organic and environmental energies and resources, given that the distinction between an organism and the environment it belongs to and contributes to constantly changing from the inside is operative, pragmatic, or functional, rather than metaphysical or ontological (Alexander 1987). I use the word *energies* in a nontechnical way and with an ontologically tolerant attitude, to mean the wide variety of resources—bodily capacities, memories, and imaginative resources from previous interactions, linguistic tools, phases, and modes of experience, as well as experienced situations, materials and things, and already existing habits, including one's own and those of other people—regardless of whether they come from the natural, social, or cultural environment or from within the organism. Consequently, a habit can be changed only if both individual dispositions and environmental factors intertwine in different ways and give rise to a new channeling of previous energies.

This definition of habit, which I derive from Dewey's legacy, is convergent with the notion supported by some theorists of the mind such as Xabier Barandarian and Ezequiel Di Paolo, who call for the recovery of a holistic concept of habit as a way of interpreting human action and of avoiding any recourse to mental representation as radically embodied, embedded, and enacted (2014). According to the idea of habit that they derive from "the organicist trend," habits are "ecological, self-organizing structures that relate to a web of predispositions and plastic dependencies both in the agent and in the environment" (2014, 1). Louis Quéré makes a similar point by stressing the difference between "interaction" and "transaction," and definitely characterizing habits by means of the latter category. In habits, as far as they are understood according to the model of physiological functions, "there is not only an interaction between the organism and its environment, but a transaction. Transaction means conjoined operations that are distributed and enacted within an integrated system, differently from the ordered composition of internal and external energies" (2016, 12–13; my translation).

This position is far from the idea of habits as primarily properties of a subject and her or his own conduct, because the agent—even the human agent is assumed to be part of the environment he or she belongs to and contributes dynamically to changing from within. As already mentioned, Thomas Alexander (1987) suggested that the same distinction between organism and environment was functional and operative for Dewey and should not be hypostatized, as has been the case throughout most of the history of modern philosophy. By adopting the dynamic system approach preferred by enactivists, it could be said that for Dewey the organism and the environment constitute an autonomous system, giving rise to a dynamically configured stable equilibrium among its different parts.

Complementarily, this kind of approach entails abandoning the idea that habits are primarily constituted by iterated associations of atomic entities or events, namely, of stimuli and responses—as was the case in most behavioristic literature (Egbert & Barandarian 2014). As early as 1896, Dewey's criticism of the reflex arc concept revealed his strategy of thought, grounded in a naturalized appropriation of Hegel's dialectic reflection, which tends to consider individual moments as events or entities isolated and abstracted from the whole process, that is, an "organic circle" characterizing the conduct of a complex living being. For sure, we can conceptualize a habit as beginning with the iterated connections of the stimulus produced by external reality on the subject and the following subjective reactions by which he or she responds. However, this picture tends to isolate certain phases of a continuous flow of transactions between the organism and its environment, and to consider the parts for the whole. This view obscures the actual conditions in which the bodily and intellectual resources of the living being operate and are embedded; consequently, it mistakenly ignores that the subject's actions are constituted by the former (the actual environmental conditions) as well as by the latter (the agent's capacities and resources). On the other hand, the above-mentioned image of habit as the repetition of a simply linear process overlooks the fact that a specific event occurring in the world can be perceived as a stimulus by a living being only if there is a selective propensity on the part of the organism itself to be touched by that event and not by a different one, because of physiological or cultural reasons.

5. A Historical Analysis: A Comparison with Conwy Lloyd Morgan

In my view, adopting an account of habit as resulting from the active cooperation of both organic and environmental energies is conceptually a crucial point that could be of value in many fields—from philosophy of mind to the theory of agency, from the cognitive sciences and evolutionary psychology to the social sciences. Its more important consequences, as already claimed by Dewey, ought to be considered on the moral and political level—whether and how changes of habits and social reform are possible was the key issue for him.

However, this was also a crucial theoretical gain from a historical point of view. In this section, I will suggest that the impact of Dewey's ecological conception of habit can be appreciated by comparing his view with the conception of habit developed by Conwy Lloyd Morgan, who published his book *Habit and Instinct* in 1896. Dewey did not refer to Conwy Lloyd Morgan's work in his *Human Nature and Conduct*—although Morgan's book was derived from a series of lectures he gave in Boston, New York, and Chicago in 1896, when Dewey was still there. Instead, he mentioned Morgan's *Instinct and Experience* (1912) in *Experience and Nature* and he was more generally familiar with the comparative psychologist's work.[9] Nonetheless, a comparison between their positions is useful, I claim, because Dewey and the English comparative psychologist share a similar naturalistic stance, relying on the assumption of a degree of continuity between human behavior and that of other animals, based on a common deflationary attitude toward the distinction between instincts and habits, as well as on a minimal notion of consciousness, on Morgan's part. Morgan was still drawing and trying to define an operative distinction between instincts and habits in his book, because he believed it to be important for solving the problem of the transmission of acquired features (1896, 23). However, he explicitly considers the distinction to be functional and based on the continuity between innate and acquired behaviors, the latter being a modification of the former (1896, 19 and 21). Basically, he draws a structural distinction of this kind: instinctive or congenital acts are ones that are grounded in inherited organic mechanisms and do not depend on learning, imitation or individual experience (1896, 25); they can be present even when an individual is isolated from the social group he or she belongs to, and they can originate an action occurring only once in the life of the organism (1896, 17). By contrast, Morgan assumes habits to be behaviors that are not inherited, but rather the product of individual acquisition, stereotyped through repetition (1896, 17). An organic mechanism is at work even in the case of habitual behaviors, but it develops in the course of one's life through the individual coordination and repetition of past experiences (1896, 17). Morgan, however, states that the purely instinctive, congenital, and completely automatic kind of action only occurs at the first occurrence, because the second time it is enacted, it is influenced by the results of previous experience that have been individually acquired (1896, 136). Consequently, there are reasons to claim that also among nonhuman animals instinctual behaviors are largely acquired, because all those behaviors resulting from the introduction of a difference by means of an individual experience are acquired: chickens, for example, very quickly learn to select their food, by eating only good worms and neglecting bad ones (1896, 19). By adopting a minimal notion of effective consciousness as the selective disposition guiding an organism on the basis of previous individual experiences Morgan (1896, 127) claims that a habit begins with a conscious acquisition based on an individualized experience and its correlative cerebral processing at the cortical level, engendering on its turn an acquired automatism through constant repetition of the same act (1896, 141). An organism's behavior transits from conscious to automatic through the association of a stimulus with a response applied to a new case similar to a previous one (1896, 151). Hence, according to the comparative psychologist, individual consciousness intervenes twice in habitual behavior: "first, it is concerned in the establishment of habits; and, secondly, in the utilization of all the active powers, including the habits so established, in meeting the varied requirements of daily life" (1896, 147).

Dewey's account of habits differs from Morgan's theory in many respects. First, Dewey, who exclusively focuses on humans, is even more radical than Conwy Lloyd Morgan in avoiding any metaphysical distinction between instincts and habits—the title of one of the chapters in his book is "No separate instincts." Nonetheless, the most insightful point for the issue at stake here is the reasons for Dewey's criticism of a traditional psychology of original instincts (1988a, 108)—reasons that could be described as holistic, transactional, or ecological in the sense discussed above. Dewey claims that "the notion of a single and separate tendency" (1988a, 104–5)—let's say hunger, sex, or fear—as a preexisting instinctual force founding human action and behavior is fallacious because it is partial and one-sided. First of all, human (but probably even animal) behavior is oversimplified when it is explained through linear causality: "no activity (even one that is limited to routine habit) is confined to the channel which is most flagrantly involved in its execution. The whole organism is concerned in every act to some extent and in some fashion, internal organs as well as muscular, secretion, etc. Since the total state of the organism is never exactly twice alike, in so far the phenomenon of hunger and sex are never twice the same fact" (1988a, 105). Dewey considered individual acts as taking place within the continuous flow of conduct; they cannot be explained as resulting either from the primacy of perception over motion (1972) or from the primacy of brain mechanisms over overt action (2004), because perception is already oriented by the movements made by the eyes, head, and body as a whole, as well as by interests, sensibility, and already existing habits—both primarily bodily and intellectual. Complementarily, brain processes are seen as one important factor in behavior together with many others—organic, cultural, social, and so on. Furthermore, as James already foresaw in the *Principles*, a plurality of nervous nets are simultaneously active when an action take place and a complex reverberation in the nervous system corresponds to the flow of thought (1981, 235).

Second, the idea of a single predisposition waiting to be expressed in a culturally habitual way is fallacious for Dewey because "the environment in which the act takes place is never twice alike. Even when the overt organic discharge is substantially the same, the acts impinge on a different environment and thus have different consequences" (1988a, 105). The crucial lesson we can draw from Dewey is a reconceptualization of behavior, understood as the result of the transactions between an organism and its environment, which exercise a reciprocal action by changing and shaping each other, although at different levels. More specifically, behaviors and habits are not properties of an isolated subject operating in a vacuum, but involve the channeling of both organic and environmental resources that are equally part of the resulting act.

Two frequent Deweyan examples are walking and seeing (1988a, 15). Walking habits cannot be considered the simple output of organic factors such as the upright posture of humans and the specific structure and dynamics of their two legs. These habits are also the result of the ground, of its being more or less sloping or slippery, and so on. Furthermore, the habit of locomotion cannot be isolated from other habits—especially seeing—since they are deeply coordinated and intertwined, "counteracted" (1988a, 26) in a unitary dynamic schema. However, this is not all, because each individual does not move and see things alone in her or his environment: the copresence of "a society or a specific group of fellow-men" (1988a, 16) affects habits in a variety of ways: from taking into account other people's walking directions, and one's own and others' peri-personal spaces, to perceiving others as implicitly assuming one's pace as appropriate or not to a specific social environment—a kind of proto-normative value implicitly related to a professional context or a more informal one.

This discourse implies that habits in Dewey cannot be considered to be separate potential dispositions waiting to be actualized in practice (see Quéré 2016). I will deal with this side of the argument in another section devoted to a comparison with Pierre Bourdieu's theory of habitus, because I think that the issue could be better presented in that way. For the moment, let's return to the discussion about Morgan's account of habits.

In addition to the different reasons for problematizing a dogmatic distinction between instincts and habits, Dewey did not share Morgan's (and Peirce's) idea that a habit is always the result of the conscious act of a single living agent. That an individual is always involved in the performance of a habitual behavior is obviously true, and Dewey never dreamed of denying this. The issue is rather that, from a Deweyan point of view, this picture of habit acquisition fails to take into account the structurally social environment where human actions occur and consequently the circumstance that many habits are already at work in the social group and that the child assimilates them with her or his mother's milk. Usual ways of doing things, engaging in certain practices and managing situations are already there and shape the child's environment; for the most part, even adults are embedded in broadly habitual practices without focusing on them. Of course, when something goes wrong or does not work, the individual is led to consider her or his habits of action reflectively, to revise and change them, as is clearly the case in the distinction between customary and reflective morality (Dewey 1978; 1985). However, this change—while crucial from a moral point of view—is always secondary, in the sense that a conscious revision of an old habit relies on an already given background of established habits, working on a more or less prepersonal level.

To sum up this point, I believe that the comparison between Morgan and Dewey is helpful to clarify the view that habits are mostly prepersonal before they have the chance to become conscious and individualized.

6. A Naturally Social Environment as the Ecological Framework of Human Habits

A further distinctive feature we can infer from Dewey's conception of habits is the overt convergence of the biological and physiological aspects of the Homo sapiens with his structurally social nature. What we find in *Human Nature and Conduct* is not a mere juxtaposition of the naturalistic and the social accounts of habits, but an explicit argument in favor of their basic intertwining within the human form of life. On this issue Dewey essentially agreed with Mead, and it could be argued that with his 1922 book he coherently developed Mead's idea of social psychology as the counterpart of physiological psychology (Mead 2011, 9)—an idea adumbrated in a germinal essay as early as 1909.

This is an important point because historically the social character of habits has been used to emphasize the divide between nature and culture, and to nourish the debate between the supporters of a universalistic idea of humanity and the champions of a strongly relativistic stance. Ruth

Benedict, who studied under Franz Boas at Columbia University (Ratner 1985, xvi) and attended classes given by John Dewey (Kent 1996), translated Dewey's concept of habit into that of custom in her *Patterns of Culture* and declared it to have been partly inspired by *Human Nature and Culture* (Ratner 1985, xvi). Although Benedict did not deny the existence of natural constraints in human culture, her proposal was not without consequences, because her strong stress on the primarily social and inherited dimension of human practices in relation to individual conduct encouraged a trend to downplay the role of biological factors in culture—a trend that had robust political implications at a time when the theory of race had become the core of fascist ideology. While it is true that "Man is not committed in detail by his biological constitution to any particular variety of behavior" (Benedict 1935, 10), one should take into account the fact that the biological constitution of human mammals entails a very serious dependency on a social group that finds no parallel in animal life. Although I am aware of the dangerous misunderstandings associated with biological reductionism (Dupré 2001), I agree with Shannon Sullivan that a biological approach to human habits could strengthen our understanding of ethical and political issues. From this point of view, I contend, human social dependency is a key aspect—probably more so than human embodiedness (Sullivan 2013). Given this caveat, we can now consider how Dewey connects the naturalistic and the social sides of habits. As we have seen in the previous section, a naturalistic conception of habits in the Deweyan vein sees habit as the result of the interdependence and mutual shaping of an organism and its environment, rather than in terms of an organism's properties. In other words, the ecological background against which a certain mode of behavior occurs is explicitly conceived as one of its constitutive factors, together with organic resources. This is true for animals other than humans, as well as for humans in this naturalistic perspective. The specificity of human behavior appears to be related to the peculiar structure of the human environment. Without any hesitation, Dewey claims that the human world is essentially social: it is more social than other animals' environment both on a quantitative and on a qualitative level (1984a), because it is characterized by forms of cooperative agency—sometimes friendly, often aggressive—that are necessary for human survival and flourishing. Hence, human "[c]onduct is always shared" (1988a, 16) and human habits are social functions (1988a, 15) because they arise out of the transactions with a naturally social environment humans are a part of and are continuously changing through their activities. Rejecting metaphysical arguments in favor of an alleged primacy of society over the individual, Dewey (1988a, 44) prefers to adopt a deflationary, antiintellectualistic stance. The philosophical problem of how society could arise from the actions of single individuals seems like a paper doubt when considering the commonplace that "some pre-existing association of human beings is prior to every particular human being who is born into the world" (1988a, 44). The artificial issue of intersubjectivity and the birth of society out of isolated, independent individuals "is not solved by reference to psychic causes," but "by reference to facts of action, demand for food, for houses, for a mate, for someone to talk to and listen to one to talk, for control of others" (1988a, 45). All of the above-mentioned needs and demands are intensified by the fact that "[e]ach person is born an infant, and every infant is subject from the first breath he draws and the first cry he utters to the attention and demands of others. These others are not persons in general with minds in general. They are beings with habits, and beings who upon the whole esteem the habits they have" (1988a, 43).

Dewey reframes the traditional problem of other minds, famously laid out by Descartes and later recovered by Husserl's phenomenology as well as by most philosophies of mind—to the point that methodological individualism has become the main trend in the cognitive sciences. Following Dewey, one should bear in mind that the whole issue is not purely theoretical and practically neutral, but has serious consequences on the ethical and political levels—with the history of modern philosophy presenting the emergence of human society as artificial and deriving from an agreement among essentially independent subjects. The alleged puzzle of intersubjectivity is not to be solved by looking into special mental processes and/or brain mechanisms. Rather, the pragmatist strategy is to regard intersubjectivity from the point of view of the conditions of life characterizing human mammals, their particularly heightened dependence on a social group to survive, live, and flourish. Dewey's reframing occurs by focusing on the banal fact of the everyday human dependence on other persons as a means to satisfy basic needs and accomplish all sorts of activities, as well as on the obvious preexistence of a social group with respect to the individual person. Consequently, I suggest making Dewey's approach more explicit by arguing that humans are bundles of habits more pervasively than other living beings, because from their very births they are embedded in a social environment of people behaving habitually. Individual conduct is habitual because it does not take place in a vacuum, according to the traditional picture of the free will of a disembodied consciousness and an essentially acosmic subject. On the contrary, each individual person's conduct is largely habitual because it derives from the transactions of bodily beings with a naturally social environment. Hence, I suggest a second characterization of habits as ways of doing things and ways in which things are done that are already there before each individual makes her or his own choices. Even much of the development of the human brain occurs within the context of a group of people acting habitually during each individual's first year of life, as Mead later realized.

From this I derive the groundbreaking idea that human habits do not begin with a conscious choice on the part of the individual agent, but rather primarily reach the individual from the group of people he or she belongs to. Habits are not private in the metaphysical sense of the term: many of them are already there before the individual takes them on, individualizing them and, at the same time, being shaped by the habits he or she adopts, rejects, or reinvents. I think that in most cases of habituation we can apply what Dewey says about artistic expression in *Art as Experience*, where he questions the traditional picture of the artist as a genius creating ex nihilo. The role of the individual in the acquisition of habits lies not at the beginning of the process but in the middle, where individuals play a crucial function in reorganizing preexisting material and experiences, both deriving from the social environment, its natural and cultural constraints, and from the individuals themselves, their organic needs, and their interests. For the most part, the individual "remake[s] and redirect[s] previously established customs" (Dewey 1988a, 44). This role can become conscious when something does not work, when the irritation of doubt rises (Peirce 1992–1998), or when an agent has to face a morally indeterminate situation (Dewey 1984c) and revise a previously established habit, but this is not always the case. Nonetheless, for the most part, habituation does not require one to be conscious, as is evident in early infancy but often happens even in adult life. This is an important difference with respect to Peirce's primary focus on the idea that the fixation of habit begins with a conscious act on the part of the subject. Dewey reframes the whole issue by shifting our attention to the other side of the process: in order to reach a new belief as a disposition to behave, other habits must be already at work within the inferential process. Furthermore, this does not apply just to habits of thought (Kestenbaum 1992), but also to the bodily and existential habits common to a social background. They can become conscious habits to a certain degree, but most of them cannot be focused on in order for the new habit of action to be explicitly reached.

7. How Does Habituation Occur?

The idea that shared habits and customs precede the process of habituation in the individual opens up new horizons and problems. One first issue regards the ways in which the individual acquisition of habits takes place; a second problem involves the traditional conception of self-identity and the individual mind as preconditions for action. I will develop this second line of thought in the next section, after I have dealt with the first aspect.

Dewey basically never inquired into the modes of habit acquisition because he probably thought—at least to some extent—that this was a false problem. Babies are born and grow up within families, villages, and institutions, that is, within social contexts where behaviors are already largely habitual, based on rules, and guided by shared norms; consequently, young men and women cannot but develop their own ways of behaving by adjusting to existing ways of doing things that are already widespread in their environmental context.

However, I propose translating this description into a general argument: (1) given a conception of behavior as the result of the structural interactions between an organism and its environment,[10] (2) and given that the human environment is naturally social and largely characterized by habitual actions, (3) an individual behavior is habitual because of the peculiar organic and environmental constraints it derives from. For example, my parents' generation in Italy spontaneously learned to remain silent and quiet in primary school classrooms, seated composedly on their little chairs, because that was the most obvious way for them to attune their context bodily, affectively, and culturally. Current generations of schoolchildren behave much more energetically in the classroom, asking their teacher questions, moving about more or less boisterously, and speaking more or less loudly according to the conduct style of their teacher. Usually, the more authoritative the teacher is, the more controlled and passive the pupils' behavior is; conversely, the more open the teacher is, the more ready to intervene the child is. In any case, the habit matured by each pupil does not consist in the imitation of the teacher's habit, but in accommodating him- or herself to the teaching habits of the adult.[11]

An important contribution to this topic derives from Mead's early criticism of imitation as a key concept used in psychology to explain language and habit acquisition (2011, 14). Mead considered this assumption to be misleading because learning to speak does not mean being able to reproduce another person's utterances, but being able to give a pertinent answer to her or his utterances. Rather than a matter of copying, learning to speak involves the capacity to attune oneself to the other's utterances, to fall into the rhythm of the conversation, and to take the other person's turn and role, by seeing one's own actions as they are perceived by the other. The crucial point in any shared activity for Mead is not the mimetic repetition of the other's behavior, but feeling the other's action as a stimulus to do something in response to him or her (2011, 14). If we consider other habits apart from linguistic ones, it seems that an analogous process frequently takes place. There are habits involving forms of attunement with a primarily physical environment and habits where the social turn- and role-taking are more decisive, but most of them occur within a framework of already existing social practices. For example, when a child learns to ride a bicycle, usually he or she has already seen other children and adults riding a bike. However, this is not the crucial point: I would say that in taking her or his first steps in bike riding, the child's eminent conscious focus is on avoiding possible falls, while learning to stay in dynamic equilibrium on the two wheels is the by-product of that primary goal. Consequently, I would argue that the dynamic body schema (Merlau-Ponty 2002) enabling the child to ride a bike should be seen as the result of the attunement between bodily resources (arm and leg length, muscular strength, readiness to react to the loss of balance, etc.) and the environmental conditions where the action takes place (wheel size, road conditions, etc.), including the social arrangement of the context (lack of cars and other dangerous vehicles, an adult pushing the aspiring cyclist from behind and gradually withdrawing her or his arms). In the case of learning to eat with a knife and fork, the social habits and constraints are evidently stronger and rest on a sort of social sensitivity (Ostrow 1990) operating on a qualitative-affective level whose significance tends to be immediately felt, rather than inferred through arguments—"I'll eat with my hands because it upsets my mum and I'm angry with her" or "I'll eat like the other children in the kindergarten because I'm a big boy too." Imitation also comes into play in the acquisition of hand, mouth, and fork coordination, but the pursuit of a goal and emotion-based behavior toward the other members of the group are likewise important features.[12] From this point of view, it seems misleading to consider habit to be a ready-made sensory-motor schema that is later exposed to a sociocultural space (Dreyfus 2005). On the other hand, the social dimension of habit is one of the factors concretely involved in the process of habit-formation, but it cannot be reduced to a rational set of norms regarded as an enabling condition for perception and habitual action (as McDowell 2013 & Shear 2013).

It could be objected that there are bodily habits that are independent of social contexts and exclusively based on dynamic bodily schemas. The point, however, is that they are very difficult to find. Habits connected to basic human needs and characteristics, such as walking and sleeping, could be seen as the best candidates. At first sight, walking seems to be simply a matter of bodily motor-coordination with dynamic ground- and space-perception. Nonetheless, Marcel Mauss's pioneering essays *Les techniques du corps* already stressed sociocultural aspects as integral aspects of habit-formation.[13] Evoking World War II hospitals, Mauss reported that nurses walked through the wards with something of a Hollywood actress's style, spontaneously different from the walking style of the nuns (Mauss 1936). Mauss's inquiry into the varied ways of sleeping—on soft mattresses, directly on the hard ground, but also standing up in the trenches during the World War I—supports his thesis that bodily techniques constitute a kind of "editing" of biological, psychological, and social factors (Mauss 1936). He strongly opposed the traditional conception of the bodily act as deriving from previous purely psychological processing, but he also denied that a habit is exhausted by a bodily schema that is only introduced into a public space at a later stage. By contrast, he spoke of bodily techniques as "social idiosyncrasies," where the naturally social human environment enters into the concrete constitution of habits.[14] Consequently, even if Merleau-Ponty's treatment of habits as dynamic bodily schemas is very helpful for understanding the bodily component of habit formation (2002), I think that his view, as well as the treatment provided by other scholars explicitly inspired by his thought (Dreyfus 2014; Nöe 2004), is a partial one insofar as it does not take into account the naturally social dimension of the human environment as a constitutive factor in the shaping of habits and behaviors. Hence, the social extension of bodily schema claimed by some of the authors belonging to the enactivist trend in cognitive science (Gallagher 2013; Fusaroli et al. 2014) should be endorsed and strengthened from a pragmatist point of view.

There is also another important consequence for the current debate that should be derived from an ecological idea of habits, and that is to say the following: the view that habits are ways of behaving constituted by both organic and environmental resources; and that, in the case of human beings, the environment is for the most part a naturally sociocultural world, laden with habits, practices, meanings, and rules. Assuming that humans find themselves in an already enlanguaged niche and that environmental resources cooperate in producing habits, my contention is that we should reject any rigid distinction between low-order cognitive processes, excluding language and knowledge mediated by mental representation, and higher-order cognitive processes, requiring this kind of mediation (Hutto & Myin 2013).[15] Habits are the active powers through which humans perceive, move, know, act, and even feel, at least partially; and they require a channeling of all the energies at their disposal in a specific situation. These energies and resources can be eminently bodily, as in swimming; nonetheless, what also comes into play in the case of swimming habits is the fact, for example, that one prevalently practices swimming as a sport in a swimming pool or that one frequently swims in the open sea. Not only the physical structure of the swimming pool, but also the sociocultural dynamics of going for a swim in an athletic swimming pool contribute to shaping one's strokes and breathing. Conversely, other mainly intellectual abilities, such as drawing inferences from a laboratory experiment, can be reinterpreted in terms of habits: the habit of selecting invariant features from background variations, the habit of treating similar aspects as identical, while disregarding small variations, and the habit of venturing a hypothesis to fill a gap in the steps of the argument we are trying to formulate; but also the habit of cooperating with other researchers in a lab, whether collaborators or seniors, as well as manual and technical habits related to the use of more or less complicated devices. From a certain point of view, habits appear to be bundles of resources of different kinds—organic, cultural, technical, and social. Sometimes certain resources seem to be predominant when it comes to doing certain things, but in a pragmatist vein I see no reason for assigning them a decisive role within the complex web of relations involved in the dynamic channeling that constitutes a habit—especially if they deal with either mental or nervous resources.

Differences of degrees are important and could be maintained when needed between more basic practices and more refined linguistic-discursive cognition. However, assuming that human perception takes place exclusively at a bodily level, apart from the naturally sociocultural context it is already embedded in is as misleading as to assume that sensibility is primarily made possible via mental representations assumed to be cognitive entities or events occurring in the mind, independently from a world of shared practices, and habits of action and communication. Considering all of human abilities to be made through habits, that is, through the cooperation of all available resources, could be a way out of an impasse that risks becoming the ultimate philosophical cramp.

8. About the Place of Mind in Habits

In the previous section, I made use of Deweyan resources to provide an account of habit acquisition as a process primarily unfolding from a social environment to the individual. This account should now be more coherently connected with the issue of the place of the mind in habits and the traditional conception of action as produced by a subject or an individual mind. As stated above, I think that Dewey's idea of the individual as an intermediate factor in habitual action, basically remaking and redirecting previously established customs (1988a, 44), should be regarded as pivotal. The self is seen as the agency reorganizing previously existing habits with old and new environmental constraints, as well as by means of organic, cultural, and social resources and energies.

On this ground, Dewey formulates his criticism of the basic premise of individualistic psychology, according to which an individual mind or subject must already be given in order for an action to take place through him or her. "The net outcome accordingly is that what can be called distinctively individual in behavior and mind is not, contrary to traditional theory, an original datum. Doubtless physical and physiological individuality always colors responsive activity and hence modifies the form which custom assumes in its personal reproductions. [. . .] But it is important to note that it is a quality of habit, not an element of force existing apart from adjustment of the environment and capable of being termed a separate individual mind" (1988a, 60).

Dewey challenges all the properties characterizing the conception of the subject in modern philosophy as well as in "orthodox psychology," that is, the idea that it is (1) independent from the world or the reality it is assumed to face, (2) separate from both nature and others—it is conceived as a mind essentially different from the body and as a mind whose relationships with the minds of others is dubious and has to be explained, and (3) prior to each empirical exchange with the outer world (1988a, 60). Instead, just like Mead, Dewey views the self as being forged through the relations it is embedded in at least from birth, if not earlier—relations with the surrounding natural environment, as well as the social relations already constituting this environment. Indeed, "For human beings, the environing affairs directly important are those formed by the activities of other human beings" (1988a, 60), from which their own existence depends and to whom their lives are exposed. Some years before, Mead had stated that "primitive consciousness even of the physical world is social" (2011, 3).

Dewey makes an interesting remark on psychoanalysis: the idea of the unconscious is "of the utmost value" because it emphasizes that the self is constituted by a mixture of conflicts and contacts with other individuals, and this is "equivalent to practical recognition of the dependence of mind upon habit and of habit upon social conditions" (1988a, 61). Nonetheless, the problem is that psychoanalysis still attributes the unconscious to a separate realm, and takes for granted the traditional assumption of the originality of the individual mind vis-à-vis society, whose institution consequently becomes a problem and is fundamentally seen as involving a repression of the subject's most private and egoistic tendencies (Freud 1919).

By contrast, Dewey and Mead adopted a view of psychology as originally social, in the sense that the individual mind looks like a result or an emergent mode of interaction with the environment basically consisting in the appropriation of already existing habits and ways of behaving, in their redirection and reorganization through a change in the environmental situation that makes a previously established habit unsuccessful or inappropriate, and affected by impulses—organic needs pushing to be satisfied and working as "the pivots upon which the reorganization of activities turn" (Dewey 1988a, 67).

Individual character is seen as deriving from the particular blend or narrative of habits the person has acquired from her or his social group and personally redirected, reshaped, or rejected. Self-identity is open, dynamic, and constituted by the continuous sedimentation and individualization of already existing habits. Hence, according to Dewey, habits primarily work "below direct consciousness" (1988a, 26), and most of them are originally acquired on a prepersonal level, in the sense that they are spontaneously absorbed from the social environment unproblematically, without any trouble or need to be focused, simply because they work. A crisis or a doubt represents a second, capital chance for habit-acquisition and redirection. It is when something goes wrong and a usual habit does not work that a specific interaction becomes conscious and the individual feels the need to respond in a different way—to take on her or his responsibility in the almost literal sense of the term.

This insight has important consequences on the ethical level, where Dewey introduced the two concepts of customary and reflective morality (1978; 1985a). In contrast to the Kantian picture, Dewey emphasized the fact that an individual's reflective and intelligent evaluations, namely, her or his conscious decisions, do not come first, that is, are not made in a vacuum. Rather, they arise out of a background of largely prepersonal and habitual, qualitatively, affectively or aesthetically configured ways of reacting to environmental circumstances and other people's conducts, which have to be taken into account as the source of more reflective behaviors, intelligent and voluntary decision-making, appraisal, and judgment, as well as their ultimate point of arrival.[16] Furthermore, morality is structurally grounded in habits, understood as the capacity to effectively do things.[17] Consequently, the will appears to be constituted by habits that are the active forces through which it can operate, because the will is conceived of as fully embodied and constrained by organic and environmental factors, rather than as the offshoot of a disembodied consciousness. Habits are not opposed to morality, but they nourish it both in its customary occurrences and when morality becomes reflective. To engage in reflection and decision making is not to abandon all the habits that governed our conduct until a moment of troubling crisis and to reach a pure choice. The point is that a moral dilemma pushes the individual to reconsider some of her or his previously established habits of conduct, to abandon them and acquire other habits, which is to say to redirect old habits and to transform her or his routine, unintelligent habits into intelligent habits or arts (Dewey 1988a, 51 and 55), that is, into more flexible and fruitful ways of channeling both organic and environmental energies. Moreover, it is clear that the reflective, which is to say conscious, transformation of an old habit is possible only against the background of other still more or less silently working habits and capacities, enacting processes of reflection as well as basically organic-environmental transactions.[18]

9. Why Are Habits Pervasive within the Human Form of Life?

It is time now to assess the peculiarity of human habits in a world widely characterized by habitual relations, as stated by both Charles Peirce and William James. Before Dewey, other scholars had emphasized the relevance of social habits in the shaping of individual behavior. However, he assigned habits a pervasive as well as constitutive role in supporting the interactions of human organisms with their natural and naturally social environment. Why such a radical position on this issue? And should we agree with it now? Dewey did not give a single explicit response to this question, but I think a cluster of answers can be gathered from his work and further radicalized within a coherent framework.

One important feature is plasticity, which was already introduced when considering James's treatment of habit. More precisely, it has to do with the fact that the human nervous system is the one with the highest degree of plasticity in nature. As already stressed (section 2), James's conception of plasticity is connected to an understanding of the world in its physical, biological, and human dimensions as basically a continuum, and it involves the assumption that human behaviors and practices can condition and reshape the physiology of the human nervous system. While James's emphasis is on neural flexibility, Dewey shifts the focus to the extreme variability of the contexts where actions take place, namely, the environment as the other crucial factor shaping behavior together with organic aspects: "the environment in which the act takes place is never twice alike. Even when the overt organic discharge is substantially the same, the acts impinge upon a different environment and thus have different consequences" (Dewey 1988a, 105).

Dewey's insight foreshadowed the contemporary emphasis on the absence of niche specialization in the human life form, originally highlighted by von Uexküll and later incorporated into Arnold Gehlen's idea of humans as still indeterminate animals and instinctually deficient beings (Gehlen 1988).[19] However, in Dewey's view, there is no emphasis on an allegedly radical break in organism-environment relations between humans and other animals. For sure, the range of possible interactions is wider in humans than in other animals, but world precariousness and stability are not viewed as exclusive human experiences, as they are according to existentialism and German philosophical anthropology. Rather, it is connected with the facts of life in general: because living beings are constitutively dependent on their environment to survive and flourish, their lives are continuously rhythmical dynamics of instability and temporary equilibrium. As stated by Frank Lorimer, habits are inscribed into the fact of life itself in embryonic form, representing its phases of momentary adaptation to those environmental conditions giving relief to organic tension (1929, 12–13). Furthermore, Dewey (like James and Morgan) adopted a more flexible conception of the differences between instincts or native impulses and habits. Assuming that behavior is always the result of the interaction of organic and environmental energies, rather than a property of the person, Dewey points out that any impulse is diversified according to the different environmental conditions in which it arises. For example, "Fear may become abject cowardice, prudent caution, reverence for superiors or respect for equals; an agency for credulous swallowing of absurd superstitions or for wary scepticism" (1988a, 69). Pure fear as a mere vital instinct never occurs as a separate phenomenon, independently from a complex situation, where both environmental factors and other organic impulses can occur and produce a different result. This is one of the reasons why Dewey claims right from the very beginning of his treatise that impulses are secondary to habits, although they are native (1988a, 3, see also 65), and why in chapter 12 he challenges the idea of separate instincts as a basis for conduct (1988a, 104 and ff.). Dewey's interest in this aspect of human conduct was far from purely theoretical; rather, he was particularly attentive to the differences it entailed in the life of both individuals and groups. Plasticity can be a powerful resource to change conducts and institutions into a more fruitful means to improve human life and mature more intelligent habits of judgment. On the other hand, it can mean docility, passiveness vis-à-vis power and authority, regressive conservatism, and the absence of critical thought (1988a, 70–71).

A second crucial aspect for understanding Dewey's emphasis on habits as something pervasive and structural in human behavior is humans' radical dependence on a social environment, especially at birth, that is before a sense of self-identity and conscious behavior emerge. As already noted, Dewey generally stressed that most human activities are shared and require a collaborative activity in order to be realized. He also focused on the peculiarity of human birth and the baby's strong dependence on the social group it belongs to because of its severe immaturity at birth. Very often, he returns to the fact that human infants begin their lives as "helpless, dependent creature[s]" (1988a, 45, see also 60) subject to the "attentions and demands of others" (1988a, 43). "Their activities could continue at most for only a few hours were it not for the presence and aid of adults with their formed habits" (1988a, 65). This is the main reason why Dewey claimed that in human beings what is acquired, namely, habits, "is the primitive" and that "Impulses although first in time are never primary in fact; they are secondary and dependent" (1988a, 65). Indeed, native impulses depend, from the very beginning, "upon interaction with a mature social medium" (1988a, 65), and consequently they are immediately exposed to and shaped by an already largely habitual social environment. There is no time for an impulse to express itself in the void, because the infant's conduct is exposed to the already channeled organic-environmental resources constituting the makeup of its own environment before its maturation occurs—on both the behavioral and the organic level (including that of the neural system).

Mead was even more explicit in connecting human immaturity at birth with the centrality of habits in human life. In an unpublished essay, whose exact date remains unknown but which probably dates back to the first or the second decade of the twentieth century, Mead devoted his attention to the relation of embryological development to education (2011, 73–82). He quotes John Fiske, one of the Darwin-inspired thinkers who influenced the Classical Pragmatists together with Chauncey Wright. "He has worked out in some detail the value of the long dependence of the child form upon the parent forms in the evolution of society. He has shown that no animal which had so long a period of dependence could possibly have survived, unless he grew up within a community in which all the essentials of our social relations were at least implicitly contained" (2011, 73).

Mead, in particular, derives from Fiske's idea of the primary social importance of infancy the hypothesis that habits can develop precisely because of the very extended period of high dependence of the child. If the baby adapted very quickly, almost instinctively, to its environment, it could not develop those valuable habits that are so favorable to the emergence of higher forms of intelligence. Consequently, Mead not only adopted a continuistic stance with reference to habitual behaviors and their connection to intelligence, but also conceived of reason as being largely dependent on habitual practices.[20] Thanks to the antidogmatic reading of Darwin in Classical Pragmatism, Dewey and Mead seem to foreshadow the evolutionist attention for processes of fetalization and neoteny in human ontogenesis and philogenesis (Bolk 1926; see also

Gould 1977, particularly ch. 9, "Progenesis and Neoteny," and ch. 10, "Retardation and Neoteny in Human Evolution"). More specifically, they already noted the strange peculiarity of the immaturity of human beings at birth compared to other mammals and their extremely long period of postfetal maturation. This was later studied by the Swiss biologist and anthropologist Adolf Portmann under the name of secondary altriciality[21] (1941; 1945) and was assumed by Arnold Gehlen. Nonetheless, while Portmann and most scholars of human evolution have focused on the long extra-uterine development of the human brain, Dewey and Mead centered their attention on the precocious exposure of the still immature infant to an already socialized and habitual environment—stressing how the infant differs from other mammals not only in brain development, but also in the ability to stand up, walk, and stay close to its mother or caregiver.[22] Habitual conditioning on individual behavior is already at work before the infant can say "I" and make conscious choices, and it appears reasonable to assume that self-identity emerges gradually out of socially acquired habits, directing native impulses from their very beginning.

There is also a third important factor that plays an essential role in the conception of human conduct as something basically enacted through habits, namely, embodiment. As strongly stressed by authors like Shusterman (2008) and Johnson (2007), Dewey considered the agent a fully embodied organism long before the embodiment turn in cognitive science. His polemical target was the leading idea of the subject as independently determined before her or his relationships with external reality are established and give rise to action through a rational, conscious act of free will—an idea that was a major trend in modern philosophy. This is particularly evident in both of his *Ethics* (1978; 1985), where Dewey strongly reacts against a formalistic conception of morality, assuming a pure imperative as the only necessary and sufficient condition for legitimate action. This view could work only for a disembodied consciousness or for a divine being, capable of giving rise to action ex nihilo. Dewey clearly assumed that the agent who feels, moves, acts, and thinks is a body, namely, a living organism. Differently from a pure consciousness, a bodily being has to channel its own energies as well as environmental resources in a specific direction, by relying on preexisting habits—that is, means and capacities—which it has found itself already embedded in. Habits are the diverse means scaffolding human perception, movement, cognition, and will, and they are not mediated by mental representations but enacted through effective powers to do something, given specific bodily and cultural constraints. For sure, an agent can reconsider, reject, or change old ways of moving, feeling, and reasoning when it becomes urgent to do so in a specific situation, but the process occurs against the background of already acquired habits that continue to support the organic and significant interactions within a given context—not in a vacuum, where reason operates as a creator ex nihilo and perception mirrors the reality out there.

Dewey is not a materialist in the reductive sense of the term. On the contrary, the point is that

> In the case of no other engine does one suppose that a defective machine will turn out good goods simply because it is invited to. Everywhere else we recognize that the design and structure of the agency employed tell directly upon the work done. Given a bad habit and the 'will' or the mental direction to get a good result, and the actual happening is a reverse or looking-glass manifestation of the usual fault—a compensatory twist in the opposite direction. Refusal to recognize this fact only leads to a separation of mind from body, and to supposing that mental or 'psychical' mechanisms are different in kind from those of bodily operations and independent of them. (1988a, 27)

The thesis that human conduct is structurally habitual because humans are fully embodied living beings emerges more clearly when considering bad habits. Referring to a remark made by a friend, the postural and respiration therapist Frederick Matthias Alexander, Dewey spoke of the traditional way of conceiving change in conduct as superstitious.[23] The false belief consists in supposing that, "if one is told what to do, if the right end is pointed to them, all that is required in order to bring about the right act is will or wish on the part of the one who is to act" (1988a, 23). This belief appears misleading when we consider a bad posture—for example, slouching. First of all, a crisis—big or small—must take place in order to produce a change of habits. In other words, something must occur in one's surroundings in order to elicit criticism of an established habit: this crisis might be brought about by a strong pain, for example; in the case of a young boy, the problem might be finding himself in a social group where he is expected to look athletic. Second, being attentive and trying to consciously keep one's shoulders back is far from easy: as soon as the person with a tendency to slouch forgets to mind her or his posture, the old habit will immediately be reestablished. In order to change her or his posture, this individual has to follow some training that will help him or her to adopt the right position and make a change in her or his environmental conditions (e.g., by swimming regularly or setting up a better workstation): this person must acquire a new habit or capacity to channel energies and find a new, more satisfying dynamic equilibrium in self-moving. A change cannot be achieved without a means or a capacity to reorganize existing resources, and without relying on a complex net of already existing habits (e.g., walking or sitting on a chair or, when writing on a laptop, seeing through glasses or being tired and frustrated) that shape each individual act. This is the sense of Dewey's statement that habits are will (1988a, 21 and ff.): they are the capacities or the active means by which will is effectively enacted, assuming that will regards a fully embodied agent, rather than a mere evanescent consciousness.

In 1926, in an essay on *Body and Mind*, Dewey declared that the concept of habit could function as a means to dissolve the enduring dualism between the mental and the bodily. Now, hopefully, this statement could appear to be a succinct formula rather than a mere slogan, coming from his nonrhetorical problematization of other dichotomies such as natural versus cultural, biological versus social, and innate versus acquired. From this point of view, Dewey largely foreshadowed the idea of the mind as something radically embodied that is now widely endorsed in cognitive science: habits are assumed to be the means by which embodied mastery is constituted. In any case, Dewey and Mead's emphasis on the bodily dimension of habit formation was integrated into the assumption that the human environment is naturally social from the very beginning—and not the other way round, as is now the case in the current debate on the mind as embodied and socially extended.

10. Refining a Deweyan Conception of Habits through Bourdieu's Account of Habitus (I): Convergences

Within the social sciences, there has been a powerful return of the concept of "habitus" after a long period of absence due to the general criticism leveled against behaviorism and the connected idea of habit as the merely mechanical iteration of a conditioned answer to a specific stimulus (Camic 1986). Pierre Bourdieu's work represented a breakthrough for recovering the concept among the basic tools of sociology, although the Latin word *habitus* was favored as an alternative to *habit*, which was felt to be a compromized term because of the use made of it by Pavlov and his colleagues (Crossley 2013b).[24] Bourdieu's concept of habitus shares some important aspects with Dewey's concept of habit but there are, I would argue, also some relevant differences. A comparison between pragmatism and critical sociology is interesting in itself, but even apart from that, I believe that an analysis of the divergences between Dewey's and Bourdieu's conception could be helpful at this point of the current inquiry into a pragmatist view of the concept of habit. It could help draw some important distinctions within the plurality of layers of the notion of habit, and hence to achieve a better clarification of this very concept.[25] A first major convergence between Bourdieu's habitus and Dewey's habit is in regard to their common understanding of these notions in terms of capacity, dexterity, acquired ability, faculty, mastery, competence, and the capacity to react. Although neither Dewey nor Bourdieu explicitly connected their conceptions to Aristotle, there is a clear air of family resemblance, documented in the case of Bourdieu through Marcel Mauss, who referred to the concept of *hexis* in his essay devoted to bodily techniques (Mauss 1936). They both struggled against a mechanistic view of habit, regarded as the repetition of a purely mechanical answer, as was already the case in psychological behaviorism. Their criticism involved more than a mechanistic understanding of habit, which is to say the idea that the overall framework of behavior is made up of simply linear associations of perceptive stimuli with correspondent motor responses. Dewey developed a decisive criticism of that view on his own, in his famous 1896 essay on the reflex-arc concept (1972), which he sought to replace with the holistic concept of organic circle. Bourdieu inherited a critical view of the associationist understanding of behavior from Merleau-Ponty, who had extensively discussed stimulus-response causal linearity as an oversimplified paradigm for understanding perception in the 1940s (1963; 2002). Although Dewey and the Pragmatists kept the word *habit*, they too distanced themselves from the common meaning of the term as routine and mere repetition. For sure, there are bad habits, namely, fixed routines that are no longer able to face a changed situation effectively; nonetheless, the common use of the term is generally negative, lacking the productive force and active capacity that both Dewey and Bourdieu recognized as crucial.

A second important point of convergence is the idea that both habits and habitus largely work on a prereflective, nonconscious and preconceptual level, although they are not opposed to cognition. Rather, Dewey and Bourdieu understood habits and habitus as entailing a kind of embodied mastery, practical knowledge, competency or expertise (see Crossley 2013a; 2013b). Bourdieu partly derived this idea from Merleau-Ponty and his category of "praktognosia," that is, the practical knowledge inhering in each body and its capacities to move and orient itself in space, to catch something, and to approach or distance itself from another body (among other things), without having to pass through mental representations and the objectification of isolated portions of perception (Merleau-Ponty 2002). In addition, from the very beginning of his ethnological studies in Algeria Bourdieu was interested in the logic of practice, which was attributed a degree of coherency and a capacity to manage experiences, while distinguishing it from discursive logic (1977; 1992).

Dewey had all the instruments required to interpret habits in terms of embodied mastery. Some he derived from James and Peirce, while plenty of others were nourished by his own naturalism. He grounded his reinscription of cognition in experience and his understanding of it as an inquiry designed to find a way out of an indeterminate situation in his idea of the agent as an organism, which is to say a bodily living being fully embedded in its own environment—an idea very far from the traditionally modern view of the subject as independent from the reality "out there." Habits are for the most part practical, embodied ways of managing both organic and environmental resources until a crisis occurs and the need to find a different way of acting elicits an intelligent inquiry and a process of inference—as stated by Peirce—incorporating a new mode of action into a new habit, namely, the changing of a past habit.

This is not the only way in which Peirce redefined the connections between habits and cognition. *Human Nature and Conduct* develops Peirce's incipient insight that the process of inference, which is to say intelligence is based and works by means of habits of thought. Selecting some aspects and disregarding others, searching for similarities and invariant features, envisaging alternatives and risking working hypothesis, among other faculties, are effective capacities scaffolding intelligence.

They are not largely unconscious because they are irrational. Rather, they are unconscious because inferential processes must be focused on the results sought rather than on the means by which they can be attained, until the moment when inference fails and the intelligent tools through which it was produced need to be revised. A third common aspect concerns habitus inscription in the social space and the placement of habits within a naturally social environment. Dewey and Bourdieu do not only embrace a general thesis on the social characterization of habits. More radically, both thinkers (as well as Mead and Mauss) never hesitate to consider embodied habits to be structurally embedded within a social medium, which comes into play in their constitution. In a Deweyan or Meadian perspective, habit acquisition in early infancy occurs within a social group of caregivers, whose already existing bodily, affective, and communicative habits shape the child's most intimate habits. For Bourdieu, bodily-cultural habits such as eating with a knife and fork, rather than with one's fingers, are incorporated through a sort of "osmosis" from the social world to the individual. For both Dewey and Bourdieu the agent or the living being never operates in a vacuum, as her or his world is a social space or a naturally social environment that is already populated with and formed by a multitude of social and individual habits that contribute to the constitution of the individual's behavior, decision making, and even character and self-identity.

11. Refining a Deweyan Conception of Habits through Bourdieu's Account of Habitus (II): Divergences

All of these convergences are significant, but there are also some important divergences. In contrast to Dewey's concept of habits, Bourdieu's habitus works as a quasi–a priori behavioral device, encompassing all of one's behavior and making it conform to a generally coherent style; it is a single principle and resistant to change. I would argue that these features are evident in the very way in which Bourdieu speaks of habitus, given that the term is used as a singular noun and, when it is used in the plural form, it is not attributed to the same agent but to a plurality of agents, each having her or his own habitus.[26] It could be claimed that there is a difference between an individual's habitus and the habitus of a social class but, given the radically social characterization of individual agency in Bourdieu's approach, the two features must be understood as strictly relational (1989), and it would be misleading to consider them to be independent from each other. Moreover, the main point is that a single agent's conduct seems to be characterized by one and only one habitus shaping all of her or his actions according to the same tacit stylistic principle, even if it can partially diverge from that of the social group he or she belongs to because of the specific composition of the capital supporting her or his movements within the social space. Of course, an agent might have more than one habitus, meaning that he or she might move from one point to another of the social space and consequently develop a trajectory habitus (1989) that is different from the habitus of the social group he or she originally belonged to. This is the case, for instance, with the construction worker in the northeast of Italy, who uses all of his resources to become a small entrepreneur and then displays new signs of distinction together with traces of his past social status as a laborer (Veblen 1899). It is also the case with the impoverished member of a formerly renowned and rich family, who has to work hard to support her or his wife and children, but is still troubled because her or his previous leisure habits demand satisfaction. In that case, there would be a struggle between the two habitus, trying to affirm themselves as the prevalent principle of the agent's whole conduct, because Bourdieu tends to see conduct as something that is engendered by a single matrix ensuring uniformity and coherence across the various actions and fields of action. By contrast, Dewey always speaks about habits in the plural and considers an individual's behavior as being characterized by many habits that are not only different but often also divergent and conflicting. He even considers the copresence of contrasting habits in a single person as a possibly fruitful event, representing the chance for a crisis, for reflective analysis on habits of conduct that were previously assumed as obvious and unproblematic, as well as an opportunity for a rejection, revision, or even strengthening and reaffirmation of habits. Dewey sees education as offering a chance for young, still flexible minds to be exposed to patterns of behavior different from their family and group customs. Play and the arts exercise a similar function, according to him. The arts are not only seen as one of the main ways in which a common sensibility and ethos is incorporated and shared by its members (1989, 10, 329, ff.). In *Human Nature and Conduct*, Dewey presents the practicing and experiencing of art as a chance to see one's own life in a different way, to consider the possibility to change, and to go in a different direction.[27] "The service of art and play is to engage and release impulses in ways quite different from those in which they are occupied and employed in ordinary activities" (1988a, 112). "They are required to introduce variety, flexibility and sensitiveness into disposition" (1988a, 111). To sum up, for Dewey habits are plural in the human world, not only in general societal life, but even within individual lives both diachronically and synchronically. The varieties of habits and conflicts between them are seen in a favorable light and should be cultivated as factors for habit-change, for their conscious assessment, and for a transition from customary to reflective morality. This last aspect represents another point of divergence between Bourdieu's concept of habitus and Dewey's view of habits. In Bourdieu's conception, a habitus tends to be resistant to change and to be seen as an agent of conservation. It is widely known that in his later texts Bourdieu attempted to partially revise his view of habitus in light of the criticism he had received on this point and to open it to change (see Crossley 2013b, 294).[28] He also recognized the existence of crises producing breaks in the reproduction of a habitus, but "[s]uch moments are relatively rare and involve major social and political upheaval for Bourdieu" (Crossley 2013a, 151). My opinion is that his openness to consider the habitus subject to change and revision is obstructed by other aspects of his theory. On the one hand, Bourdieu regards self-reproduction, extension, and duplication into different activities, as well as the transposition of the same structure into different fields of agency as basic traits of the habitus, which tends first of all to last, to be durable, and to resist any change. The conservation and imposition of the same seems to be the mark of the habitus. On the other hand, Bourdieu never developed any hypothesis about the process of a habitus changing, unlike Dewey who strongly focused on the dynamic processes related to the acquisition, revision, modification, denial or new acceptance of habits, and the replacement of routine habits with more intelligent ones (and vice versa). Crises in conduct occur continuously in ordinary life and are factors of change as well as chances to reorganize existing resources in more favorable (or indeed worse) ways, to behave more intelligently and more responsibly, or even only differently, in the face of a changed existential situation. As channels of both organic and environmental energies, habits are certainly relatively stable—channels usually have banks and a bed, and they can be more rigid or more flexible. However, the banks and bed of a channel can be modified and disappear, as well as be strengthened. Furthermore, there are channels that are not supported by any structure but are simply based on production of waves—be they electric or magnetic. They only exist when they are produced.

This last point, again, allows me to touch on a crucial divergence, represented by Bourdieu's quasi–a priori view of habitus.

A couple of definitions might be useful to help illustrate what I mean. In his first attempt to outline a theory of practice out of his inquiries into Kabylian ethnology, Bourdieu defined the habitus as a "system of lasting and transposable dispositions which, integrating past experience, functions at every moment as a matrix of perceptions, appreciation and actions, and makes possible the achievement of (an) infinitely diversified task, thanks to analogical transfers of schemes permitting the solution of similarly shaped problems" (1977, 82–83).

Some years later, in *Distinction: A Social Critique of the Judgement of Taste*, Bourdieu characterized the habitus as "the generative formula which makes it possible to account both for the classifiable practices and products and for the judgements, themselves classified, which make these practices and works into a system of distinctive signs" (1984, 170).

And furthermore:

> The habitus is necessity internalized and converted into a disposition that generates meaningful practices and meaning-giving perceptions; it is a general, transposable disposition that carries out a systematic, universal application beyond the limits of what has been directly learnt of the necessity inherent in the learning conditions. That is why an agent's whole set of practices (or those of a whole set of agents produced by similar conditions) are both systematic, inasmuch as they are the product of the application of identical (or interchangeable) schemes, and systematically distinct from the practices constituting another life style." (Bourdieu 1984, 170)

Bourdieu's different definitions of habitus, although more or less rich, always seem to converge with the idea of the habitus as a unique structure or enabling device, shaping and governing every empirical action of an individual. Bourdieu speaks of a "system" of enduring dispositions, of a unique "matrix" forging and giving uniformity to one's own perceptions and expectations, of a "generative formula" producing further similar modes of action and ruling our classification of actions, of "necessity internalized," capable of giving our behavior the coherence of a unitary system of practices. Lexical choices are unambiguous when it comes to this issue and clearly introduce a distance between habitus and single habits, between a quasi–a priori enabling device and its a posteriori instances. The gap between a habitus and "a whole set of practices" engendered by the habitus itself is similar to—albeit less extreme than—the difference between a transcendental condition and its empirical occurrences. Ironically, Bourdieu did not give up the Kantian effort to find a principle governing "the fertile *bathos* of experience" (Kant 1997, 125), although the habitus as a quasi–a priori principle is nonpure, fully embodied, and embedded in the largely opaque logic of practice. With regard to this point, Foucault was right in claiming that the distinction between a transcendental and an empirical level continues to govern modern episteme about humans, as Nick Crossley recalls (2013a, 145; 1971). These remarks are convergent with Louis Quéré's criticism of Bourdieu's dispositional conception of habitus (2016); by conceiving the habitus as a system of dispositions and a system of schemes, Bourdieu would fall into the kind of dispositionalism criticized by Wittgenstein (see Chauviré 2002). Dispositionalism is the idea of a permanent potentiality considered as a hidden and underlying mechanism explaining reality—grounded in the assumption that reality (the wide range of human practices in this case) needs to be explained by having recourse to an additional level (namely, a habitus), and cannot be taken as such, for what it is.

I agree with Quéré and Crossley that this is not the case with Dewey's conception of habits, which is foreign to the logic of searching for a principle explaining human practices on a deeper level. Habits are effective capacities to do things and manage surrounding circumstances, but there is no preestablished mechanism explaining them. Not even a mental representation or a neural path works as a naturalized enabling condition because, in a Deweyan vein, it must be seen as one of the resources that are channeled in a specific practice, together with other organic resources, as well as with environmental energies and conditions. This point can be assessed in light of a passage from *Human Nature and Conduct* on the possibility of understanding habits as means or tools. Dewey states:

> We may think of habits as means, waiting, like tools in a box, to be used by conscious resolve. But they are something more than that. They are active means, means that project themselves, energetic and dominating ways of acting. [. . .]

Even the saw and hammer are means only when they are employed in some actual making. Otherwise they are tools, or potential means. They are actual means only when brought in conjunction with eye, arm and hand in some specific operation. [. . .] And whenever they are in action they are cooperating with external materials and energies" (1988a, 22).

Habits are not identical to predefined schemes of action, deposited within the body as neurological programs or within the mind as mental representations. Rather, habits are ways of organizing preexisting resources—physiological mechanisms as well as already existing ways of doing, speaking, and thinking: for, according to Dewey, this is what the human environment and consequently the human mind are largely composed of, together with material conditions. Drawing a distinction between the potential and the effective use of a tool is legitimate and helpful, but it is a functional, operative, and contingent distinction, not a dogmatic and hierarchical one. This deflating way of thinking is also evident in Dewey's openness to consider the words *attitude* and *disposition* possible synonyms of *habit* (1988a, 31–32). The important issue for him is to maintain the projective, dynamic, and operative quality of the word *habit* together with its reference to a capacity to retain prior activity and acquired sense. "Attitude" and "disposition," instead, "suggest something latent, potential, something which requires a positive stimulus outside themselves to become active" (1988a, 31). In other words, these terms tend to leave out the fact that a habit is not simply established by a subjective mechanism, but consists in the effective organization of already existent behavioral resources (both bodily and intellectual) with ecological features and conditions.

To return to the possible definition of habits as a relatively flexible channeling of both organic and environmental resources, I would stress two aspects of the connected metaphor. As mentioned above, channels—water channels as well as tunnels dug underground—usually have banks and a bed. But there are even channels—electric or magnetic channels—that have neither banks nor a bed, as well as channels—such as those dug by children building of a sand castle on the seashore—that have a bed only for the time in which a stream of seawater keeps flowing through them. In any case, banks and beds can change, usually less rapidly than streams of water, be they natural or made by human hands (see Boncompagni 2012). There is no ontological difference between the former and the latter, but only a functional and open distinction within a context and a natural history of acquisition, stiffening, revision, and change of habits. This is the reason why I prefer to speak of "channeling," in order to emphasize the dynamic structures of habits, their being processes, although they often become stiffened and compulsory.

The above-mentioned quasi–a prioristic (or "dispositional, in Quéré's words) nature of Bourdieu's habitus can be seen even by considering the role that is attributed to the body. For sure, as noted before, Bourdieu characterizes the habitus as strongly embodied and acted on through the body. However, the body tends to be considered the place and the means for the sedimentation and reproduction of the habitus, rather than as an active factor in the organizing of both organic and environmental resources. In his account, the movement occurs from the social space to the bodily dimension and then extends to other practices via bodily means. Bourdieu's example of learning to eat with a knife and fork and then extending the same lifestyle to handwriting is a clear case illustrating the function of the body as a fundamental means of habitus reproduction.

To conclude this chapter, it may be useful to mention one last difference between Dewey's and Bourdieu's view of habitus, related to the prereflective as the general background of habits. Probably influenced by the phenomenological tradition, Bourdieu considers the logic of practice to be structurally alien to the typical intellectual need to give reasons for practices—a peculiar practical logic that in his view is inevitably transformed and betrayed by theoretical procedures (1992). A Deweyan conception of the relationships between the prereflective, qualitative phases of experience and more conscious, reflective movements and choices is more complex, circular or at least bidirectional. As has been emphasized with reference to sensibility, Dewey always points to a "vast complex of other qualities and things that in the experience itself are objects of esteem or aversion, of decision, of use, of suffering, of endeavor, of revolt," in which "the intellectual element is set" (2004, 3). However, the results of intellectual analysis are sedimented in unreflective experience, in the very fabric of human sensibility and emotional structures, contributing to redirecting and reshaping them.

12. Habits and Change

Can we derive any practical difference from comparisons of this kind? I think that these distinctions between habits as a plural matrix of behavior and the habitus as a single one, between a quasi–a priori conception and a naturalistic, contingent, and reviewable one, are not of merely theoretical import. It can make a great difference to consider habits as primarily acquired at a prepersonal level. In other words, the point is the typically pragmatic issue of the consequences of a specific theory on our lives at a more or less close level. Briefly, what I mean is a conception of habits as plural and provisional, as involving a channeling of resources coming both from the organic and intellectual factors of the individual and from the natural, as well as the naturally social and largely habitual environment that he or she is interacting with, rather than as hidden devices at work behind empirical practices. I think that such a conception has at least one important consequence for the way in which we relate to the life and actions of others, both individually and as group, as well as for our own ways of acting and behaving. The point is that this Deweyan approach to habits can be helpful for viewing and using them not only as the main means for moral and political conservatism but also as agents of change. At the same time, the view that habits are mostly acquired prereflectively from one's social group and consciously considered only when they no longer work could encourage us to focus on the ways in which a critical revision, rejection, reappropriation or transformation of habits takes place.

In a genuinely pluralistic vein, Dewey avoided painting a picture of habits as something exclusively dominated by power relationships. Habits are more than just ways of shaping and maintaining asymmetrical social relations and inequalities. Rather, they always involve power in the sense of the capacity and effective ability to do something, to organize and manage resources, even if very often they enter into crisis and need to be revised.[29] Habits do not always work in a regressive direction, be it on the epistemic or the political level. This does not mean, of course, that Dewey was not conscious of the enormous weight of habits on societal life—inquiring into the possibility of reform or revolution, he said that institutions are stiffened and externalized habits (1988a, 76).

It is unquestionably the case that habits can become the mere confirmation of a social order, can become regressive and prevent the critical evaluation of a given political or economic context. In any case, Dewey's approach is not one-sided: habits are plural and often divergent; they primarily derive from the social group a person belongs to, but people do not belong to only one social group. Habits are acquired and integrated by passing through an individual filter that is made of a peculiar mixture of stories, relations, and impulses. Habits are not irreversible because they are imposed by the social context. Rather, the individual is an integral part of the social context itself and can contribute to changing it from within by means of her or his actions and reflective choices, as well as by means of new habits, even though there are certainly very significant differences of degree regarding the capacity of individuals to revise old habits and collective customs—economic behaviors and political practices being among the most challenging contexts, of course. There is no doubt that the channeling of organic and environmental energies through habits and the plasticity of impulses can turn into a socially and politically regressive forces and can ensure largely predictable and controllable behaviors for marketing experts as well as for politicians eager to win votes.

In any case, in light of the above-discussed approach, crises appear to be important: changes in the material constraints affecting the way a habitual action takes place tend to open a gap through which a native impulse can arise and elicit either a rejection or modification of a no longer effective habit. Individual impulses are not necessarily negative or antisocial (as was held to be the case from Hobbes to Freud). They could also represent chances to introduce greater flexibility within behavior. Exposure to a large variety of different and sometimes diverging habits and customs can be a means for the reflective reappropriation, denial, or reshaping of previously established habits. Dewey mentioned education, play, and the arts as a means to expose oneself to pluralism, but the current widespread multiculturalism could be taken as a much stronger challenge. Could the disruptive effect of the frequently abrupt present-day exposure to other cultural, religious, and political customs be channeled into a more critical reconsideration of the habits opaquely ruling our own forms of life? Certainly, there is no guarantee of success, but I have the impression that there are not many other democratic alternatives open.

An interesting example suggested by Dewey pertains to human work and the chance for men and women to find satisfaction and to enjoy their own work, instead of considering it mere drudgery, as has been the case from the famous episode in Genesis to the current exploitation of labor in both postindustrial societies and so-called economically developing countries. Considering work to be mere toil performed to bring some money home is a clearly regressive habit, confirming social distinctions based on economic power and legitimizing, among other things, the deletion of any aesthetic quality in work and the complementary confinement of the arts to the sphere of leisure time and entertainment (Dewey 1989, 15). "The existing psychology of the industrial worker for example is slack, irresponsible, combining a maximum of mechanical routine with a maximum of explosive, unregulated impulsiveness. These things have been bred by the existing economic system. But they exist, and are formidable obstacles to social change" (Dewey 1988a, 89).

Nonetheless, the distance from an idea of habitus as a single matrix generating a whole lifestyle makes quite a difference, as do the criteria by which other lifestyles can be classified.

Dewey thinks that some habits can be criticized, rejected, or transformed if something changes in the real-life conditions where they take place, whether this change comes from the context or from the agent. Of course, a critical appraisal of a previously assumed habit can only occur against the background of other habits operating at a prereflective level. Dewey reminds us that "no adult environment is all of one piece. The more complex a culture is, the more certain it is to include habits formed on differing, even conflicting patterns" (1988a, 128). Considering the case of industrial work, if one of the industrial crises we are acquainted with in our days were to occur, it might lead to the bankruptcy of a certain company or its acquisition by a larger corporation, to the detriment of the workers. Nonetheless, such a crisis could also open up other avenues: for example, the workers might become involved in the management of the enterprise and turn it into a cooperative business in the best-case scenario, as happened in Germany in the 1970s or with the Mondragon cooperatives in the 1950s (Stikkers 2011). In other, less frequent cases, deciding to change one's life and to follow one's own personal aspirations can lead someone to find a more satisfying, if less profitable, career. These are very partial and maybe overly optimistic answers, but they remain faithful to the idea that the social fabric and the shared environment are the only immanent resources we can count on.

A similar case may be represented by ways of consuming food within different cultural contexts and in different economic systems. Researchers have discovered that most food production and commercialization across the world is dominated by just a small number of international corporations controlling the market. In Italy, we suffer less from the consequences of this—starting with the consumption of low-quality, unsafe food—because of our habits connected with the preparation and shared consumption of food. Italians tend to expect high standards when it comes to nutrition, but this seems to be becoming more and more a privilege of the culturally conscious middle class, while broad segments of the population are increasing their consumption of junk food. However, because of the enormous public health cost of poor nutrition, educational programs promoting safer approaches to eating are now being provided to children from the kindergarten level up. There is no guarantee that future adult generations in Italy will be able to resist the increasing power of the international corporations controlling the food market. Nonetheless, working on previously established habits and the chance to transform them into more critical choices and new, more intelligent habits, seems like an affordable strategy.

To conclude, a few words more must be added in relation to the idea that habit acquisition occurs mostly at a prepersonal, unreflective level. Adopting such a view, I think, could help redirect our approach to the issue of the popular support of regressive policies both in Europe and in North America in recent years. Deliberative democracies and communicative rationality are valuable goals we should pursue in most cases. Nonetheless, they should not make us forget that a much more opaque mix of sensibility and prereflective habits is what shapes people's preferences and aversions, needs and fears. Disregarding these behavioral mechanisms could mean adopting an overly intellectualistic stance toward decision making and letting cunning political figures manipulate people's *sensus communis*.

13. Conclusion

The comparison with Morgan's natural-continuistic conception I proposed in the first part of this chapter has shown that it is not enough to adopt a view of habit as something characterizing all animal forms to varying degrees, although it is important to adopt and to further develop a deflated distinction between innate and acquired traits in animal behavior.

I have radicalized Dewey's conception of habits by emphasizing his shift away from methodological individualism and associationism as the traditional framework for interpreting habit, seen as the automatization of a primarily individual way of responding to a stimulus. A more promising alternative is to adopt an ecological or holistic approach to habits, considered as ways of channeling both organic and environmental energies. I have suggested that the ecological background should be regarded as an integral part of human behavior and the constitution of habits, rather than as a further or external dimension to which an independently predetermined way of behaving becomes adjusted only at a later stage, either by means of a subjective act or through a neurological process.

Given the naturally social characterization of the human environment, habit acquisition appears to mainly occur at a prepersonal and prereflective level, deriving from the need for each human being to accommodate her- or himself to the already largely habitualized social niche in which she or he is embedded. From this point of view, habits appear to be ways of doing things and ways in which things are done that are already there before each individual makes her or his own choices. This means that the individual mind and consciousness cannot be assumed to generally lie at the beginning of the process of habit acquisition. Rather, individuals play a crucial role in rejecting, reappropriating, or reshaping a previous habit when there is a crisis—be it a practical problem or a real moral one. In this case, one's own behavior must be analytically considered and a reflective choice must take the place of a previous habitual aversion or preference.

Focusing on the structurally social characterization of the human environment in relation to the shaping of habits involves two further consequences with reference to current debates. On the one hand, most human habits cannot be seen as taking place at a purely bodily level, by means of dynamic motor schemas; rather, it is necessary to consider the environment shared by other acculturated bodies—sometimes a happily shared environment, more often a contested one—where human movements occur as part of habit shaping. On the other hand, it seems more fruitful to avoid any rigid distinction between different orders of cognitive processes in favor of an interpretation of human behaviors as involving a variety of organic and environmental factors. Sometimes bodily factors are more pervasive than intellectual features, other times social and cultural resources represent more compelling constraints in the determination of a habit than natural impulses. Nonetheless, habits appear to occur through the interaction of mutually constitutive organic and environmental factors and not within the (representative) mind or the (computing) brain of the agent.

Finally, I have drawn a detailed comparison between a pragmatic conception of habits and Bourdieu's notion of habitus. The discussion proved challenging because the two views share an idea of habitual behavior as involving bodily mastery, a prereflective and strongly embodied capacity to manage one's own position within a structurally social space. However, I have argued that Bourdieu's conception of habitus as a single matrix of behavior is too monolithic and tends to maintain a gap between the habitus as a quasi–a priori condition and its empirical instantiations in human actions. Instead, I have suggested endorsing Dewey's pluralistic view of habits, as well as the view that they have a natural history of relative fixation, crisis, and change. Some habits tend to become mere routine habits and even regressive customs and prejudices, insofar as they seem to resist changes in the material scenarios where human practices occur; other habits are more intelligent, flexible, and open to changed conditions. In any case, both kinds of habits are part of the contingent form of life humans continually contribute to shaping and are in turn shaped by.

Even Dewey's theory of habit changes shows that his antiintellectualism is not dichotomistic. For sure, routine habits and customary morality are largely prereflective and unconscious, and operate at a quasi prepersonal level. An individual's action can become reflective when a previous habitual mode of conduct no longer fits a new situation, namely, when a practical difficulty arises, when it enters in conflict with an opposite habit of action, or when a strongly emotive reaction reveals the limits of a habit. These kinds of circumstances make an old habit explicit or conscious and create the need for a process of revision, refusal, or reappropriation. A routine habit can turn into a more flexible, intelligent habit, and a customary prejudice can be abandoned in favor of a more responsible moral choice. However, this is not the end of the story, because there is no guarantee that a new intelligent habit will maintain the capacity to respond to each situation and reflective morality will not become customary and mechanical in its own turn. The flow from more prereflective phases of experience to more intelligent, conscious, or reflective ones is continuous and open to change—as seen, for example, when quasi-instinctual aversions and preferences become emotionally conscious through the breaking of a habit of selection; or when, to mention another example, an institutionalized habit undergoes a crisis and becomes subject to a revision and to transformation into a new explicit norm of behavior and judgment. Furthermore, each explicit revision and reform of an old habit remains supported by habits of thought, action, and practice that continue to work silently or operatively. Consequently, "'Consciousness' [. . .] is a very small and shifting portion of experience" (Dewey 2004, 4), but there are no sharp, fixed boundaries between reflective, intelligent behavior and the space of demanding and giving reasons, no division between these two separate realms or reciprocally impervious logics.

Chapter 5

Human Experience as Enlanguaged Experience

1. Enlanguaged Experience: A General View

According to a leading account of the relationship between the so-called Neo-Pragmatists and Classical Pragmatism originally developed by Richard Rorty (1982), one of the most important divides between the two is represented by the still metaphysical anchoring of Dewey's and James's philosophies in experience, considered as the basic ground for philosophical inquiry. On the contrary, contemporary Pragmatists such as Rorty himself, Robert Brandom, and Huw Price (Hildebrand 2014) have decisively rejected any appeal to experience in favor of language. Consequently, they have been able to definitely abandon any empiricist dogmatic residue.[1] This picture of the state of the art within Pragmatism is certainly an oversimplified one, as David Hildebrand has sought to explain (in Hildebrand 2014), by showing that the positions we find are more nuanced; among current Pragmatists, there are some scholars who still assign an indispensable role to experience in philosophical inquiry, such as Richard Bernstein, Thomas Alexander, and Richard Shusterman, although they do so with different emphases and in pursuit of different goals. Other scholars, such as Mark Johnson and Joseph Margolis, support a continuity thesis between experience and language—again, in different ways and for different reasons. Rosa Calcaterra has claimed that, in spite of his aggressive style, Rorty himself did not give up experience for language as the key concept for a postmetaphysical Pragmatism. On the contrary, he tried "to transfer the distinction discursive/non-discursive to the level of that between different and yet inter-translatable linguistic games" (Calcaterra 2019, 35).

It is not my intention to enter this debate. Rather, a first claim I am going to make is that the picture of Classical Pragmatists as thinkers exclusively focusing on experience—regarded as the still metaphysical ground of philosophy (Rorty 1977)—at the expense of language is not only simplistic but indeed false. A serious analysis of their texts shows that their attention to language is a decisive factor in their understanding of human experience and of the peculiarly human form of life.

On a more theoretical level, my contention is that the Classical Pragmatists have developed interesting insights and arguments with regard to the role of language in the configuration of human experience that can be brought together within a comprehensive framework, by carrying them to their ultimate theoretical consequences. Building on this work, I wish to advance the notion of "enlanguaged experience" as an attempt to make the outcomes of their reasoning more explicit and coherent, and to move—once and for all—beyond the alleged dichotomy between language and experience, and the idea that these are basically two independent realms or fields within the human world. Certainly, they can and must be dealt with separately for specific reasons and within specific inquiries, yet humans primarily encounter language as an integral part of their experience, which has already been shaped through communicative interactions.

The Pragmatists took language to be primarily part of behavior and a mode of acting within the naturally social human environment, rather than an external cloth of thought used to convey a primarily internal product of the mind to outside reality. They also highlighted the qualitative, aesthetic, and pragmatic features of language by considering them a constitutive part of doing things together and sharing common goals through words, rather than merely suprasegmental aspects of speech, within a conception of language chiefly understood as a means of reference or as a potentially independent syntactic structure. By contrast to what has become the prevailing attitude in analytical philosophy of language, linguistic practices in concrete existential situations are considered to play a structural role in the shaping of typically human forms of life.

While the idea of a close intertwining of experience and language in the human world had long been clear to me (Dreon 2007), I first came across the adjective *enlanguaged* in relation to the human world, culture, understanding, and knowing in Joseph Margolis's *Toward a Metaphysic of*

Culture (2016, ch. 1). I then chose to adopt it to characterize my own idea of experience, derived from the Pragmatists.

The notion of human experience as "enlanguaged" should suggest that words, utterances, discourses, and chats are an integral part of the human experience of the world: they are ingredients of our shared practices that are already there before each individual takes the floor for the first time. Conversely, human experience, which is to say humans' interactions with their natural and naturally social environment, find themselves contingently, if irreversibly, embedded from each person's birth within contexts made up of linguistic practices, more or less meaningful relations, and questions and answers that contribute to continuously redefining what happens. In other words, linguistic practices are both some of the ways in which humans experience their environment and a vital part of the environment humans experience and pass down through countless generations.

Furthermore, in contrast to "linguistic experience," "enlanguaged experience" refers to the fact that human beings do not primarily encounter language in an isolated or pure form—whatever this might mean—the mere logical structure of language, a transparent device for making univocal references, a series of distinct and clear definitions, the product of an innate grammar, and so on.

Language is part of our conduct: it is deeply mixed with other communicative components of our behavior, which could roughly be characterized as multimodal and are continuous with more strictly linguistic aspects—where "continuous" means that there are no sharp boundaries but only fuzzy limits, an overlapping and intertwining of verbal and gestural features.[2] Language is part of the thick fabric of our experience, as well as of the human world. For the most part, it works in a "mongrel" (Margolis 2017, 63 ff.) way, and this is exactly why it fits the majority of situations humans have to deal with. Language serves—and has always served—several functions with respect to human experience and behavior: for sure, it is a very powerful device to refer to things and events that are not present; it is an amazing tool for selecting and making subtle distinctions, as well as for making more or less risky inferences. It is a remarkable epistemic tool: while relying on manipulative, sensorimotor competencies, it enhances and reshapes them through its capacity to operate virtually and to make cross-references, avoiding the need for continuous experimentation. Language, however, is also an impressive means to establish more or less intimate bonds, to maintain, enhance, and manage them, as well as to manipulate other people's actions, habits, and beliefs. Language can also be enjoyed in itself, either in poetry and literature, or in infantile babbling. Through role-taking and narrative, it definitely contributes to the development of consciousness and personal identity. In some situations, it functions in a formulaic and holistic way, while in other contexts it works more analytically. The Pragmatists, I would argue, help us appreciate language as something that is concretely experienced in our conduct, namely, as a complex, multifaceted, multilayered cluster that serves many different functions, by working sometimes mainly aesthetically, other times mostly analytically, and for the most part flexibly shifting between the two extremes to suit specific contexts. In brief, aside from being an incomparable epistemic tool, language enters the constitution of humans in a variety of ways, including as a constitutive part of the human environment.

It should be clear that, by following the Classical Pragmatists, I am adopting an empirical or natural approach to language by envisaging it as part of what humans do and experience. Nonetheless, to be clear, I must explicitly add that while favoring the idea of a constitutive function of speech within human ontogenesis and phylogenies, I do not consider it a transcendental (or quasi-transcendental) condition of possibility of experience. Rather, I seek to interpret language as the completely fortuitous and contingent product of a natural history, even though it causes irreversible changes and has a disruptive effect on the previous organization of transactions between nonhuman forms of life and their environment. Although human speech arose out of preexisting physiological resources and modes of intelligent behavior, I think language should be regarded as an emergent phenomenon, causing a degree of discontinuity in the continuum of life forms. While language emerged from the reuse and co-optation—for different purposes—of an already existing range of structures and resources (White 1985; Snowdon 1993; Fitch 2010; 2012; Parravicini-Pievani 2018), it caused a retroaction or loop effect on the previous organization of experience. Probably because of their closeness to open-minded Darwin scholars such as Chauncey Wright and John Fiske (Parravicini 2012), the Pragmatists were able to foreshadow and make use of concepts such as exaptation, which was famously redefined by Gould and Vrba (1982) and also used to consider the mutual, dynamic, and open-ended adaptation between organisms and their environmental niche (see Laland, Odling-Smee, & Feldman 2000 on the concept of "niche construction"; Sinha 2009 and 2015 on language as a "biocultural niche").

Dewey and Mead strongly emphasized that the human mind and selfhood should be considered the exceptional, albeit fortuitous, consequences of the advent of language (see also Margolis 2017). To this important insights, I would add that verbal communication has also had a profound impact on—and caused a reshaping of—already existing forms of nonhuman animal sensibility, as well as the already habitual structures of many animal behaviors. This phenomenon occurred and continues to occur in the maturation of human beings simply because our natural environment is already profoundly linguistic before our birth. At least from the very first days in their life, human beings are systematically led by other people to get on the train of the human mutual adjustment of behaviors by means of cross-modal communication activities (Stern 1985; Trevarthen 1979; Dissanayake 2000; Falk 2009). Words constitute but one important feature of this process of adjustment, although over time they have become more and more crucial. These kinds of proto-linguistic forms of interaction are fundamentally *phatic* in character (Malinowski 1923; Jakobson 1960), which is to say that they are mainly focused on maintaining and managing intimate social bonds. They are also chiefly holistic and formulaic, and largely based on prosody and communicative rhythm—as claimed by supporters of a common evolutionary origin for language and music (Mithen 2006; 2009; Brown 2000; 2017), as well as by Alison Wray's holistic proto-language hypothesis (Wray 1998).

I would argue that the idea of a completely prelinguistic human infant is a myth, if it is understood in terms of a purely perceptive bodily experience of the world, completely disconnected from surrounding linguistic behaviors. Already before birth, humans are exposed to the linguistic world of the community they belong to; their first cries and requests for food and attention are embedded in an enlanguaged environment, even if they are not verbal (Dreon 2007, 16, ff). The human niche, while remaining largely undetermined compared to the usual living conditions of other animals, is somehow an already linguistic niche, and this circumstance cannot but make a difference also with respect to primarily nonverbal forms of behavior.

Imperative orders, joyful exclamations, vivid invitations to behave in one way or another, words, chats, and narratives are already part of everyday experience and constitute the background even of dull pain and a mute sense of solitude, as well as more private pleasures. Words—mostly uttered by other people—are already there and surround even nonprimarily linguistic experience, from organic events to mystic union in religious or artistic experience. This de facto condition is the rather obvious but often neglected fact supporting my proposal about human experience being enlanguaged.

The standard for this argument is Dewey's argument for human sociality in *Human Nature and Conduct*. Philosophers have long tackled the problem of whether to support the claim that society is the product of a conventional agreement between individuals or indulge in a metaphysical conception of society as prior to the individual. Dewey suggests the following way out of the problem: "But to say that some pre-existent association of human beings is prior to every particular human being who is born into the world is to mention a commonplace. These associations are definite modes of interaction of persons with one another; that is to say they forms customs, institutions. There is no problem in all history so artificial as that of how 'individuals' manage to form 'society'" (1988a, 44).

Similarly, to say that language as a metaphysical or purely logical entity is an a priori condition of human experience is to indulge in "nonsensical metaphysics" (Dewey 1988a, 44). However, to say that some preexistent linguistic and communicative practice within a human group is prior to each particular human being's experience of the surrounding environment is to mention a commonplace. These linguistic and communicative practices are modes of social interaction between persons, serving a variety of different functions; they are both based on and give rise to habits, whether behavioral or more specifically linguistic habits. The problem of how individuals manage to jump from purely perceptive or even sensorimotor experience to linguistic practice is artificial, because it assumes a merely perceptive dimension that is never primarily given in the human world. These are the reasons why I suggest we speak of human experience as "enlanguaged experience": not because we ought to consider language the quasi-transcendental condition of human experience (Apel 1972), but because it has always been the case that we live in a linguistically shared world that inevitably affects the ways in which our living form interacts with its environment.

2. Some Promising Convergences

Within the field of radical embodied cognitive science and enactivism, Di Paolo, Cuffari, and De Jaegher speak of "linguistic bodies" to support the idea of continuity between life and language (2018, 3, ff.), as well as the notion that human sense-making is enacted by bodies that are always already embedded in a linguistic world (2018, 165, ff.). Hence, the whole debate about the categorical gap between sensorimotor skills and language is not only "largely uncharted" (Di Paolo, Cuffari, & De Jaegher 2018, 4), but has been framed in misleading terms.

The idea of "enlanguaged experience" that I derive from the Classical Pragmatists converges in many respects with that of linguistic bodies coming from the more progressive trends in cognitive studies—which still remain minority trends, as far as I am aware. Di Paolo, Cuffari, and De Jaegher have developed an idea of human bodies as linguistic bodies, that is, as material networks of relations and processes that have grown within linguistic communities (2018, 7; see also 196). They also embrace a very open, empirical, and pluralistic conception of language, as something that has "no abstract, self-standing theoretical center," but is rather "a concrete open totality embedded in networks of material, biological, and sociocultural codetermining relations" (2018, 107; see also 116 and ff.). Moreover, they acknowledge that language, understood as a shared lifeworld of socio-material practices, is already there when individual sense-making practices enacted by human beings emerge and develop (2018, 165).

These scholars' views basically converge with the Pragmatists' cultural-naturalism because they support the continuity between life and language, while at the same time emphasizing that human bodies are deeply embedded in a linguistic environment. However, with the Pragmatists I will radicalize this move by explicitly arguing that, within the context of the continuity of life with language and inherited culture, the emergence of language and shared cultural practices, while fortuitous and unexpected, has a disruptive impact on mainly organic-based forms of experience; it has a loop or feedback effect on previous forms of experience, producing changes and the reconfiguration of human experience in comparison with "hypo-symbolic" (Lorimer 1929) forms of interactions.

Moreover, the Pragmatists preferred to speak of "experience," rather than "bodies," and I personally think that their choice was a better one: for the Pragmatists (see Dewey 1981, 18–19, quoting James 1976) the word *experience* encompasses everything occurring in the world, including both organisms, that is living beings or bodies, and the environment they belong to, which they contribute to changing from within, and which they must interact with in order to preserve their life and possibly flourish. Dewey and the Pragmatists, in other words, did not overlook the importance of the body for understanding human cognition, but they preferred not to set out from what is still a one-sided perspective. Rather, they set out from the fact that human beings find themselves embedded in a natural and naturally social environment, which literally gives rise to their bodies and contributes to shaping them as human bodies. The human environment has become naturally social and linguistic in a broad sense; consequently, human experience, understood in terms of organic-environmental interactions, can no longer be the same, because both human organisms and the human environment have deeply changed.

Another interestingly convergent field of research gravitates around the concept of "languaging" advanced by Stephen Cowley, Thomas Wieben Jensen, and Sune Vork Steffensen from the Center for Human Interactivity at the University of Southern Denmark and previously defined by Thibault. By adopting the word *languaging*, they focus on language by primarily viewing it as an activity and a kind of behavior developed within social interaction. Language is seen as an activity, or more precisely a group of activities, that is "materially emobodied, culturally/ecologically embedded, naturalistically grounded, affective-based, dialogically coordinated, and socially enacted" (Thibault 2011). The distinctive feature of this notion is that it involves abandoning the traditional distinction between a language system—whether an autonomous *langue* à la Saussure or a specific innate module in the brain à la Chomsky—and its use or application in current speech. More specifically, supporters of this view reject the idea of a hierarchical order between language as an autonomous system and language as use, which is to say the very idea that the former is the deep hidden structure underlying the use of the latter, and that using a language presupposes an already defined language system, where *already* means before and independently of linguistic practices and interactions. Instead, they suggest an ontological inversion of the above-mentioned order, by considering "first-order languaging behavior" the real ground out of which language derives as a "second-order construct" (Jensen 2014—that is, as a symbolic and rule-governed system. As pointed out by Jensen, this approach involves a form of nonreductive naturalism, as well as a stimulating emphasis on the continuity and intertwining between affective and cognitive linguistic features (Jensen 2014), to which I am very sympathetic. However, I would argue that the notion of "enlanguaged experience"—which I developed before coming into contact with the "languaging" approach[3]—is better because of its "double-barreled" status, as originally suggested with reference to "experience" by James in his essay "Does Consciousness Exist?"

(1976) and later by Dewey in the first pages of *Experience and Nature* (1981). Far from regarding experience as a merely subjective realm, as is usually the case in modern philosophy, the two Pragmatists stressed the relational structure of the word *experience*: the latter includes both the individual who is doing something and the effective conditions in which her or his action takes place, as well as the result of her or his action. In my proposal, "enlanguaged experience" has the advantage of involving not only languaging as a behavior performed by humans, but also the idea that language is an intrinsic part of the human environment where each new languaging intercourse takes place. Not only are the practices by which human organisms interact with one another and with their natural environment enalanguaged, but so is the environment itself, including previous human practices, words, and meanings, that is, the linguistic habits accumulated by previous generations and continuously reconfigured by new individual and collective contributions.

This stress on the linguistic structure of the human *Umwelt* leads me to one last point of engagement with current debates on language from an anthropological perspective.

While I was working out my claim that human experience is de facto, and irreversibly, intertwined with language—understood both as a way of experiencing the environment and as a constitutive part of the human environment itself—I found a further stimulating point of convergence with the conception of language as a biocultural niche within current studies in language evolution. Chris Sinha proposes a conception of language as a biocultural niche and social institution developed at the epigenetical level through the bidirectional interactions between organisms and their artifactual niche. By applying to language the conception of "niche construction" formulated by Laland, Odling-Smee, and Feldman, linguistic practices can be envisaged as environmental factors playing a constructive role in selection processes, which is to say in favoring the emergence of human cognitive-symbolic capacities at both the phylogenetic and the ontogenetic level (Sinha 2009). In Sinha's view, language and culture are an integral part of human ecology, because linguistic and cultural practices, together with organic processes, are seen as the set of activities through which human organisms transform their environmental niche and contribute to constructing it. Consequently, they in turn represent environmental constraints on human experience across different generations (Laland, Odling-Smee, & Feldman 2000). One element of convergence with the view of language that can be derived from

Classical Pragmatism, I think, is partly connected to the reemergence of a "Darwinian framework of evolutionary theory" to the detriment of the neo-Darwinian emphasis on genes as the allegedly ultimately site of selection processes (Sinha 2009, note 2). A certain degree of convergence also comes from the emphasis on the problem of the relative discontinuity of the human mind and human conduct against the background of the basic continuity with other forms of life—an issue that Sinha refers to as "the paradox [. . .] of discontinuity in continuity" (2009) and which the Classical Pragmatists constantly had in view, as will become clear in the last sections of this chapter (especially 5 and 7).

However, the approach I am suggesting here is a peculiar one, because it mainly consists in the exploration of some prescient and still challenging insights suggested by the Classical Pragmatists with regard to language as an integral part of human experience. In this chapter of the volume, I will try to explore some important contributions to the understanding of the interdependence of experience and language in the work of Dewey, Mead, James, and a minor but important figure for the issue at stake, namely, Frank Lorimer—a demographer who initially studied under Dewey and completed a PhD under his supervision. I will reconstruct their arguments as carefully as possible, by referring to their texts. However, I am not proposing this kind of investigation from the perspective of philosophical history or philology. Rather, in what follows I deliberately make use of the Pragmatists' insightful yet fragmentary insights and arguments with regard to language, cognition, and emotions as contributions to the conception of human experience as enlanguaged I am advancing here.

In any case, I wish to make it clear that this chapter should not be regarded as an attempt to formulate a theory of linguistic meaning or to investigate language as a system of signs—although some interesting contributions on such subjects can be found in the Classical Pragmatists' works. Considered from the point of view of the standard analytical philosophy of language, the object of my investigation might seem to be ill-defined and based on a lack of discrimination between syntax, semantics, and pragmatics. Moreover, it could be objected that my analysis conflates empirical inquiries and a logical, timeless approach to the basic rules of language.

In fact, my purpose is to explore the intertwining of experience and language or the broadly linguistic environmental niche that for the most part characterizes human forms of life. My research focuses on enlanguaged experience, considered as primarily defining the current material conditions of human life. A sharper definition of the borders of strictly linguistic phenomena—as well as of human sensibility—can and should be pursued for specific purposes. However, it is my contention that they should be regarded as analytical distinctions drawn within the original entanglement of "enlanguaged experience" characterizing human lives and the human species—at least, for the moment.

For the sake of clarity, I will divide my exploration of the resources derived from the Pragmatists as contributions to my own conception of "enlanguaged experience" between two different chapters. In the present chapter, I will focus on Dewey's insights into language, cognition, and the mind, suggesting that his theory must be integrated and made more coherent through Frank Lorimer's clearer account of preexistent organic forms of intelligence. I will devote the next chapter to arguments derived from Mead, James, and Lorimer in order to support my thesis of the continuity between sensibility and language—a claim I already explore within this chapter with reference to Dewey's thought and further develop in a more comprehensive way in the following chapter.

First, from Dewey I will derive an account of the natural genesis of the human mind out of previous forms of animal behavior and human association: according to Dewey, feelings for favorable and unfavorable environmental conditions become sense and meaning through the loop effect of the appearance of language on sensibility (sections 3 and 4). Section 5 provides a caveat on Dewey's choice to employ the word *mental* exclusively with reference to humans, which is to say to forms of intelligence involving language. Lorimer's work is drawn on in order to deal more coherently with organic forms of intelligence (section 6). Section 7 engages with both pragmatist (Lorimer and James) and current (Dreyfus and Hutto) debates on nonlinguistic behaviors, supporting my argument that the often neglected linguistic environment should be envisaged as a constitutive factor of behavior.

3. Dewey on the Emergence of the Mind out of Language and Human Association[4]

In *Experience and Nature* Dewey provides a succinct account of the natural genesis of the human mind out of previous forms of animal behavior, as well as of the appearance of language. While not always detailed, this can be adopted as a good point of departure for a theory of human experience as enlanguaged, to be later integrated and developed through the contributions of other Pragmatists—especially Frank Lorimer and George Mead—as well as through an engagement with the current debate in evolutionary sciences, linguistics, and developmental psychology.

From the very beginning of the chapter "Nature, Communication and Meaning," it is clear that the main issues at stake are the relationships between mind and thinking, on the one hand, and language, on the other hand, within a basically continuistic framework. Dewey is going to reverse the traditional mentalistic approach as well as the leading individualistic philosophical stance, according to which "Social interaction and institutions have been treated as products of a ready-made specific physical or mental endowment of a self-sufficing individual, wherein language acts as a mechanical go-between to convey observations and ideas that have prior and independent existence" (1981, 134).

The complementary conception that Dewey criticizes is that language "expresses" thought as a pipe conducts water, where the pipe/language remains inert and has an "even less transforming function than is exhibited when the wine-press 'expresses' the juice of grapes" (1981, 134). Conversely, Dewey maintains that speech, that is, linguistic utterances and exchanges, are the fortuitous but now necessary conditions for the emergence of the mind as well as individual identities.

Of course, this is a challenging perspective, posing at least a couple of potential philosophical problems. One of these problems is represented by the possible underestimation of previous nonverbal forms of intelligence—in the next section Dewey's way out of this problem will be dealt with, but it is the work of Frank Lorimer, I suggest, that should be investigated to find a more coherent and better developed treatment of the subject.

Here I wish to tackle another significant difficulty connected with the conception of the mind I derive from Dewey, namely, a view of the mind as emerging out of language and meaning. The difficulty is represented by a misleading understanding of the relations between the two (i.e., language and the mind) from a transcendental perspective that is very far from Dewey's sensibility. He clearly states the need to consider language from a purely naturalistic perspective, and I think that this approach to language as part of human natural history should be embraced, avoiding any temptation to interpret language as a kind of quasi-transcendental horizon for the possibility of meaning. Dewey says that language, like gestures and cries, is primarily a mode of behavior, just like walking or grasping (1981, 139); and he states this in a sentence that sounds very similar to Wittgenstein's passage on speech as a natural activity among humans.[5] Dewey recalls that language is primarily a "natural function of human association" (1981, 139); it should not be underestimated that speech is primarily a powerful tool for establishing, maintaining, and enjoying social bonds, as noted by Malinowski (Malinowski 1923, quoted in Dewey 1981, 160) and Jakobson (1960)—and as more recently confirmed by a range of different scholars such as Colwyn Trevarthen (1979), Ellen Dissanayake (2001), and Deane Falk (2009). Moreover, Dewey states that language and meaning did not emerge intentionally, out of a preestablished independent mind, but "by overflow"; they are "by-products" (1981, 139) of preexisting organs and activities that happened to be reused for different purposes.[6] Incidentally, Dewey's capacity to anticipate more recent conceptions of language evolution here seems quite astonishing. In his important book *The Evolution of Language*, Tecumseh Fitch claims that language should be understood as deriving from a plurality of preexisting processes, activities, and functions; it "is not a monolithic whole and from a biological perspective may be better seen as a 'bag of tricks' pieced together via a process of evolutionary tinkering" (2010, 6). Consequently, when Dewey affirms the primacy of language over mind, understood both as thinking activity and as a function of individual identity, he is considering the advent of language as a completely fortuitous and contingent event that could also have not taken place. Nonetheless, given the advent of language out of preexisting resources developed in unexpected directions, it had a disrupting effect by comparison to other forms of animal life. In Dewey's eyes, the main consequence of the emergence of language has been the emergence of meaning and symbolic activity in organic-environmental interaction, in addition to its huge contribution to the rise of a new form of commonality or shared experience. In other texts (Dewey 1984a, 253 and 250; 1988a, 44), Dewey acknowledges not only the social nature of human beings, but also the fact that many other species are already social. Consequently, his main aim is to understand how and why human sociality is comparatively so profound or, to use Michael Tomasello's formula, how and why it humans have developed a kind of collective or Joint-Intentionality (1999, ch. 3; 2008, ch. 3).[7] Speech proves to be a very strong tool to make something common, to share common intents and purposes because, within conversations with others, humans have the chance to shift from "coexistence into participation" (Dewey 1981, 138). "Something is literally made common in at least two different centers of behavior. To understand is to anticipate together, it is to make a cross-reference which, when acted upon, brings about a partaking in a common, inclusive, undertaking" (Dewey 1981, 141). Language gave humans the chance not only to do something in common by pursuing a shared goal, but also to distinguish each person's role and contribution within a shared activity. Verbal communication or conversation is the place where responsibility emerges literally by means of one's act of responding to another person's utterance. As is well known, Mead further explored these aspects, but it is worth noting that Dewey had already emphasized the fact that, within the linguistic exchange, an individual can distinguish what one is saying and doing from the words and acts of one's interlocutors by means of role-taking and the rhythmical alternation of voices and pronouns. Human collaboration, unlike hens' "ego-centric" coworking, is "participative" for Dewey (1981, 140) because each individual involved in some work in progress can recognize the part he or she is taking as well as the job the other person is doing; each individual can perceive, enjoy, or suffer this commonality, as well as try to influence others' conduct. Hence, Dewey emphasized Malinowski's thesis of language as "a piece of human behavior" (Dewey 1981, 160, quoting Malinowski 1923, 474) that plays both the instrumental role of converging on a common goal and the consummatory role of an "enhanced sense of membership" (Dewey 1981, 160). Dewey (like Frank Lorimer, as will be explained in the next section) always highlights the fact that language within human practices cannot be reduced to its instrumental character, although it is fundamental for him to assume that speech is an extremely powerful tool for doing things together. The words of the other speaker or my own, the utterances of my friend or my enemy, as well as the poet's verses, are also immediately enjoyed or suffered in themselves. Tangible human speech can never be reduced to merely instrumental discourse, reflective inquiry, and cognition for Dewey, as it also belongs to the qualitative or aesthetic background of immediate human experience. This is an important point, I contend, to avoid the sterile opposition between experience or perception, on the one hand, and language, on the other, as well as a foundational paradigm of the relationship between the latter and the former. I will return to this issue in the next chapter. To sum up the provisional result of this Deweyan approach to language, it could be argued that language grew out of previous forms of animal coexistence but—and this is the point where I radicalize Dewey's legacy—retroacted or had a loop effect on previous forms of animal sociality, which were profoundly reorganized by the advent of human speech. Participation in the sense of taking a distinct part in a shared activity was thus made possible, as was an enhanced sense of community (or hostility, I would add).

4. Dewey on the Emergence of Meanings out of Feelings and Previous Forms of Sensibility

A second disrupting consequence caused by the advent of language on previous forms of organic-environmental interaction is, of course, connected with the introduction of meaning within life: "Language is a natural function of human association; and its consequences react upon other events, physical and human, giving them meaning or significance" (Dewey 1981, 137). Here, as will become clear from a few sentences, Dewey does not assume that animal life is foreign to meaning, but that its ways of being significant are qualitatively different.

Readers familiar with Wittgenstein's *Philosophical Investigations* (Black 1962; Cometti unpublished manuscript; Faerna 2018; Steiner 2019) have rightly emphasized that already in 1925, Dewey provided an antimentalistic conception of meaning, far from any attraction for the myth of private language. He clearly rejected as a "heresy" the idea of meanings as private, "as a property of ghostly psychic existences" (1981, 148). Rather, meanings in his view must be understood starting from shared forms of action and, consequently, as not private in essence and not primarily corresponding to an entity—whether it be a mental state or an isolated object, "a thing in separate singleness" (1981, 146). Seen from the perspective of humans taking part in participatory activities in view of an end, meanings are "a method of action, a way of using things as means to a shared consummation" (1981, 147). Dewey even says that "[m]eanings are rules for using and interpreting things," where interpretation is in turn understood as a practical activity, that is, as "the imputation of potentiality for some consequence" (1981, 147). Meanings are primarily "the standardized habit of social interaction" (1981, 149); therefore, they can become privileged modes of referring to certain things toward which action is directed or with which action is concerned. As crystallized habits of conduct within social activity, meanings do not primarily occur within the mind, but in real contexts of exchange between persons. This does not prevent us from talking about mental images but, from a Deweyan perspective, these images should be regarded as deriving from common speech and shared experiences rather than as the solitary products of each individual mind and/or of neural computing, understood as independent from social intercourse, or as conditions of language as the mere conveyor of thought (Steiner 2019).

This conception of meaning as habit within a social context of action is confirmed in Dewey's *Logic. A Theory of Inquiry*, particularly when Dewey considers an example clearly drawn from an anthropological context—an example similar to Quine's famous "*gavagai*" case, but much older. The case (taken from Ogden & Richards 1923) regards a foreign visitor to a tribe of "savages" who wishes to know their name for "table." Tapping on a table with his fingers, he asks a group of young men what this is and receives different answers: one boy utters the word for the action of tapping, a second one says the word for the material out of which the table is made, a third one answers with the word for the object, and so on. The point for Dewey is that the translation is indeterminate because the word is detached from a shared context of action—a communicative practice both practical and linguistic—which would make it meaningful.

> [T]here is not possible any such thing as a direct one-to-one correspondence of names with existential objects; [. . .] words mean what they mean in connection with conjoint activity that effect a common, or mutually participated in, consequence. The word sought for was involved in conjoint activities looking to a common end. The act of tapping in the illustration was isolated from any such situation. It was, in consequence, wholly indeterminate in reference; it was no part of *communication*, by which alone acts get significance and accompanying words acquire meanings. (Dewey 1991a, 59)[8]

Although this idea was a breakthrough, I contend that it is only part of a wider conception of meaning sketched by Dewey. The complementary and usually neglected part of this conception is his idea of the genesis of meanings out of previous forms of feeling and sensibility in nonhuman animals. Beyond treating meanings as standardized habits of action within shared contexts, Dewey provides an initial outline of a natural history of meaning according to which the latter emerged out of previous forms of animal sensibility in a basically continuistic way, while still considering the loop effect of language on preexisting form of sensibility. Further and more detailed contributions to such a theory could be found in the reflections by Frank Lorimer and George Mead, as I will show in the next sections.

Dewey notes that, compared to inanimate beings, living beings are characterized by the fact that their relations with the environment in which they exist are always biased (1981; 197) or self-interested, in the sense that living beings always tend to remain alive—they are not indifferent to the way environmental actions affect them, or to the consequences that their own activities have on their lives.[9] Ultimately, perspectivism with respect to meanings is rooted in life, namely, in living organisms' instability and biological tension—Dewey speaks about precariousness in *Experience and Nature*, as do the enactivists, as I have noted in the chapter 2. Living beings always find themselves anchored in a certain environment and dependent on the circumstances unfolding within it. Obviously, this occurs to more or less complex and refined degrees, depending on the form of life under consideration. Dewey notes that one important element of differentiation within the continuum of life is represented by the emergence of the capacity for (self-) motion and locomotion, which makes the first forms of postponement of satisfaction possible, and consequently the reference to something else that is not immediately present in the proximity of the organism. Like the enactivists, and Merleau-Ponty before them, Dewey assumes motor-activity to be of primary importance for living organisms when it comes to making reference to something else, whether present or not. In its turn, this kind of capacity is interpreted as an active intervention in the environment or as an embodied semiosis. Selectivity and partiality, therefore, do not apply only to human beings, but also to animals—that is, to animals capable of locomotion, because they are strictly connected to the practical capacity to reach something or someone that is not close. These animals develop a sort of sensibility that also involves a temporal structuring of interaction: instead of occurring immediately, interaction unfolds through a preparatory stage of tension and anticipation, and a stage of accomplishment (fulfillment), in which the action is completed (consummation). It is important to note that the first reason to distinguish between different phases of experience—between anticipatory and consummatory phases, as well as between immediate, qualitative, or aesthetic moments, on the one hand, and reflective phases, on the other—is rooted in the naturally rhythmic course of life within an environment that is peculiar to self-moving animals.[10] This way of structuring interactions is typical of more complex organisms, yet it cannot ensure reflection—in other words, according to Dewey, it is not mental, although it clearly implies various degrees of intelligence. It involves what the American philosopher calls "psycho-physical" activities and behaviors, insofar as the biological structures themselves entail a subtle selective sensibility, whereby things are discriminated and felt to be favorable or unfavorable, good or bad, even though, strictly speaking, they are not known. As I have already claimed in the chapter 2, sensibility primarily reveals itself as the capacity to discriminate between favorable and unfavorable aspects of the environment, rather than as the purely sensory perception of things. Feelings become meanings in typical human interactions—but this does not mean that the process can be described as a teleological development from the inferior to the superior, which would be entirely out of keeping with Dewey's Darwinian interpretation (2007; see, too, Cometti 2016, 60), and with the emphasis on chance that is typical of all Classical Pragmatists (cf. Calcaterra 2011).[11] Feeling becomes sense in man by means of language, because it is in a communicative context that a vague feeling of the situation takes on a specific objective reference: it does not remain submerged in an indistinct whole, but emerges with a clearer outline and a broader possibility of articulation, even in view of further ends, by postponing actual enjoyment or suffering. Among humans, language retroacts on animal sensibility, refining the capacity to discriminate a whole situation as favorable or unfavorable and to break it down into more specific details that can be focused on as being more important or urgent than others. By way of example, Dewey mentions the distinction that may be drawn between experiencing a certain disturbing or disgusting situation and smelling a foul odor or seeing some red blood. In order to be specified as disgust or as uneasiness, these feelings need to be "designated as signs." In short: "The qualities of situations in which organisms and surrounding conditions interact, when discriminated, make sense. Sense is distinct from feeling, for it has a recognized reference; it is the qualitative characteristic of something, not just a submerged unidentified quality or tone" (1981, 200).

But, Dewey continues, "Sense is also different from signification": whereas the sense of something is a kind of "immanent meaning" that is immediately enjoyed or suffered, signification implies the use of a quality as a sign or index for something else, for a further, temporally deferred possibility of consummation. By disentangling the different levels that Dewey succinctly sketches out, it could be argued that animal sensibility—understood as the capacity to feel a situation in its entirety as favorable or unfavorable—is reshaped by the advent of language among humans at a double level. On the one hand, it passes from a holistic feeling to the capacity to focus on a specific thing or part of a situation that is still primarily enjoyed or suffered; on the other hand, that thing becomes a sign for a further reference to something else—that is, a chance for postponed enjoyment or suffering. Consequently, words are not only a means (the most powerful means) to make references, but they enter our sensibility by making it select and focus on specific objects, individuals, and parts or phases of a more complex situation. Consequently, language is seen both as the instrument of reflective experience and as a crucial factor in primarily qualitative, aesthetic experience.

As regards Dewey's position on making reference to something that is not present, he says that human beings are capable of changing mere suggestions—whereby something present suggests something absent, of which it is a sign (smoke suggests fire and is a sign of it)—into meanings by means of language. In passing, it may be interesting to note that Dewey speaks of "suggestions," rather than indications in the 1916 *Introduction* to his *Essays in Experimental Logic* (2004): he seems to foreshadow the idea that certain things are perceived as suggestions, which is to say as incitements or invitations to act in a certain manner, anticipating James Gibson's conception of affordance (Gibson 1979; Dings 2018). In any case, the transition from sign to meaning—that is, from a two-way relation to a three-way one—is not allowed by the intervention of a mental image of the absent thing. In other words, the external event of smoke does not become mental because an alleged psychic image of it is produced in the mind, understood as an inner space; there is no need to posit the duplication of smoke into an internal representation that corresponds to the external phenomenon. In the concrete communicative exchanges in which it appears, the word *smoke* becomes part of mental behavior, namely, of a meaningful behavior for Dewey, in relation to an obstacle or uncertain context. Because of the impasse about what to do, smoke—the sign suggesting fire—becomes a crucial tool within a reflective process of inquiry, whereby it is analytically distinguished and fixed by means of gestures and words that guide the interlocutors' actions. Consequently, it is clear that according to Dewey, the emergence of forms of mental interaction between human beings and their environment is de facto based on language, understood as a meaningful exchange between speakers: not only are words a far more stable means of discriminating and sharing the "suggestions" of signs than gestures, but the natural environment of human beings is social, insofar as their destiny or history depends not just on their individual actions, but also—and especially—on shared activities, on their (peaceful or conflicting) participation in associated forms of life. Verbal language (1981, 213) is not a means to convey inner representations, but primarily a means allowing interlocutors to mutually regulate their conduct in view of action: language itself is a kind of communication consisting in vocal gestures, which extends and transforms previous forms of gestural communication, yet still remains—at an embryonic level—a kind of gesture itself, that is, a kind of action, whose meaning is shared by the speaker and the listener in view of a common practice (Dreon 2012a). Words allow us not just to retain the consequences of our previous actions and to anticipate the results of future ones, but also to recall and foresee the effects of other people's behavior: what language conveys is the world of others, of our fellow-humans, rather than a thought activity occurring primarily within our own minds or the neural computation of a brain cut off from the rest of the body and the world.

To briefly sum up my argument, Dewey did not provide only a conception of meaning as connected with habit and use in social practices, but also an idea of meaning as stemming from previous forms of animal sensibility, which were profoundly reshaped by the discriminating and universalizing power of language within the human form of life. "Esthetic and affectional meanings"—bonding intended to establish and maintain social relations and the enjoyment or suffering deriving from them—became "scientific meanings," that is, terms "defined for their consequences with respect to one another" (1981, 148).

In a nutshell, sensibility became enlanguaged in humans, by comparison to nonhuman animals. As already noted, however, this does not entail a hyperlinguistic or inferential idea of sensibility, because Dewey affirms the double nature of language, which in his view is both instrumental and consummatory, part both of the immediate suffering or enjoyment of the conditions of life—for it enhances sensibility and directs it toward specific aspects of a situation—and of the reflective efforts by which humans try to face indeterminate situations.

5. Dewey on the Mental as a Peculiarly Human Affair

As I hinted above, a further outstanding as well as problematic contention is represented by Dewey's decision to reserve the word *mind* and *mental* for characterizing typically and exclusively human forms of behavior and connecting their emergence with the advent of language.[12] Dewey considers it misleading to use the word *mind* to refer to some sort of entity (1989, 267–68) and instead uses it to describe the character, mode, and quality of certain kinds of interaction between the specifically human form of life and the environment to which it belongs and on which it depends. From this point of view, Dewey rejects both the Cartesian tradition of the mind as a sui generis ontological substance compared to the extended substance, and the British Empiricists' conception according to which the mind results from the association or combination of different perceptions, and their mutual relations.[13] Rather, the term *mental* describes the kind of behavior based on meanings, which is to say standardized habits of action as well as discriminating tools for reflective experience and triadic reference. Human behaviors are mental for Dewey because by means of broadly linguistic practices human beings can analytically return to experiential situations that are primarily enjoyed or suffered for their impact on the life of those individuals who are involved in them and make reference to other signs, delaying the consummation of actions in progress.

By reserving the word *mental* for a typically human form of experience, I believe that Dewey was emphasizing the relative discontinuity introduced by the emergence of language in organic-environmental interactions. He was taking very seriously the idea that "the paradox is one of discontinuity in continuity" (Sinha 2009).[14] Language emerged fortuitously as one mode of behavior among others, relying on previous physiological and intelligent—yet not "mental," according to Dewey's use of the term—resources. Nevertheless, the advent of speech among groups of humans caused the emergence of meaningful or mental behaviors, which is to say that it had a disruptive effect on previous forms of organic-environmental interaction eminently guided and controlled by a mainly holistic sensibility. In other words, I believe that Dewey wished to point out the transformative effect on previous forms of experience and feelings caused by the emergence of language: its irreversible feedback or loop effect on already existent modes of organization of organic-environmental exchanges. Of course, this is a crucial but dangerous move, because it runs the risk of being translated into the misleading thesis that the emergence of mind and thinking is the product of language *tout court*. At the same time, this thesis involves the false assumption that Dewey was denying the existence of any form of intelligence among nonlinguistic animals. Both of these theses are erroneous in general as well as with reference to Dewey. *Mental* was not a synonym for *intelligent* for Dewey, who already understood sensibility as a rich and complex capacity to orient oneself within the environment, as well as a more or less habitual way of responding to environmental solicitations, among nonlinguistic animals. On the other hand, Dewey realized that mental behaviors are rooted in previous forms of organization and not merely in language. Nonetheless, he did not explore this aspect in detail. Frank Lorimer, I would argue, clearly saw the potential danger in Dewey's account of the origin of the mental through linguistic practices. Consequently, in the next section I will suggest integrating Dewey's thesis with Lorimer's more careful formulation.

For the moment, I wish to emphasize that the coherent consequence of adopting a Deweyan view is the idea that human experience is structurally enlanguaged, that is, embedded in broadly linguistic and meaningful practices, in shared meanings and in a cultural environment, constituting the background of every human gesture, from a newborn's first cry onward. This does not mean that each human experience is strictly linguistic or always mediated by inferences. I am not trying to substitute the "linguistic" element for the "mental" as a feature pervading all human experiences. On the one hand, from a Deweyan perspective, the linguistic element is never a mere inferential tool; rather, it is assumed to be a qualitatively rich as well as practical, fully embodied, and socially embedded feature of experience. As I have already stated, for Dewey language belongs both to the more reflective and instrumental phases of experience, in virtue of its powerful discriminating function, and to the consummatory phases of experience—words in themselves as well as "communion actualized" (Dewey 1981, 160) can be primarily enjoyed or suffered for the impact they have on our lives. Discourse is the most powerful tool for discrimination, analysis, inference, and abduction, but speech also works as a qualitative source of experience because of its material qualities—rhythm, tones, timbres, pauses, hesitations, and melodic lines—and, above all, because of its power to establish and enhance bonds, both friendly and hostile ones, as well as to share situations, goals, and things. Far from cutting off humans from their sensible roots, language enhanced sensibility, by enriching it with the power of discrimination between the subtler nuances of feeling and their intentional objects. Language, as I have argued in the second chapter (section 6), is also important for the development of our so-called "interior life"—contrary to the commonplace, according to which our experience of ourselves is ineffable in essence, but also to the behavioristic denial of any interior process.

On the other hand, Dewey conceives of the relations between consummation and instrumental inquiry as circular and interdependent. His distinction between primary and reflective experience is not foundational[15] or hierarchical, because human beings are animals who, from the very beginning, find themselves caught in the core of a culture, that is in the middle of communicative and linguistic interactions as well as inferential processes, which belong to a community more than they do to any individual speaker and knower. All of this interferes with and has consequences for qualitative experience, which incorporates the results of previous inquiries and is modified by them. Incorporation takes place by means of habitualization, through the sedimentation of the results of previous inquiries as largely unconscious habits of action, as well as by means of a continuous reconfiguration of human sensibility—whether by practices of expansion or of impoverishment. There is a kind of circular process that moves from qualitatively thick experience to analysis, the formulation of hypotheses, and inference each time a difficulty arises about what can or should be done in a specific context. On the other hand, the outputs of reflective experiences cannot but return to the primary experience out of which the need for them emerged and through which their strength will be tested. Consequently, language and sensibility should not be seen as two separate and hierarchically ordered levels of cognition but as elements that are intimately intertwined in the human world. Old habits of feeling are reshaped and new modes of sensibility are set by linguistic and cultural practices; meanwhile, ordinary language absorbs the outputs of reflection and becomes an integral part of the experiential fabric.

6. Frank Lorimer on the Growth of Intelligence Prior to Verbal Activity

To the best of my knowledge, Frank Lorimer remains a widely neglected figure within Classic Pragmatism, probably because, after obtaining his PhD under John Dewey's supervision at Columbia in the late 1920s,[16] he quit philosophy and specialized in demography, focusing particularly on the connections between reproduction and marriage in different cultural settings.[17] Nonetheless, his book *The Growth of Reason* (1929) deserves attention, because it can be considered an attempt to provide a more detailed elaboration and a more coherent account of the insights on language and thought that Dewey presents in the central chapters of *Experience and Nature*. After all, the subtitle of Lorimer's volume is *A Study of the Role of Verbal Activity in the Growth of the Structure of the Human Mind*.[18] Frank Lorimer's work is important for the project of developing a theory of human experience as enlanguaged because his reflection sets out precisely from the troubling problem I have hinted at above, namely, the danger of conflating the thesis about the decisive role of language in the emergence of mind with the unjustified assumption that language is the only enabling condition of intelligence. Even though we finally move beyond the view of the mind as a unique kind of substance, completely discontinuous with respect to natural processes and prior to language, considered as a mere means to externalize thought, we still run the risk of considering one only possible alternative. According to this opposite hypothesis, human thought as a whole should be regarded as an entirely linguistic behavior and the whole structure of human mental life should be viewed as relying exclusively on the social organization of words, gestures, and symbols (1929, 4). This picture of the debate tends to limit the interpretation of the relationship between language and thought by framing it in the oversimplified terms of what comes first: either—as has been conventionally maintained—thought is already defined in the interior theater of the mind prior to any linguistic cloth it could wear, or language as a social and symbolic practice is the only condition of thought and of the emergence of mental behavior. Even if I think that this dichotomistic way of posing an alternative is not in accordance with the Deweyan perspective, there are good reasons to support Lorimer's claim that the presentation of the issue at stake in *Experience and Nature* tends to "overstate the extent to which the structure of human thinking is derived from discourse and fails to give adequate recognition to the *organization* of intellectual processes prior to verbal activity" (1929, 85). Relying both on studies on animal behavior and on investigations on the acquisition of language in young infants, Lorimer focuses on organic, prelinguistic forms of intelligence as one of the sources out of which human "free intelligence" emerged. The point is to understand that the shift from organic to free, symbolic, or social intelligence in humans has been made possible by the profound reorganization of previous organic modes of intelligence caused by the advent of language.

I would argue that this is a good point, providing crucial support for a coherent application of the double-barreled concept of emergence to the arising of human intelligence: (1) a phenomenon is emergent if it counts exclusively on already existing resources without invoking the intervention of extra-empirical agents or nonnatural kinds of substances and (2) if it involves new forms of organization of preexisting resources that are irreversible and irreducible to the mere association of the elements out of which they arose. Dewey's emphasis on the second aspect might seem like an underestimation of the first one: speech played a disruptive role in the arising of symbolic behavior, but we should not underestimate the fact that, on the phylogenetic level, language reshaped and profoundly reorganized already existing forms of organic intelligence. Lorimer's point is that from an evolutionary perspective, human reason cannot be reduced to preexisting forms of organic intelligence plus their externalization via language, because speech elicited a symbolic transformation of intelligent behaviors that were, however, already given.

Consequently, we need a conception of organic intelligence prior to symbolic intelligence in order to see this last, peculiarly human form of intelligence as both continuous and emergent. Coherently with his naturalistic commitment, Lorimer refused to approach the issue of intelligence from the standard starting point of on an isolated, representational subject, separated from the reality "out there." Instead, he preferred to approach intelligence through a "working formula," namely, an operative concept, about organic life. An organism, he says, "is a tensional dynamic system, determined by the interaction of innate and environmental factors, and maintaining a more or less constant pattern in the midst of incessant changes within and without" (1929, 8). As stated in chapter 2, every living organism is structurally exposed to an environment and continuously tries to maintain a dynamic equilibrium with its surroundings by interacting with them at multiple levels. Thus, thinking and cognition do not basically consist in mirroring external reality, but rather have to do with tension and the reestablishment of an equilibrium between the organism itself and the environment of which it is a constitutive part. Using words that sound very similar to the enactivist concept of sense-making (Thompson-Stapleton 2009; Di Paolo & Thompson 2014), Lorimer claims that "[t]he first stage of intellectual activity may now be defined as the tensional organismic correlation of vital processes and adaptability, the capacity to restore equilibrium in relation to quite a wide range of environmental change" (1929, 10). However, I would argue, a first difference between "sense-making" and "organic intelligence" is a nuance between philosophical lexicons: speaking of "making sense" entails, if only involuntarily, the risk of still conveying the idea of intelligence as a projection of the subject on a reality that in itself is devoid of meaning. On the contrary, "organic intelligence" directly has to do with the structures of life, the practical hindrances or resources that can help a living being more or less successfully face the situations in which it happens to find itself and to be exposed to. A further difference is that Lorimer (like Dewey and Mead) does not see a simple continuity between sense-making and human cognition; rather, he leaves the door open for a relative discontinuity or profound reshaping of organic intelligence into symbolic intelligence.

As stated in the previous chapter of this book, Lorimer sees organic intelligence as having to do with the close relationship between each organism and its environment: it pertains to the rhythmical alternation of "organismic tension" and "habit formation" (1929, 13), and in this sense is "relatively independent" of social factors (1929, 7). According to this view, habits play a central role in experience, representing the (both biological and intelligent) adaptive answer of the organism to the environment, provisionally configured in such a way as to relieve the organic tension that is constitutive for a living being—a relatively stable channeling of organic energies in a field of continuous transitions with a natural environment scaffolding a kind of associated behavior, which however does not yet coincide with the kind of cooperative behavior we find in the human world.

A second important aspect is that organic intelligence and habit formation are seen to consist of both "*minute* and *implicit* processes" and "*gross* and *overt* processes" (Lorimer 1929, 19), which is to say both of psychological and neurological processes and of movements of the body as a whole. The point is twofold for Lorimer: on the one hand, one could get rid of a long series of philosophical problems by refusing to consider "minute processes" private events that take place within the mind and are therefore "discontinuous from the realm of observable things" (1929, 19). On the other hand, these processes are some of the components of integral intelligent behavior, together with other more visible events.[19] One should avoid reducing intelligent action to computing processes occurring within the nervous system and should instead regard them as events happening within a more or less complex nervous network, that is, as some of the important factors at work in an integral form of behavior that concerns the organism as a whole in its action within an environment. For example, speaking about a donkey, its capacity to make decisions, and to behave more intelligently than an amoeba, Lorimer emphasizes that the "excellent intellectual apparatus" of the donkey "is not isolated from the other physiological processes of the donkey" (1929, 16). I will not reconstruct the various phases of organic intelligence suggested by Lorimer. What deserves to be mentioned here is that, in his view, the progressive physiological differentiation and centralization of the nervous network is correlated with the differentiation of organism-environment interactions into two rhythmically alternating phases: a preparatory phase, which indirectly contributes to restoring the equilibrium of the organism, and a consummatory phase, where a new form of equilibrium is gained, enjoyed, or suffered. This is an important distinction that clearly anticipates, I would argue, the one between so-called immediate or primary experience—where human beings feel things aesthetically or qualitatively, in terms of how such things directly affect them (Dewey 1981, 73)—and reflective experience, namely, cognition—where human beings postpone the consummation of an act and experience things in terms of the import they can have on other things rather than directly on their own lives.

In comparison to organic intelligence, human intelligence is free because it is not necessarily anchored to situations that are immediately perceived. While in organic intelligence the crucial connection is between the organism's body and the natural environment, in free intelligence the main tension and the consummatory phase of experience take place between the organism and the naturally social environment it shares with others. Lorimer's (but also Dewey and Mead's) contention is that the profound reorganization of organic intelligence into free intelligence is connected with the advent of symbolic activity (1929, 23), it is "dependent upon the acquisition of words, or other symbols which are derivative from linguistic culture" (1929, 31).

I will devote section 8 of chapter 6 to Lorimer's treatment of symbolism and syntax as characteristic features of free intelligence that are due to language. For the moment, I wish to focus on the way in which he addresses cases of nonlinguistic behavior among humans, because I believe that this can provide an important contribution to the comprehensive picture of enlanguaged experience I am advancing.

7. NonLinguistic Behaviors: The Neglected Linguistic Environment as a Constitutive Factor in Behavior

Is there any space for proper reflection without words among adults? This is a question that can be addressed with Lorimer's help. He clearly had this issue in view and could resort to two alternative answers coming from the Pragmatist tradition: Dewey's answer was negative, while James's was positive, as it is evident in his treatment of the deaf-mute case. This is an important point in the current debate, connected with a cluster of notable philosophical issues I have already hinted at in section 6 of chapter 2. I am thinking of Hubert Dreyfus's phenomenological claim in favor of a skillful, primarily embodied being in touch with the world, which would be essentially independent of conceptual rationality (2005, 47), but also of the discussion within Enactivism about ways of scaling up processes of embodied coping with the environment to so-called higher cognitive processes (Hutto-Myin 2017), or—to put it differently—of scaling down the imagination, memory, and so on to embodied and enactive terms (Gallagher 2017, 189). To me, this is an important point for stating a clearer pragmatist argument in favor of the structurally enlanguaged character of our experience.

Let's begin with Lorimer's discussion of the deaf-mute case presented by James both in *The Principles of Psychology* (1981) and in an essay, "Thought before Language" (1983b).[20] James referred to the case of Mr. Ballard, a deaf-mute individual whose narrative has been collected and published by Samuel Porter, to show that this man was able to develop some complex abstract conceptions about the world around him before acquiring the language of signs. In Lorimer's treatment of the case, two aspects deserve attention: first, even if the deaf-mute child did not acquire a standardized language of signs until he was older, he already made gestures and signs that could be understood by his mother, whose intimacy with him enabled her to understand his needs and desires and to communicate with him, although not properly by means of words. Second, Ballard had to acquire the language of signs after his mother's death, that is, when he could no longer count on an intimate bond but had to deal with adults who had neither a close relationship nor much acquaintance with him.

The first argument that I suggest, which derives from Lorimer, is that even apparently idiosyncratic human behaviors involve at least basic gestural communication, relying on individuals' "co-operation with their parents and friends" (1929, 27), or depending on speakers' capacity to attune with one another. More radically, I would reformulate this thesis by emphasizing that, even before acquiring a language of signs, the deaf-mute already finds himself within a speaking environment—both verbally and by means of gestures—that will try to entrain him on an (at least very basic) conversation. Therefore, he will feel disoriented in the case of any real difficulties in allowing him to take part in a shared activity (however elementary it may be). This support from the social environment he belongs to—"the co-operation of intelligent adults" (1929, 28) with a deaf-mute child—is a constitutive factor of his behavior that cannot be disregarded. An already given network of communicative and linguistic practices is prior to the child's first utterances, regardless of whether he is able-bodied or deaf-mute. His first cry or first tentative look, I claim, cannot be regarded as isolated from the broadly linguistic environment where they occur, if one considers behavior—as I do—not simply as the result of one's own organic dispositions but as the complex outcome of both organic and environmental factors. The behavior of the deaf-mute child is not simply the product of his allegedly merely innate organic endowment (or lack of endowment); rather, his acts will result from his (more or less difficult) interaction with an already linguistic and communicative medium that works as a structural element in the configuration of his behavior. As already stated in the previous chapters, it is crucial to realize that behavior is a function of the structural relationship between an organism and its environment, not the mere result of some of the organism's properties (whether they be innate or acquired). To put it another way, my contention is that if we take seriously the thesis according to which the mind is structurally embedded in an environment, we cannot disregard the linguistic niche in which our more or less intelligent behavior unfolds.

A second important argument I wish to make more explicit is that the transition from mainly gesture-based communication to strictly verbal conversations is deeply connected with the kind of social environment the agent is interacting with: a conversation of gestures, idiomatic utterances, and idiolects can work very well within a group of intimates, but when the community becomes larger, when it is also composed of foreigners, interlocutors need a relatively more stable tool to interact with a "generalized other," to quote Mead's formula, as well as a more clearly structured form of communication. Hence, I contend, different affective connotations of the social environment (small groups of intimates or larger groups of strangers pursuing a common goal) can make a big difference in the use of language. On the other hand, the process of discrimination of single relatively stable names and verbs within language—Lorimer speaks of "nominal integration" (1929, 50)—and the arising of syntax appear to be not primarily constitutive linguistic elements, but processes occurring within a primarily holistic-working and affective-based form of speech, as emphasized by Alison Wray (1998; 2002).

For the moment, I suggest applying the first argument to the case of solving spatial problems via perceptual-kinesthetic schemata (Lorimer 1929, 23). Even if we maintain that no linguistic form of reasoning enters the process of solving problems of self-orienting in space among humans, we should not overlook the broadly gestural and verbal activity with which self-orienting is intertwined in the human world—from considering the position of the sun or other significant points with reference to one's own body, to looking at a map, not to mention the use of a mobile phone. When Lorimer says that even kinesthetic experience among humans "is dependent upon verbal or gestural activity" (1929, 24), this thesis should not be read as involving a transcendental claim—as if language and conceptual rationality were the enabling conditions of human motor-sensibility. His statement, I argue, should be read as a different claim: (1) assuming that each behavior is the result of both organic and environmental factors, namely, of their constitutive relationship, and that (2) it is empirically, yet irreversibly, the case that the human environment is already highly communicative and linguistic before each individual's birth, and (3) each human behavior must be regarded as the complex result of organic factors occurring within a broadly linguistic niche. Consequently, although one cannot deny that human sensibility, perceptual, and motor capacities are largely based on organic resources already found among nonlinguistic animals, in human behavior sensibility and language hold together—or, as I have already often stated, the advent of speech caused and continues to cause a profound reshaping of previous forms of sensibility, feeling, habit formation, and sense-making.

Let's now consider two other important cases regarding language acquisition in humans and among bonobos.

"Vocal activity," Lorimer says, is a "spontaneous feature of the infant's career" (1929, 33). However, "this vocal activity does not play any particular role in the child's social relations and intellectual habits until it has been transformed by the operation of social processes into verbal activity, that is, into an instrument of communication and speech." My contention is that the above-mentioned argument should also be applied to the first cries of the child—which, incidentally, are deeply cross-modal, involving as they do both vocal features and bodily agitation. Lorimer is right to emphasize that the cries of a small child originally had an organic function and basis, being but a transformation of its breath; however, my point is that not even the neonate's first cry takes place in a pneumatic vacuum. On the contrary, it occurs within an already (mainly affectively) communicative and linguistic social environment to which the infant is exposed from the very beginning. Even a suckling wails and fidgets differently depending on whether it hears its mother's voice or that of someone else, and its response varies depending on the tone of the person's voice, the melodic line of her or his speech, proximity or distance, and whether the setting is a familiar or unfamiliar one. It could be stated that very early on the original organic function of the cry is transformed, reshaped, or exapted (Gould & Vrba 1982) into a communicative function, but honestly, it is difficult to register the merely organic function of cries among humans. In other words, the purely organic function of the human cry seems to me to be an abstraction one makes a posteriori in order to distinguish between the different analytical components of a primarily integral act within a complex form of life.

A similar line of argument, I suggest, could even be useful to explain why superior anthropoid apes have failed to develop a symbolic culture, in spite of their "splendid brains" (Lorimer 1929, 32). For sure their "vocal equipment" is not so fitted to articulate speech: the human voice represented a clear advantage because "[n]oises made in the throat and head are peculiarly fitted to become instruments par excellence of social life and rationality, because of their production and social efficacy" (Lorimer 1929, 32).[21] Once again, however, we should not overlook the influence of the environment as a crucial component in the configuration of animal behavior. Behavior should be regarded as a function of the relation between each organism and its environment rather than as something deriving from a mechanism within the organism itself: while the first cry of the child is already embedded in a linguistic niche, the first wail of a little ape is not, and this circumstance makes a big difference. This thesis could help explain why in the famous case studied by Sue Savage-Rumbaugh (Savage-Rumbaugh & Lewin 1994), the mother ape Matata (born and raised in a nonlinguistic environment) found it so difficult to acquire just a few words from humans, whereas Kanzi, her baby ape, was able to develop more complex linguistic capacities, thanks to being exposed to verbal conversations from birth. Consequently, Tim Ingold correctly emphasizes that according to Sue Savage-Rumbaugh (Savage-Rumbagh & Rumbagh, 1993), where an intelligent creature is placed in a developmental context that imposes a situational need for complex communication with similar intelligent creatures in the social environment, syntactic structures are *bound to emerge* as necessary solutions to the communicative problems. Thus, language is no more given *in* the environment than it is *in* the organism; it emerges in the relational context of the organism in its environment and is therefore a property of the developmental system constituted by these relations (Ingold 1993, 41).

Chapter 6

Exploring the Continuity between Sensibility and Language

1. On Continuity and What It Means

As already stressed, in my opinion a view of human experience as enlanguaged involves the idea of a strong continuity between sensibility and language, where "continuity" includes various different aspects. First, it refers to the fact that most ordinary conversations do not only function via syntactic structures and objective references, which is to say through the objects they are about. They also work through mainly affective-laden features, such as the mutual regulation of timbre, rhythm, melodic lines, intonation, and gestures between the speakers, who more or less dialectically share suffering and enjoyment through their speeches, pursue their interests and goals, and try to understand one another's dispositions to act. Linguists and grammarians can and must distinguish between those different aspects for specific purposes, but one should not forget that discrimination occurs within the primarily thick—that is, not discrete—fabric of enlanguaged experience. Second, continuity means that linguistic practices in humans should be regarded as having their roots in the qualitative-aesthetic sensibility, which human beings share with other organisms, because living structurally involves being exposed to an environment, be it favorable and welcoming or menacing and adverse, as I claimed in the chapter 2 of this book. Third, continuity between sensibility and language requires us to consider how the human linguistic niche or our culturally laden environment produces feedbacks or loop effects on animal sensibility, reshaping it and transforming it into a distinctively human sensibility—given the contingent outputs of our natural history. In the last section of chapter 2, I already mentioned the growth of self-oriented sensibility and affectively based consciousness as rooted in linguistic tools for ascribing actions and responsibilities—from pronouns to storytelling. Another disruptive effect of human linguistic capacities on previous forms of organic sensibility I have mentioned is the wide and nuanced variety of human affective responses, which decisively goes beyond the mostly binary reactions—acceptance or refusal—among animals.

Guided by this view, in section 1, I have discovered further important hypotheses among the Classical Pragmatists that I regard as significant contributions to my own proposal and would suggest integrating with one another. From Frank Lorimer I derive the idea that language functions in a continuous and holistic fashion before it becomes subject to analytic distinctions—as originally foreseen by James and Dewey, and currently assumed at both a phylogenetic and ontogenetic level by Alison Wray (section 1). Section 2 claims that James was considering the idea of language as a continuous flow of relations, in contrast with a simplified view of James as the supporter of the primacy of experience over language. In sections 3 and 4, I make use of Mead's reflections to complement Dewey's and Lorimer's accounts on the growth of language out of already existing forms of organic intelligence through a theory of the genesis of verbal gestures out of communicational contexts that—I would argue—are based on a primarily affectively based mutual regulation of actions. Comparisons are provided with both historical hypotheses (Wundt) and contemporary theories (Tomasello, Tattersall), as well as with the literature on language acquisition among infants (Stern, Trevarthen, Krueger). In section 5, I further develop an idea of primarily affectively based self-reflectivity. Section 6 then explores the possibility of feedback reactions between language and animal sensibility.

Finally, in sections 7 and 8, I will examine Mead's and Frank Lorimer's reflections on the transition to properly referential and symbolic language, with marked cognitive powers. I suggest considering their two approaches as complementing each other. Lorimer provides an account of the emergence of human reason out of animal intelligence by means of words, focusing on signs as devices used to refer to something absent toward which an action is directed. Mead explains the transition to verbal gestures and significant symbols through the social extension of the conversational context—from a small group of intimates to a larger group of nonacquainted, more distant people, consequently providing—I suggest—an affectively oriented reading of the generalizing process involved in linguistic interchanges.

2. The Aesthetic-Affective Tissue of Speech and the Birth of Nomination

As hinted above, in Frank Lorimer's book I have found a clarifying account of the genesis of language—with its symbols and syntax—out of the preliminary aesthetic-affective tissue of speech. This hypothesis, I contend, should be adopted within an approach to human experience as enlanguaged, namely, as involving continuity between sensibility and language, as well as a loop effect whereby language reshapes human sensibility. Lorimer's idea was probably influenced by the work of Jespersen (1922), and possibly also by an early Deweyan essay titled "The Psychology of Infant Language" (1971b). Now, this notion seems to agree with Alison Wray's hypothesis of a holistic protolanguage preceding analytical, compositional language from both a phylogenetic and an ontogenetic perspective. In Wray's view (1998; 2000), this holistic and largely formulaic protolanguage has eminently affectively based social functions: from enhancing bonds to excluding others, from managing other speakers' behavior to maintaining the fluency of rhythmical alternation within conversations. Compositional, analytic language, made up of distinct words, would have arisen via the segmentation of the holistic language, which would still continue to represent the background out of which more analytical linguistic utterances emerge in current verbal exchanges. According to Wray, this transition was influenced by a change in the socio-affective conditions of human environments, namely, the transition from small groups of intimates to larger communities with more solid relationships and exchanges on a larger scale, also involving strangers.

Lorimer stresses the fundamental continuity of breathing, out of which language would have emerged via exaptation of the organic function toward a social aim. Speech, he says (1929, 36), is primarily a "continuous flow" and "cannot be considered as made of separate elements placed side by side as letters." "Nominal integration," that is, the distinction of names and verbs within the continuity of speech, would be a subsequent phenomenon within the development of language in the child. Dewey's very short article dating back to 1894, already went in a similar direction: considering the result of an empirical survey on the frequency of the various parts of speech among different children, Dewey argued in favor of "the gradual *differentiation* of the original protoplasmic verbal-nominal-interjectional form [. . .], until words assume their present rigidity" (1971b, 69). Lorimer goes much further, by explicitly arguing that nominal integration must be understood in terms of action and behavior: it is not a kind of initial baptism through which a name is correlated to a referent (Kripke 1980), but "the integration of phonetic elements as fixed conditioned reactions to specific situations as conditioned stimuli to specific types of social and personal behavior" (Lorimer 1929, 50).[1] This insight already includes a conception of meaning, but for the moment let's focus on the linguistic material preceding integral nomination according to Lorimer. The primary organic source is represented by cries, wails, and vocal reflexes that, although clearly connected to biological needs (hunger, thirst, fatigue, or pain), already have the social function of drawing attention. This rough kind of social function is destined to acquire more complex and nuanced meanings through the following phases of language development. Early infant speech will remain for the most part regulated by emotions and affects, connected to the baby's dependence on the bonds of a community of caregivers—although Lorimer does not provide an account of the expression of emotions of the sort to be found in Mead. A second step toward the development of language is constituted by a period of babble, characterized by a considerable degree of free experimentation with vocal variations. On the one hand, Lorimer observes that this represents a crucial moment for organizing the kinaesthetic and vocal-auditory features that are bound together in linguistic utterances. On the other hand, he claims that babbling is a form of free expression of "the energy of life" and of exuberance enjoyed as such, it is a playful activity and a first chance for aesthetic pleasure, giving support to the thesis upheld by some anthropologists concerning the festive origin of language.[2] Lorimer also emphasizes that the ludic dimension of babbling and the baby's enjoyment of sound variations are a form of "primitive poetry" (1929, 65), which lies at the basis of artistic activities among adults: "Eventually *lallen* becomes a joyous activity, an end in itself, an infantile art—a joy which is the common joy of the most primitive and the most sophisticated peoples, and which is basic in more elaborate arts, song, symphony and poetry" (1929, 41). Incidentally, I would note that this claim is at least partially convergent with the current thesis of the first exchanges between infant and mother as the predecessors of poetry and artification (Dissanayake 2011). Nominal integration, understood in the above-mentioned way, will develop out of this "protoplasmatic," affectively regulated and aesthetically rich form of language. Hence, Lorimer concludes the following:

> One of the immediate conclusions to be drawn from this study of the growth of verbal activity in the life of the child is the artificiality of making any rigid distinction between the affective and the referential relationships of words. Symbolic structure is a gradually differentiated structure within the total physiological and social context of linguistic activity. This is, of course, no disparagement of the normative value of insisting upon the differentiation of strict symbolic reference from vague fancy and emotive connotation. It is simply a protest against the assumption of such a division as pointing to factors originally isolated in the rise of symbolic activity or as involving an absolute metaphysical distinction. (1929, 63)

The image of language I derive from Lorimer strongly emphasizes that language does indeed play different functions in human lives, both functions primarily oriented at maintaining and controlling affectively based social relations and ones oriented at making reference to objects in the context of actions or behavioral goals. Functions of the latter kind are no more essential to the definition of language than functions of the former sort in human experience; on the contrary, the former emerge from the need to attract the attention of the other speaker, who is already involved in primarily holistic, largely affectively based (proto-) language. Furthermore, I contend, more referentially oriented aspects and qualitative devices continue to overlap in ordinary conversations, by responding to different needs through a different logic, conditioning one another via loop effects and feedback actions, and generally complementing one another.

Before dealing in greater detail with Lorimer's account of the emergence of meaning, symbolism, and syntax, I should say something about his criticism of the "instinct of imitation" (Lorimer 1929, 44) as a key to understanding language acquisition among infants. Instead of evoking an imitation instinct, Lorimer considers the common features of empirical practices that are connected to language acquisition among adults and outlines that almost none of them coincide with the mere repetition of a word or a sequence of words proffered by another speaker. There are cases of social conditioning where an adult repeats an isolated item of the baby's utterance and in this way reinforces attention and the reuse of the item within the infant's further utterances. There is also a basic sense of rhythm and prosodic gait of the conversation that tends to entrain the baby's utterances within the rails of the verbal exchange. Dual rhythmical alternations of utterances between baby and caregiver should also be mentioned, as they are not merely an acoustic phenomenon but a complex cross-modal one (see Stern 1985). Here sounds are accompanied, enhanced, and clarified by bodily and facial movements, together with which they constitute an integral communicative behavior. Cases of authentic echolalia or vocal imitation of the phonetic patterns uttered by an adult can be found at the end of the first year in a child's life or at the beginning of the second one. Finally, there is also a further interesting phenomenon, namely metalalia, whereby the baby seems to develop the capacity to complete an adult's expression in situations that are similar to those in which the child originally heard them.

This is an important point for the Pragmatists, who agreed about the limits of imitation as a fundamental concept to understand social behavior, habits, and language acquisition, as I have argued with reference to Dewey's conception of habit acquisition. I will be returning to this issue later on with reference to Mead's analysis of language.

3. James against the Language of Names: A Digression

Before addressing the issue of the emergence of meaning, symbolism, and syntax out of a primarily social-organic form of linguistic communication in light of Lorimer's and Mead's work, I suggest focusing on some interesting insights coming from William James's treatment of language.[3] For sure, James's case is very challenging for my enlanguaged experience thesis because he is the only Classical Pragmatist who remained a supporter of the primacy of experience over language. In his *Principles* he clearly maintained an idea of thought as basically prior to language. Moreover, it cannot be denied that his chapter on the stream of thought is still marked by solipsism and methodological individualism. Thinking is seen to occur within the interior theater of the mind: James overtly speaks about consciousness' "absolute insulation" (1981, 221) and the divide between different personal minds as "the most absolute breaches in nature."

This approach to thought is evidently very far from the strongly social perspective later adopted by Dewey and Mead, but James's contribution should not be underestimated, because he proved capable of looking at speech from a different perspective and of providing a richer and more nuanced conception of language. More specifically, I suggest we regard James as a critic of the prevailing habit of considering language to be basically composed of names and of favoring a conception of thinking as composed of discrete units rather than as a continuous flow. By criticizing associationist theories of thought and language, James shifts the focus to relations and continuities in language, suggesting we view language too as a stream, rather than as a sum of discrete names with sharp boundaries.

This is a rather controversial issue because, according to a traditional understanding of William James's chapter on the stream of thought, James formulated an idea of linguistic meanings as private feelings occurring within the speaker's mind and Wittgenstein implicitly criticized the conception of meaning presented in *The Principles of Psychology*: in section 11 of his *Philosophical Investigations*, he accused James of confusing meanings with feelings (Goodman 2002, 119).[4] According to this standard view, James would be a supporter of the claim that the meaning of a word is something, namely, a kind of mental or psychic entity preceding the linguistic exchange within a given practice. James would have supported the assumption that the meaning of words such as '*if*,' '*and*,' or '*Wait!*' consists of the correspondent feelings occurring within the speaker's mind. In his *Brown Book* (Wittgenstein 1964, 78), when speaking of St. Augustine's view of language, Wittgenstein concedes to James that we can think of the meanings of words in two ways: either as states of mind or "as the role[s] which these signs are playing in the system of language." According to Russell Goodman's reconstruction of the standard interpretation (2002, 121), Wittgenstein attributed to James a failure to distinguish between these two meanings of meaning, suggesting that James was conflating the psychological and the grammatical dimensions of meaning. James's polemical target is an atomistic conception of thought as primarily composed of discrete units, while "what we experience are things in relations," says Henry Jackman, "and we typically no more have a separate experience of things than we do of the relations themselves" (2017, 180). At first glance, James's position seems to be a clear condemnation of language, whose structure leads us to think that thought is the sum of discrete units—namely, either sensations or mental states corresponding to things in the world. The leading assumption of James's argument is a criticism of the atomistic conception of the mind as consisting of simple mental states, such as sensations, whose composition would give rise to higher levels of mental activity. Already in *The Principles*, as well as later on in the *Essays on Radical Empiricism*, James proposes his critique of the empiricist assumption as a critique from within this tradition—by assuming an associationist conception of the mind, traditional empiricism would not be faithful to the empirical method. Considering the way in which thought proceeds in us, according to James it must be acknowledged that one never experiences simple sensations in themselves, but rather an incessant flow of thought, which certainly dwells on substantive parts, but also proceeds from one part to another and these transitions are also integral parts of its continuous flow.[5] "The things are discrete and discontinuous; they do pass before us in a train or chain, making often explosive appearances and rendering each other in a twain. But their comings and goings and contrasts no more break the flow of the thought that thinks them than they break the space and the time in which they lie" (1981, 233). Well, James claims that the misleading belief that ideas or mental representations—which he even defines as mythological entities (1981, 230)—constitute thought and correspond to things in the real world is due to the "whole organization of speech" (1981, 230). Since people use names to indicate things, they tend to assume that ideas correspond to names or representations in the mind and that thought consists of a series of discrete representations. For example, thunder is never an isolated phenomenon within a storm. Rather, it occurs as a boom breaking the silence and contrasting with it. However, "[h]ere, again, language works against our perception of the truth. We name our thoughts simply, each after its things as if each knew its own thing and nothing else" (1981, 234): the *belief* that thought results from the sum of discrete entities (such as representations or mental states) arises from the way people talk, namely, from the *habit* of naming things.

However, if we read James's text more carefully, it seems to me that he is not actually criticizing language as a whole, based on the belief that it causes an artificial fragmentation of thought. Instead, I would argue, James's criticism concerns a prevailing conception of language as consisting essentially of names. Paying attention to this important specification, it becomes clearer why there are so many positive appreciations of language within the chapter, despite James's criticism of the associationist view of language and its noxious influence on the conception of thought. Therefore, I think it is possible to keep together the two different approaches to language in James's philosophy, which are characterized as mutually opposed by William Gavin in his book *The Reinstatement of the Vague* (1992).[6] It could even be said that James here is suggesting that the reader *observe* a series of ways in which language and verbal structures work, by looking at them from a different perspective. This change of perspective on language is not sufficient for a theory of human experience as enlanguaged, but represents a decisive step toward a nonreductive view of the wide range of functions that language plays in human lives. In spite of the compulsory habit of segmenting thinking into a series of representations corresponding to the names of things, James presents a series of observations on feelings of relation and tendencies in speech, as well as on linguistic fringes accompanying only apparently sharply defined names. Hence, he compares the tendency to look almost exclusively at names to the artificial concentration we might exercise on a drop of water, forgetting that it derives from a snowflake one has grabbed with one's warm hands and that it is going to evaporate in a few seconds (1981, 237).

After the famous passage comparing the flow of consciousness to the life of a bird, with its alternation of flights and rests (James 1981, 236), a shift occurs in James's perception of language. Language no longer appears to constitute an obstacle for the continuity of thought because one's attention moves from nouns to linguistic rhythm, to the flow of sentences and clauses: in other words, it is not considered a merely optional or supra-segmental element, but something which contributes to making names meaningful.[7] James invites the reader to shift his attention to conjunctions, prepositions, adverbial phrases, syntactic forms, and voice inflection (1981, 238). He says that through these different linguistic aspects, "it is the real relations that appear revealed" (1981, 238). Evidently, a focus on conjunctions, for example, does not fit the habit of pairing a separate name with a separate thing and a separate representation. When adopting a conception of language as primarily consisting of names, conjunctions create some problems and must be reinterpreted as playing a merely ancillary role. By contrast, focusing primarily on conjunctions, adverbial phrases, and so on could help us dismantle substantivizing and hypostatizing habits of thought.

For sure, James's formulas on a "feeling of *and*" and a "feeling of *if*" (1981, 238) were slippery and could prove misleading, as they could be taken to suggest that James supported the theory that the meaning of words consists of feelings. According to this view, meanings would primarily coincide with states of mind, even though in certain cases they are not representations of things but feelings—and of course, this is the source of the standard view of James as the "whipping boy" of section 11 of the *Philosophical Investigations*. However, I think that this kind of reading is inconsistent with the general anti-atomistic view of thought that James was supporting here. A similar interpretation would mean indulging in the tendency to privilege names, to hypostatize them, and to believe that thought is composed of an association of mental states—of discrete feelings in some cases and mental representations of things in other cases—criticized by James himself in these pages.

A theory of linguistic meaning as consisting of feelings within the mind would also be difficult to reconcile with James's treatment of feelings and emotions in *The Principles*, which denies the existence of any "mind-stuff," as has been said in the third chapter, section 2.

In a nutshell, James was not interested in a conception of meaning as consisting of feelings within the mind. Rather, he was trying to argue that in speech one hears or feels—note the use of verbs rather than of names—the relationships and transitions between things and events, relationships that are not entities at all, yet exist: "[N]amelessness is compatible with existence."[8] James also suggests we pay attention to expressions like "nothing but," "not yet" and "when?" which he considers to be "signs of the direction of thought" (1981, 244): they do not match sensory images of relatively stable things. Rather, they are signs of the functioning of language, revealing the direction of the discourse. This kind of function is evident, according to James, when reading a text: an expert reader is able to read a text at first glance with expressiveness, the right emphasis, and appropriate pauses, even though he or she may not always understand its content in detail (1981, 245).

James is also interested in the chance to adopt a different approach to names. Already at the beginning of his speech he points out that we should pay attention to agglutinative languages and to declensions in Latin and Greek. Linguistic phenomena of this kind show that even names are not unalterable, but change to match the context in which they appear and from which they are not independent (1981, 230). This is a further chance for James to emphasize the relations existing between words, rather than isolated words considered as self-standing. There is a difference between using "man" as a universal term and speaking about that solitary "man" who is facing us: even when dealing with names, their relations within a given context play an important role in determining their meanings (1981, 248).

At a certain point, James seems to push this contextualistic view of names even further (see Gavin 1992, 72); he also assigns names a halo of implications, of relations with other words. James speaks of "long association fringes of mutual repugnance or affinity" between words (1981, 251).[9] The "fringe" or "suffusion" is not only a character of thought and brain processes. For James, it is also a linguistic character, which plays a role in the process of determining the meaning of words. One vaguely perceives a "train of words" involved in the utterance of a single word; in spite (or because) of their vagueness, they mark the difference between the use of a word in a given context compared to a different situation. Here James suggests the famous comparison with harmonic sounds in music: even if the note is always the same, each musical instrument has a different voice because the fundamental note is merged with a series of harmonics that always give it a particular timbre or character. I wish to point out that this Jamesian insight is not simply equal to the idea of the semiotic chain of references or inferences illustrated by Peirce: there is a difference between a word's intimate connections with other words within one's own mother tongue or jargon, on the one hand, and the explicit descriptive knowledge of the relations within a chain of words and thoughts, on the other hand—that is, a kind of linguistic knowledge about something distinct from linguistic acquaintance. Here James is emphasizing the role of the only vaguely felt relations involved in a word, whose boundaries are not sharply defined because they are ruled by affectively or aesthetically based repulsions and attractions. For sure, there are situations requiring an analytic explication of the chains of references involved in a word, but this is a further possibility of experience.[10] For this reason, James introduces a distinction between two kinds of meaning, one dynamically taken and the other considered statically or without context:

The "meaning" of a word thus taken dynamically in a sentence may be quite different from its meaning when taken statically or without context. The dynamic meaning is usually reduced to the bare fringe we have described, or felt suitability or unfitness to the context and conclusion. The static meaning, when the word is concrete, as "table," or "Boston," consists of sensory images awakened; when it is abstract, as "criminal legislation" or "fallacy," the meaning consists of other words aroused, forming the so-called definition (James 1981, 255).

Certainly, the meaning of a word can be considered to be a static entity, corresponding to a perceived image when isolated or abstracted from the context out of which it arises. Incidentally, it could be observed that in the case of abstract names, even the static meaning is not a pure concept, for James, but a series of words.

However, meaning can and probably should also be considered primarily a dynamic process or verb—rather than as a mental state preceding a linguistic utterance. In this case, a word means according to its capacity to suit or to fit a given context, as well as some expected conclusions.

Certainly, James's focus on the continuities within language is still far from the continuity of communicative behaviors and verbal utterances I find in Dewey's and Mead's conversation of gestures and human interactions. Nor did he formulate Dewey's and Lorimer's idea of a gradual emergence of names out of a primarily holistic structure of human utterances. Nonetheless, James was already able to see continuities and relations as constitutive linguistic features at least on a par with names. Moreover, the path was already open to an understanding of the meaning of a word not as an entity, but as something dynamically occurring within the circumstances of speech.

4. Mead on the Genesis of Verbal Gestures out of Emotional Conversations

The work of George Herbert Mead is crucial for focusing on another form of continuity that was very important for the Classical Pragmatists and is pivotal for the theoretical proposal I am presenting. This is the continuity between sensibility and language. Underlying this hypothesis are two basic assumptions: on the one hand, a conception of affectivity and the emotions as a function of organism-environment relationships rather than as a private dimension—more specifically, as a function of organisms living in a naturally social and shared environment; on the other, an idea of language as a form of social behavior largely based on affective and qualitative resources, rather than as a primarily cognitive medium to refer to objects "out there." Language enables humans to keep in touch with others, to maintain and regulate social bonds, to act on others' behavioral tendencies as well as their own, to do things together, to select some shared privileged references within primarily holistic situations, and so on. In other words, language is primarily seen as enacting a phatic function in which a referential function is anchored, giving rise to more cognitively oriented activities. I would argue that Mead, like Dewey and Lorimer, adopted a primarily anthropological approach to language, rather than framing language within a mainly epistemic background. Language is seen as a typical feature of the human way of life, connected with the organic-environmental constraints characterizing human life, while at the same time shaping it from within.

Nonetheless, it is clear that, by comparison to Dewey and Lorimer, Mead paid much closer attention to the intertwining between language and human sociality. Consequently, I wish to make use of his insights to develop my own account of human experience as enlanguaged from the point of view of the peculiarly enhanced human sociality, which I consider mainly from an affectively based point of view. Mead adopted a relational and conversational idea of language as a powerful means to manage social conduct and to mutually regulate social behavior. Speech, utterances, and conversations are constitutive features of the human way of life within the continuum of already existing forms of animal communication—an assumption that is very far from the traditional and still prevailing image of language as a powerful cognitive device for transmitting information already determined within the mind or processed within individual brains.

By considering some Meadian texts dating back to the first decade of the twentieth century, I will recover his ideas about the connections between sensibility and language, because in those years he took a keen interest in the continuity between emotive gestures and verbal conversations. By contrast, in the following years he was to devote considerable efforts to explaining the crucial transition from conversations of gestures, which are already to be found among nonhuman animals, to properly symbolic or linguistic exchanges, based on the sharing of a relatively stable reference. I will return to this important transition in the penultimate section of this chapter, but for now I will focus on those parts of Mead's production offering a richer idea of his conception of language, understood as key means of social interaction.

As is always the case in this book, I will not simply reconstruct Mead's thought concerning the above-mentioned topic. My goal is to rely on Mead's suggestions to develop some theoretical insights that are not fully expressed in his work—the genesis of self-reflectivity occurring within the mutual turn-taking between the newborn and the adult through timbre and prosodic resources, as well as gradually through syntactical devices; the feedback of language on sensibility and the consequent sui generis shaping of human sensibility with comparison to other forms; an idea of attention sharing that is not primarily cognitive and, above all, the thesis of the linguistic nature of human ecology, that is, the assumption that human ontogenesis occurs in an environment already characterized by shared linguistic practices in which every young individual is already entrained from birth, if not before.

On the other hand, Mead's communicative perspective affords an understanding of animal sensibility, and not only of human sensibility as a form of mutual regulation of social behavior, as opposed to a set of mental states and processes that take place in the allegedly interior theater of the mind. This view of sensibility as involving attunement with the disposition to act of another animal pulls the rug out from under the sterile opposition we often witness in philosophical circles. What I am referring to, once more, is the contrast between those who support a foundation of language in sensibility, interpreted as the hard, prelinguistic bedrock of human experience, on which language would intervene only later as a tool to express it externally, and those who tend to consider language an eminently inferential tool or a quasi-transcendental enabling condition of human experience (as exemplified by the debate between Dreyfus and McDowell, now illustrated in Schear 2013), a space of reasons detached from the space of natural causality (McDowell 1996; Brandom 2000).[11]

Furthermore, I believe that Mead's approach to the genesis of language is still stimulating with respect to the recently developed perspectives in the field of evolutionary psychology speculating on the development of human communication—although Mead did not provide a detailed account but rather a series of promising insights. More specifically, I believe that some of his hypotheses could provide a useful tool to overcome some of Tomasello's mentalist hesitations in the interpretation of shared intentionality, that is, with regard to the issue whether so-called ultrasociality was established earlier than human language and whether it is an enabling condition of verbal communication. Joseph Margolis quite rightly wondered whether shared intentionality could effectively have developed without relying on already existing linguistic resources (2017). By radicalizing the Classical Pragmatists' insights, I suggest that the qualitative leap in the human form of sociality and the rise of language may be connected to each other by mutually constitutive relationships, rather than by a one-way founding connection. To put it differently, our peculiar form of life, characterized as highly shared and linguistically interwoven, has been configured through the reciprocal pushes and adjustments of these two components.

5. Emotive Communication as an Antecedent to Verbal Interaction[12]

In 1888, Mead attended Wilhelm Wundt's lectures (Huebner 2014, 43), where the German psychologist formulated the thesis that human language found its evolutionary origins in the expressive acts triggered by emotions and that communication based on emotional gestures should be considered the primary basis from which the complex syntactic structure of language later developed (Blumenthal 1973, 15).

Having adopted a continuistic perspective on human development from nonhuman forms of life, Mead shared Wundt's idea that verbal communication had an emotional origin. However, Mead radically reformulated Wundt's thesis by adopting a completely different approach to emotional gestures, namely, the pragmatist approach to emotions I have reconstructed in the chapter 2 (section 10) of this book, and which was profoundly critical of both Darwin's and Wundt's assumption that changes in the body and face should be understood as the external expressions of preexisting internal psychic states.

According to Mead, it is unnecessary to assume a conceptual framework separating bodily movements from allegedly internal or mental states, by considering the former a means to communicate what occurs in the private theater of the individual mind to the outside world.[13] In other words, Mead rejects Wundt's dualistic parallel between physical and psychic features to describe emotional processes. This kind of interpretation appears problematic if one considers the emotional exchanges occurring between nonhuman animals—the case of aggressive barking dogs being one of the most widely cited by Mead. The image of a double-layer phenomenon constituted by a mental state and its outer expression through bodily movements appears questionable even when looking at human babies, who respond very early on to the smiling faces of their caregivers. In both cases, it seems somewhat strained and misleading to attribute to an animal or a newborn the ability to decode its interlocutor's mental states based on what are allegedly mere externalizations.

Instead, Mead believes that in conversations between human beings, bodily attitudes, facial expressions and the tone of one's voice are felt as dispositions to act in a certain way, that is as gestures, which constitute the "earliest stages of acts" (2011, 5) or even of "syncopated," "truncated" acts (2011, 15). Their meaning for the interlocutor is represented by the possible behaviors they announce, as well as by the impact they could have on her or his actions and reactions. Bodily changes such as contracting the forehead, opening one's own eyes wide or smiling are gestures, that is, they represent the initial phases of acts on the part of the agent that are "already significant" for the interlocutors "in the sense that they are stimulated to perform reactions before they have significance of conscious meaning" (2011, 23). Very succinctly, it could be argued that for Mead emotional behaviors immediately have a communicative nature because they occur within a shared context, where they produce a form of reciprocal regulation of interlocutors' actions.

Furthermore, the meaning of emotional gestures, as Dewey had argued (in 1971a), is not primarily cognitive, like the content of a judgment. Rather, it involves a primary form of sensibility that does not distinguish between presumed purely descriptive-perceptive first phases, followed by a secondary evaluative act. For Dewey as well as for Mead, a certain gesture enacted by a partner is felt (and not known, as already stated) for its favorable or harmful impact on the lives of those who perceive it.

In the first decade of the twentieth century, Mead adopted Dewey's position and developed it in a more decisively social direction: emotions are not primarily subjective mental images, but crucial features of the behavior of a human being rooted in a naturally social environment that is already shared before birth. The mutual and dynamic regulation of the interactions between human living beings and their environment is primarily realized through a sort of affective proto-evaluation of the possible consequences of a certain disposition of the interlocutor toward her or his partner within a conversation of gestures. Mead speaks of "attitudes" and "dispositions" as parts of an action rather than as mental representations: in attitudes and dispositions the action is only partially outlined and inhibited during the exchange, but it could evolve in one direction or another according to the mute or verbal answers of the other person taking part in the communicative process.

In summary, a first central aspect of Mead's approach to emotional gestures compared to Wundt's is the rejection of the dualism between internal and external, mental and physical, private and public. The second peculiar element of Mead's approach concerns his interpretation of emotions as primary factors of social and communicative behavior—which avoids the possible opposition between sensibility and language, by regarding both as involving as set within communicative contexts. From his point of view, emotions are fundamentally relational gestures, whose meaning is constituted by the affective relevance of the other speaker's behavior for one's own actions and reactions. Far from being considered something essentially private that must be conveyed by other means in order to become accessible to others, emotions are seen to play a pivotal role in the mediation of social behavior and cooperative action. They contribute to configuring a form of reciprocally affective tuning of the gestures of the interlocutors taking part in a conversation of gestures—be they mute or verbal gestures.

> Such beginning of acts and organic preparations for actions, which have been called expression of emotion, are just the cues which have been selected and preserved as the means for mediating social conduct. Before conscious communication by symbols arises in gestures, signs, and articulate sounds, there exists in these earliest stages of acts and their physiological fringes the means of coordinating social conduct, the means of unconscious communication. And conscious communication has made use of these very expressions of the emotion to build up its signs. They were already signs. They had been already naturally selected and preserved as signs in unreflective social conduct before they were specialized as symbols. (Mead 2011, 5)

To be honest, this argument is even more radical than it might seem at first, because Mead supports the theory that individual selves emerge and take shape during conversations of gestures. This assumption pulls the rug out from under the presupposition of an interiority considered to be determined before any communicative interaction and limited to the translation of private mental states. In other words, we should not adopt the idea of a completely determined individual mind as the precondition for emotional exchanges. On the contrary, according to Mead, the dynamic and structurally social condition of a conversation of gestures is what allows individual identities to shape one another, by feeling the behavior of the other as significant for their own actions and as relevant to their own existence.

By combining Dewey and Mead, it could be argued that it is the feeling of one's partner's attitude—as threatening and aggressive or friendly and generous—with respect to one's own conduct that brings out the sense of one's own self as different from others. In other words, it is the socially extended environment (to adopt a formula coined by Shaun Gallagher in 2013 and 2017) where humans are embedded since birth that brings out the feeling of one's own self as different from the other's self.

Mead concludes that affective sensibility is the matter out of which individual selves are primarily constituted: "so must we not assume that the stuff out of which selves are constructed is emotional consciousness?" (2011, 5). While my interlocutor's experience is as immediate as my own in the exchange of gestures, a more reflective process of differentiation can develop starting from this primitive form of coexistence and mutual conditioning, leading to the configuration of the sense of my own self as distinct from that of my interlocutor.

Consequently, a comparison with the two main positions on the problem of other minds shows that Mead's perspective unhesitatingly rules out the so-called Theory Theory, based on an understanding of the other's intentionality as involving an inferential process. Nonetheless, it would also be misleading to interpret Mead's position as a variant of the so-called Simulation Theory, based on an analogy between bodily sensibilities, if the starting point remains an allegedly strictly individual experience that should be projected from one's own body to the other's body (Stueber 2006). If anything, it could be claimed that from Mead's point of view the experience of the other as another me is not a problem at all and the whole question is based on an artificial doubt—on a "paper doubt," to quote Peirce's well-known formula—and epistemological fallacy assuming knowledge as a fundamental form of experience, to use Dewey's vocabulary (Dewey 1988). The reason is that at least from birth the newborn is embedded and exposed to an already participated environment, in which its individual identity and 'interiority' gradually takes shape through the process of differentiation of its own answers from the responses of others and through the appropriation of common experiences from a personal perspective. All of this happens, according to Dewey and Mead, because of the natural conditions of human life: given the marked immaturity of the human newborn at birth, each member of the human species is particularly vulnerable and dependent on the social group to which he or she belongs from birth, and cannot survive without support from her or his intimates. Thanks to Fiske's studies (Mead 2011, 73) and their adoption of some Darwinian insights, both Mead and Dewey decisively overcame philosophical individualism, both in its methodological and in its metaphysical implications.

This range of insights from the two Pragmatists could be translated into the language of evolutionary psychology by claiming that they already recognized the connection between the highly social configuration of the human natural environment—in which ontogenetic processes are enacted—and the strongly marked neoteny of human beings. These aspects prove to be important, in my opinion, in light of Tomasello's theses about the genesis of the peculiar sociality of human beings, based on their exclusive ability to share attention to something with others. The convergences with Mead's thought (Nungesser 2015) are numerous and explicitly acknowledged, starting from the common biosocial approach (Baggio 2015) to human development—from the very idea of "cultural naturalism," namely, the idea that cultural development grows out of biological development and contributes to reshaping it. However, there is a problem related to the constitution of shared attention that, I would argue, could be solved through arguments derived from the Pragmatists. Tomasello's insistence on understanding others as intentional agents sometimes leads him to adopt the misleading approach of the recent debate on the experience of others: shared intentionality is considered by asking how it is possible to attribute "intentional states" to others (1999), and linguistic communication is translated into the ability to "read others' mind" and to "attune" with it (2008). For sure, Mead's approach is much less detailed than Tomasello's. Nonetheless, Mead's philosophical move has a disrupting effect on the classical problem of other minds, as this has been defined at least since the phenomenological revival of its Cartesian formulation. Mead subverts the whole issue by claiming that both individual minds and one's own interiority grow out of a primary shared context of mutual adjustment of behaviors, where the various interlocutors find their place by taking turns in conversation with others.

Mead was able to derive this idea not only from theoretical arguments but also from his early interest in infantile psychology.[14] Mead considered the first forms of infantile interaction with caring adults as privileged contexts for the investigation of the formation of individual identity, the birth of intelligent human behavior, and the origins of language. This happened many decades before Stern (1985) and Trevarthen (1979), whose research is now rightly referred to by scholars who endorse the idea of the social extension of the mind, after having previously emphasized its embedment in an environment (Fusaroli et al. 2014; Gallagher 2013; 2017; Krueger 2013). Given these assumptions, Mead could only reject the picture of the child as a "solitary epistemologist" (Spurrett & Cowley 2010).

To conclude this section, an important aspect—also with respect to the contemporary debate on this topic—is represented by Mead's criticism of Wundt's use of the concept of imitation. This is actually a recurrent criticism among the Classical Pragmatists, as has already been noted with reference to Lorimer's thoughts. According to George Mead, imitation cannot be considered a key category for understanding gestural communication (on this see Joas 1997, 99), because the ability to take part in social interactions, both silent and verbal ones, does not consist in miming or reproducing the utterances of one's interlocutor. If someone is aggressive toward me, I can certainly answer her or him aggressively too, but I can also leave or react with an ironic smile to that person's belligerent disposition. The point is that I am not simply reproducing the other's behavior, but I am responding through the adoption of a certain attitude or a certain role that is relative to the way in which I feel her or his disposition toward me. The emphasis on feeling the attitude of others as crucial to the way I react is important for Mead's thesis about the continuity between silent gestural conversations and linguistic exchanges, because verbal communication seems to continue and intensify a capacity to grasp the thread of the conversation hinging on forms of emotionally anchored communication (on this point see the interesting considerations in the chapter 3 of Cook [1993]).

6. The Transition to Linguistic Gestures: The Affective Dimension of Self-Reflectivity

A further section of this chapter will be devoted to the transition to properly linguistic utterances, involving Mead's explication of the emergence of linguistic reference. For the moment, I am interested in focusing on a series of aspects characterizing the relations between sensibility and language that I derive from Mead's texts and wish to make more explicit, in order to incorporate them into my own view of human experience as enlanguaged, thereby deeply intertwining qualitative-affective and linguistic features.

The first relevant aspect in this regard is to be found in some essays that date back to the early twentieth century—such as "Emotion and Instinct," "The Problem of Comparative Psychology," and "Concerning Animal Perception" (Mead 2011). Here Mead attributes an essential role to the emotional components of the interactions between an organism and its environment with respect to the development of intelligent behavior. Rejecting the traditional dualism between emotion and cognition,[15] the American Pragmatist emphasizes the role played by obstacles in the development of intelligent behavior; for Mead, the emotional dimension of an act can vary to a great extent but is never absent. While a behavior characterized by the "immediate grasping and enjoyment of the object sought" (2011, 27) may be regarded as instinctively emotional, interest arises when there is an obstacle preventing the achievement of an end that would allow the act to reach its consummation.[16] According to his view, human instrumental reason appears to emerge from more instinctual modes of behavior along a continuum, when hindrances and impediments come into play. On the one hand, Mead emphasizes the emotional-appetitive connotation of interest, which is nourished by desires and rejections. On the other hand, when some kind of resistance prevents the immediate satisfaction of a certain need, sensibility continues to be crucial within conduct, but changes its function and place within the process of action. In two famous essays (Dewey 1984; 1988), as well as in *Art as Experience* (Dewey 1989), Dewey will argue that in the course of intelligent behavior qualitative or affective thinking becomes a sort of criterion for the selection, evaluation, and control of the whole action.

However, inhibition is not sufficient to explain the transition from intelligent behavior—which for Mead, as for Dewey and Lorimer, humans share with other animal forms—to mental and reflective behavior. In fact, Mead and Dewey reserve the terms *mind* and *mental* for specifically human experiences, which are characterized by significant exchanges and linguistic interactions between human organisms within their naturally social environment—as has been emphasized in the previous sections of this chapter with special reference to Dewey and Lorimer's caveat. Vocal gestures seem to represent a difference with respect to this relative discontinuity in the animal world. In order to consider the affective value of reflectivity, I believe we should focus our attention on the lessons devoted to "[t]he vocal gesture and the significant symbol" in *Mind, Self, and Society*.

According to Mead, the human voice is particular with respect to other gestures, because it can be perceived by the person who utters a word as well as by her or his interlocutors, differently from facial, hand, and bodily movements. For example, I can perceive myself when engaged in a heated discussion with a colleague, and this allows me to adopt a disposition in response not only to my partner's utterances, but also to my own words, as if they were directed at me by another interlocutor. In other words, within the vocal conversation I do not only take into account the attitude of the other person, but I can focus on my own disposition from the point of view of the other, precisely on account of its significance for the other's conduct. "It is this which gives peculiar importance to the vocal gesture: it is one of those social stimuli which *affect* that makes it in the same fashion that it *affects* the form when made by another. That is, we can hear ourselves talking, and the *import* of what we say is the same to ourselves that it is to others" (Mead, 2015, 62, italics mine). I suggest reading Mead's conception of reflectivity in primarily affective terms by relying on his original idea that verbal communication developed out of emotion-based forms of reciprocal attunement. Words can be *felt* by the speaker who utters them as well as by her or his interlocutor, not in the sense of mere sensory perception, but because they can have an impact on the situation or on the speaker's life, in addition to having an emotional effect on the ways in which the interlocutor will react. Although this intuition is not further expounded on in Mead's texts, its consequences are stimulating: from the point of view I am suggesting, it can be inferred that typically human phenomena such as self-consciousness and metalanguage cannot be limited to higher forms of cognition, because they also involve an emotional capacity to be affected or touched by others' actions and to feel oneself as one is felt by others.[17]

This does not mean that Mead's emphasis on the properties of vocal gestures is unproblematic. I believe that Mead's hypothesis cannot be reduced to the position of the supporters of a vocal origin of language, as opposed to the supporters of a transition from hands to words (see Corballis 2002; Tomasello 2009), as if the whole issue of language phylogeny boiled down to the question of whether human verbal language evolved from the songs of birds or from the grunts of apes. Rather, I suggest that in Mead's philosophical framework, vocalizations are understood as peculiar bodily gestures already developed within animal communicative exchanges.

Gestures are considered holistic behaviors: when preparing for a fight, a male dog moves his legs, straightens his tail, and grinds his teeth, and these actions are not separate from the aggressive barking of the dog, but are all part of a cross-modal behavior—to employ an interesting adjective used to describe proto-conversations between infants and their caregivers in the current literature (Stern 1985; Trevarthen 1979; 1998; Dissanayake 2000; Falk 2009). The alternative between gestural origins and a vocal genesis of language appears too rigid when seen from such a holistic perspective on communicative behavior.

However, a serious objection comes from the case of nonhuman vocal gestures, such as the singing of birds. Bird sounds apparently do not give rise to forms of reflectivity, despite being audible to those who emit them as well as to other birds around them—certainly, they do not give rise to a form of reflectivity comparable to the human one. To respond to this type of objection, it obviously seems necessary to emphasize the difference between hearing sounds and hearing words, that is, to refer to the idea of the emergence of symbolic stimuli out of aesthetic ones presented in the short yet dense work A *Theory of Emotions from the Physiological Point of View* (Mead 1895). The next two sections of this chapter explore this transition from Lorimer's and Mead's complementary perspectives.

For the moment, I suggest taking conversational turn-taking, the mutually dynamic adjustment between questions and answers, and the rhythmic alternation of voices in human conversations as important features for focusing on the affective dimension of reflectivity. While Mead did not explicitly address these topics, I believe that his original insights must be further developed in that direction.

No doubt, reflectivity—which is to say the ability to hear even one's own words as they are felt by the other—finds exceptional instruments in linguistic syntax and the logical structure of language. These tools are not available in nonhuman communication contexts: what I primarily have in mind are verb conjugations *in primis*, which clearly determine the need to attribute the action to someone, while also allowing the replacement of one subject by another one, including the speaker him- or herself as an effective or possible agent. However, it seems to me that the ability to produce a highly coordinated vocal exchange precedes both the ability to conjugate verbs and the development of the powerful referential function of language—as stated by Dewey, Mead, and Lorimer, but also by Malinowsky and Jespersen. Indeed, the coordination of conversational turn-taking is already present in the early exchanges between mother and newborn, in which the coordinated alternation of the utterances appears to be functional to the maintenance and strengthening of relations between interlocutors (Trevarthen 1979; Falk 2004; Dissanayake 2011), privileging the phatic as well as affective-relational dimension of communication, rather than the referential function. Mutual attunement seems to be produced by an emphasis on prosodic features and timbre aspects of communication, as well as through an enhancement of melodic lines, suggesting that the newborn has a sense of its own turn within the conversation and of its own role in the communicative context. The extreme flexibility of rhythms, timbres, and tones can partly explain the reciprocal entrainment that is already established in the communication between mother and infant, and which—to the best of my knowledge—finds no parallel in the nonhuman animal world. However, this flexibility is not sufficient in itself: while primates' grunts are conditioned by a physiology that makes the possibilities of phonation rigid and limited, this does not apply to the singing of birds. Another element missing among nonhuman animals, I contend, contributes to explaining humans' highly developed capacity to coordinate their utterances to those of others and to find their place in a discourse. This element is the already linguistic characterization of the environment in which the newborn is immersed at least from birth, if not before, and within which it undertakes its first exchanges, or, to put it differently, its linguistic habituation and cultural heritage, which precedes every first inchoative attempt to take part in a conversation. The utterances of the adult who takes care of the infant lead the newborn along the tracks of human conversations, through the spontaneous recourse to a range of multimodal tools that are both embodied and embedded in a linguistic context—the tone of the voice, the melodic line of utterances, the speed and articulation of words, and the expressive rhythm, but also arm and face movements, nodding, and so on (Stern 1985; Trevarthen 1979; Krueger 2013).[18] In other words, a deeply embodied linguistic niche, strongly intertwined with linguistic and shared practices, could help explain the discontinuity of the human voice with respect to nonhuman forms of gestural communication. From this point of view, it would be appropriate to speak of cultural-linguistic practices as shaping the peculiar human ontogenetic niche (Gauvain 1995), in which human experience—even silent experience—occurs, as I stated in the second and the last sections of the previous chapter.[19]

7. Feedback Effects of Language on Sensibility?

It is evident from the final remarks made above that Mead's insights into the origins of human language in emotion-based communication need to be further integrated—and not merely because of his very succinct style of writing and reasoning. There are important theoretical aspects that must be explicitly taken into consideration in order to adapt some of his ideas to a theory of human experience as enlanguaged.

First, it is important to consider the consequences of the above-mentioned "reflective device" that is characteristic of human verbal communication for previous, nonlinguistic forms of communication between individuals. It is clear that Mead's discourse on the transition from bodily gestures to vocal and symbolic gestures represents an opportunity for the emergence of human selves and reflective behavior along a continuum of animal life. For sure, teleological or deterministic implications should be excluded, given the antimetaphysical reading of Darwin shared by all Classical Pragmatists. Probably, a completely random variation in the vocal and auditory apparatus of some primates (without considering changes in brain size, or the exceptional strengthening of neural connections, regarding which see Deacon [1998]) transformed previous conversations of gestures into linguistic conversations, whose collateral products were human selves and their mental and reflective modes of conduct. Language gave rise to people "as natural artefacts," as Joseph Margolis puts it in his *Venetian Lectures* (2017).

This means that Mead should have explicitly considered the consequences of his hypothesis for his linearly continuous approach: while completely fortuitous, the emergence of new forms of interaction with the environment—involving behaviors capable of (self-)reflexivity—ought to have elicited the question of the relative discontinuity represented by human conduct within animal life (for a similar question see Cahoone [2013], as well as Sinha [2009] on the so-called paradox of discontinuity in continuity). As I have already stated, the adoption of an emergentist perspective is not only based on the assumption that new forms of organization of preexisting vital and environmental resources cannot be reduced to the mere sum of the elements composing them. Emergentism also involves the assumption that novel forms of living and experiencing the world have an impact on previous modes of organization, producing a feedback or loop effect on preexisting conditions. Today, Gould and Vrba's concept of exaptation (1982) can be used to explain the impact of language on the reshaping of previous organic-environmental interactions—probably random and soft at first, and later disruptive with respect to previous forms of communication. As already noted, the Classical Pragmatists could rely on the idea of the co-optation of previous traits of a given body developed by Chauncey Wright—one of the members of the legendary Metaphysical Club—and apply this theory to completely different goals and functions, as clarified by Parravicini and Pievani (2018).

A second important aspect, which deserves attention from a post-Meadian perspective, more closely concerns a central aim of this volume, namely to highlight the mutual shaping of sensibility and language in the human world. Mead did not explicitly consider the impact of language on previous forms of emotional communication. Nonetheless, if we accept the idea that verbal exchanges engendered reflectivity and symbolic intelligence, we should also address the question of their impact on previous, not yet human, forms of sensibility. In other words, I believe that it is plausible to assume that linguistic gestures involved a profound reorganization and reshaping of emotional and bodily gestures. Some interesting observations concerning the ways in which language exerts its impact on affective experience have been suggested by Giovanna Colombetti in the context of an enactivist approach in the so-called affective sciences (2009). However, I believe that the question of the effects of verbal communication on emotional exchanges should be radicalized by adopting a coherent pragmatist approach to the problem. The grinding of teeth is already a primitive means of mutually coordinating behavior among dogs and, at the same time, a useful tool for orienting them in their environment. Nonetheless, human sensibility has also come to be directed toward the utterer her- or himself, who feels her or his own actions as they are felt by the other and is aware of this exposition not so much from a cognitive as from an emotional point of view: the speaker feels that the exchange affects her or his own life, chances, and relationships with others. To sum up, it could be argued that in humans emotions become feelings and affective self-awareness, or that through the development of emotional exchanges in a linguistic direction, they undergo a reconfiguration or a reorganization such as to bring out a new function with respect to previous ones: besides representing a crucial medium for coordinating social behavior and orienting oneself in the environment, sensibility became (on a phylogenetic level) and becomes (on the ontogenetic level) a tool to check one's own position and role in the shared world and to detect the impact on oneself of events happening in the surrounding environment.[20]

Cultural naturalism—that is, emergentism as I understand it—does not endorse an interpretation of the relations between sensibility and language according to a phenomenological model, involving the assumption that a purely sensible bodily experience represents the primarily nonlinguistic basis of our exchanges with the environment and that language constitutes a further, higher layer of explicitly reflective and inferential experience (as Madzia 2016 claims in relation to Mead, or as Dreyfus emphasized in his debate with McDowell in Schear 2013).

I think that both human reflectivity and the peculiarly human forms of intelligent behavior, as well as the linguistic dimension of human ecology, support the thesis of a decisive retroaction, reorganization or reshaping of the already existing ways of moving in the world that are typical of non-human living beings in virtue of all the contingent yet irreversible effects of human language. Instead of suggesting the existence of a foundational or hierarchical order between sensibility and language, these should be understood as structurally intertwined aspects, shaping each other, within peculiarly human life forms. This does not mean reversing the founding order so as to make language an almost a priori condition of human experience, because its appearance is envisaged as being entirely contingent and as deriving from the fortuitous mixture and unpredictable reuse of previous affective, cognitive, and communicative abilities (Parravicini & Pievani 2018).

A coherent development of cultural naturalism, I argue, involves the rejection of the dualistic alternative, according to which either language is the enabling condition of sensibility or sensibility is the bedrock on which higher cognitive processes can develop and become consolidated. In order to overcome this alternative, we should not adopt too partial an image of human language as an eminently inferential instrument (Brandom 2000). Rather, language as a whole should be seen to involve the qualitative and affective dimension highlighted by James, Mead, Dewey, and Lorimer. Language should be regarded as serving a range of different functions in human life and as operating in hybrid and approximate ways that can be further refined yet always overlap and which, for the most part, work well in human lives because they maintain a flexible, "mongrel" character (Margolis 2017)

8. Lorimer on the Emergence of Symbolic Intelligence: Words, Syntax, and Logical Structures

Now that the deep intertwining between language and sensibility has been illustrated, the major problem that remains to be tackled is the transition to the properly symbolic and referential function of language, that is, to its brilliant cognitive power. Two strategies can be borrowed from the Classical Pragmatists within a view of human experience as enlanguaged: the first one is represented by Frank Lorimer's account of the origin of human reason out of organic intelligence by means of words, which could be considered a development of Dewey's proposal in *Experience and Nature*. It is mainly centered on the notion that symbolic language requires a distinction between the sign and the further reference to an absent thing or event that is the goal or the focus of an action in progress. Dewey stressed the shift between considering things and events as having a direct impact on one's own life and considering things and events as referring to other things and events, thereby delaying their affections on the agent's life conditions. On the other hand, Mead gave his own radically social account of the transition from mute gestures to verbal gestures through the idea that significant symbols arise out of a social extension of the conversational context.

My suggestion is to consider those two hypotheses as complementary approaches to the issue at stake—namely, how language was able to become the most reliable tool for coordinating social action and our highly complicated cognitive enterprises.[21]

In this section, I will focus on Lorimer's theory, while the next one will be devoted to George Mead's proposal.

As has already been suggested, symbolism appears as the key moment in the transition from broadly vocal activities to verbal ones, but Frank Lorimer emphasizes that this change relies on previous forms of organic intelligence and on already preexistent modes of sociality. I will note in advance that, personally, I would have placed greater emphasis on the complementary aspect of the feedback effect caused by the advent of symbolism and language on already established forms of organic intelligence. As already stated, I think that, in a radically cultural-naturalistic vein, the disruptive reorganization of previous forms of organic intelligence caused by verbal activities should clearly be highlighted.

However, Lorimer's position deserves a detailed exposition, as it contains many interesting suggestions: from a theory of symbolism to a conception of concepts, to an emphasis on the continuity of logical operations with biological dynamics.

He begins his investigations from "words," which he considers to be rooted both in organic activity and in a socially shared environment. When dealing with the two different sources, however, the two sides of the coin seem difficult to disentangle. Vocal activity is obviously already present in many nonhuman forms of life, where it appears to be anchored in basic organic needs—to relax after an effort, to avoid pain or enjoy pleasure. However, as Lorimer acknowledges, vocal activity already has the social, albeit primitive, function of attracting others' attention. I would argue that if this is true in the case of animals like birds or apes, it is all the more true in the case of human neonates: for instance, the organic need for nutrition manifested in crying seems capable of attuning the human newborn to different kinds of interlocutors very early on—the breastfeeding mother, other intimates who cannot feed the baby but can take care of it, and strangers. Even babbling as the disinterested enjoyment of free vocalization seems to originate primarily in the proto-conversations between mother and infant.

On the other hand, Lorimer is open to the idea that "[s]ocial organization is also prior to verbal activity" (1929, 74): as already clarified at that time by Wolfgang Köhler's investigations (1925), apes are apparently able to welcome newborns through acculturation, by introducing them both to patterns of instrumental behavior and to quasi-ritual actions, such as playing, dancing or miming. "It would, however, be a great mistake to minimize the difference between animal-society and human society" (1929, 77), because the social dimension of apes' life is much more limited than that of human life: much of an ape's life is organically regulated, "whereas to be 'human' is essentially a social process" (1929, 77).

In any case, Lorimer believes that the transition from vocal to verbal activities is enacted through the arising of words or other symbols. Along a continuum of mainly phatic-oriented communication, words and symbols emerge as relatively fixed reactions to environmental situations. I wish to emphasize that this idea entails a couple of interesting consequences: first, words or symbols do not stand primarily for things but for patterns of action or reaction to specific natural and social contexts. They enable complex extensions and differentiations of the already social function of vocal activity, consisting in directing others' attention toward some event, thing or circumstance that is pivotal for action. Hence, "[f]unctionally, the word become the *tag*, or *handle*, of a whole behavior complex in social and personal adjustments" (1929, 79). Lorimer's example is greetings among infants, who gradually became capable of varying them according to different social settings (greetings among pairs, greeting an adult, bidding an object farewell). In the same vein, Lorimer defines a concept as "an implicit behavior pattern focused on a word or other socially established behavior" (1929, 82) and does not interpret the generality of ideas as deriving from the individuation of common, invariant properties among different things. Instead, he regards ideas as "response patterns which function in relation to varying situations" (1929, 90) and appear applicable to a variety of contexts.

Second, symbols are characterized as involving a difference between themselves (or between themselves as signs) and what they symbolize—a distinction that is always socially or institutionally established, according to Lorimer. It is precisely this kind of distinction—involved in the intimate structure of symbols themselves—that elicits a deep transformation within already existing forms of organic intelligence. Indeed, symbolism enables and enhances both the analytical process of isolating a phase or part of a behavior, when tension arises, and the synthetic process of considering the previous analytically isolated moment as part of an overall situation, when an action comes to its fulfillment or, in Dewey's words, to its consummation. In other words, symbolism and the advent of relatively fixed patterns of reaction to different (socially and linguistically established) situations cause a deep reorganization of previous forms of organic behavior: these become rational or free intelligence because through words and symbols humans are able to discriminate elements within a primarily experiential continuum, to postpone enjoyment or suffering, to refer to other signs and symbols, to find a new synthesis, and to solve states of tension and crisis.

In turn, syntax—which is to say the internal organization of symbolic structures and the mutual relationships between signs—is rooted in what are basic tension-consummation processes characterizing organic life in an environment. According to Lorimer, syntax emerges out of primarily holistic as well as emotively managed forms of social interaction, by means of the gradual differentiation of words-sentences—where a single word refers to a whole situation—into verbs and nouns—that is, into actions and objects or ends in view of an action, which gradually come to be discriminated within the overall utterance. Lorimer emphasizes this transition from a more holistic and emotively regulated use of speech to a more instrumentally directed discourse: he considers it to be continuous, ever happening and bidirectional. This idea is convergent with contemporary researches on holistic speech and utterances (Wray 1998; 2002; Mithen 2009; Brown 2017), as already noted, and could be interestingly applied to poetry and fiction (Dreon 2016b), as well as to the thick fabric of ordinary conversations.

Finally, the continuity between reason and organic factors emerges, even with reference to logical operations: if only in passing, Lorimer suggests we could identify the organic root of logical implication in the transmission of excitation as one of the fundamental patterns of behavior. At the same time, logical negation should be interpreted as the extension of an inhibitive pattern of behavior on the symbolic level (1929, 152). Clearly emphasizing the continuity between different forms of intelligence, Lorimer prefers to speak of hypo-symbolic and symbolic forms of intelligence rather than of prelogical and logical behavior (1929, 151).

Lorimer was even able to foresee that cultural evolution and an already shared cultural environment are an integral part of the individual ontogenetic process: humans are "heirs of the symbolic accumulation and organization of vast ages of human conversation and conjoint activity" (1929, 151). What this means, I would argue, is that mere organic intelligence among humans is an abstraction that is difficult to isolate in real life. This position is not far from Michael Tomasello's thesis that cultural transmission and cumulative cultural evolution constitute a foundation for the development of human cognition (1999). There is, however, a difference between Tomasello's and the Pragmatists' embryonic insights into sociality and language, as I have already argued in the previous section. In contrast to contemporary evolutionary anthropologists, Lorimer, Dewey, and Mead basically believed that the peculiar structure of human sociality—so-called joint or We-intentionality—was not the prerequisite for verbal communication and language development (Tomasello 2008). Their incipient intuition was that typically human ways of being social developed together with the gradual growth of symbolic and verbal forms of interaction by means of bidirectional actions and reactions, which is to say through a mutual configuration occurring dynamically and continuously. In the child's life and in the life of humanity, Lorimer says, "there is the same fundamental relationship between language processes and patterns of social activity: words are gradually fixed by the operation of social patterns, as they become more and more definite through accumulation in primitive behavior or they exist ready-made in civilized society—and in either case, the verbal processes contribute to the further definition and elaboration of modes of social activity" (1929, 79).

9. Mead's Theory of Reference

As already stated, Mead's inquiry provides a further contribution to explaining the transition from more qualitative, socio-affectively based, as well as holistically operating forms of speech to analytic discourse and objective reference. Whereas Lorimer highlighted the continuity between organic, hypo-symbolic forms of intelligence, and free symbolic intelligence via language, Mead focused on the emergence of conversations of linguistic gestures as connected with an extension and a change in the social contexts where communication occurs from the very beginning: a shift from groups of intimates to larger communities, where the mutual regulation of conduct must be connected to more generalized and relatively stable habits of action. This shift, I should point out, involves a change with regard to both the affectively based meanings of social relations and the different goals toward which their actions are directed.

Evidently, neither of these theories is regarded as providing an exhaustive interpretation of linguistic symbolism and verbal reference that makes it possible to develop a proper philosophy of language. Rather, both Mead's and Lorimer's accounts are meant as contributions to an approach to human experience as enlanguaged, that is, to linguistic practices and utterances considered as an integral part of ordinary human experiences, neither primarily isolated nor always easily detachable from other human actions and reactions.

As I have shown in the previous sections, Mead emphasized the continuity between conversation as the emotive-based coordination of conduct and verbal conversation, by adopting an externalized conception of sensibility. He even strongly challenged methodological individualism as a suitable approach to understand the mind and meaning: "Significance," he argued, "belongs to things in their relations to individuals. It does not lie in mental processes which are enclosed within individuals" (1922, 163). This does not mean that he completely rejected the distinction between inner processes and external ones, or between private and public phases of experience. On the contrary, he tended to view these distinctions as functional, contextual, and changing over time, and not as divided by ontological or epistemic gaps (1934/2015, 41).

Mead's radically social perspective on human experience led him to state in a very early essay that "the earlier history of the race and the history of childhood shows us that primitive consciousness also of the physical world is social and only becomes a physical consciousness with the growing power of reflection" (2011, 3). If we adopt this conception as a basic framework, we should explain how the transition occurred from conversations of gestures, even of verbal gestures—mainly concerned with establishing social bonds, maintaining them, and mutually coordinating social conduct—to a "physical consciousness" of the world. In other words, we need to explain how human consciousness became mostly focused on things and the common references in our speeches.

This transition does not undermine Mead's social characterization of human experience; rather, as hinted above, it appears to involve a shift from more intimate social bonds to a wider society of agents, whose behaviors should be—and indeed are—generalized in order to be taken into account by the speaker. In Mead's discourse, a key role in the whole process is played by the notion of "significant symbols," which is given an interesting, albeit very succinct treatment, in an essay dating back to 1922, "A Behavioristic Account of the Significant Symbol."

As is usually the case in Mead, the point of departure is a comparative one: the hen pursuing an angleworm indicates it to the chicks; although the hen has no intention to communicate something, her gesture is the beginning of an act pushing the chicks to behave like her. An animal in a herd feels some danger and begins to move away; its disposition to flee is a gesture for the rest of the herd, which will be led to move away too. In both cases, animals select an object as the goal of their action or an event as crucial for them, and the beginning of their action serves as a gesture for other animals, who are directed toward the same object (food) or led to avoid the same event (danger). However, there is no shared attention for the same object or event on the part of the first agent.

On the contrary, in the eyes of the intelligent observer, a gesture becomes a significant symbol, that is: "the gesture, the sign or the word which is addressed to the self when it is addressed to another individual, and is addressed to another, in form to all individuals, when it is addressed to the self" (Mead 1922, 162).

Through the arising of significant symbols, I suggest, two complementary stabilization processes are enacted. I use the verb *enact* because it clearly describes a context of action and a shared practice (be it aggressive or friendly in nature): what Mead provides is a "behavioristic account of the significant symbol." On the one hand, the speaker envisages the object or the event he or she is selecting as the focus or the goal of one's action and as requiring the same kind of conduct on one's own part and on that of the interlocutors. An object or an event is pointed out in its shared meaning, that is to say—according to Mead—as primarily affording or requiring a specific action, and as demanding that the action indicated be the same for both the speaker and her or his partner. In contrast to the mute gesture, the significance of the symbol is relatively fixed and made common through the sharing of the kind of activity that is involved by the symbol itself. I would contend that the originally affectively based capacity to attune to another individual's disposition to act, that is, to adopt this other person's attitude, is reconfigured into the faculty to converge on a commonly pointed out object or event. This context of "shared attention" is characterized by Michael Tomasello (1999, ch. 3) as being peculiar to human sociality, but in Mead's approach it is not understood as a primarily epistemic device. Rather, I would argue, it is primarily affective and pragmatically oriented, while also giving rise to the distinction between one's own identity and the identity of others through turn and role taking within the conversation.

Through this change, I suggest, the context of signification becomes structurally multireferential: there emerges a double meaning of meaning, having "two references, one to the thing indicated, and the other to the response" it requires from the speaker and her or his interlocutor (Mead 1922, 162). Mead calls the first reference the "name" and the second reference the "concept." In other words, the meaning of a name or the concept is a habit of conduct and the process of stabilization regards the object only insofar as it is the common focus or reference for a future action.

Nonetheless, reference is not only object and conduct related. There is a further reference to the interlocutor and to the speaker him- or herself, felt as her or his own interlocutor: it is this web of mutual connections that enables a name to stand for a specific object or event requiring a specific kind of behavior. This process of fixation of the symbolic reference demands a multiplication of references and is realized through the advent of speech: to make Mead's argument more explicit, I propose the thesis that the advent of language is pivotal for the emergence of symbolic activity, because language is able to produce relatively stable references through its capacity to support such complex webs of connections—whereas conversations made up of mute gestures are not. In any case, it is clear that Mead claims that the symbolic process occurs within a communicative space from the very beginning and not in the alleged interior theater of the mind. Furthermore, from a Meadian point of view, even some previous forms of organic intelligence (to use Lorimer's formula) already take place in a social context, though they remain opaque and do not give rise to properly shared actions.

On the other hand, a process of generalization occurs with reference to the interlocutor. Within verbal interactions, speakers becomes able to feel and look at themselves through the eyes of the other, which is to say that they become able to take into account the potential consequences of their own actions as if they were enacted by their interlocutors. Gradually, speakers become able to generalize both their own attitude and the other's disposition to act as the object, event or situation at stake requires, by "taking the role that is common to all" (Mead 1922, 161). In other words, there is a process of progressive generalization that leads a habit or attitude to behave in a specific way when dealing with an object or event, as the same mode of response is gradually extended from the "specific group" to the "vox populi" and "vox dei" (1922, 162), acquiring normative value. This process mostly occurs via education and play, that is, through enculturation, or exposition to already established habits of conduct and customs, meaning through entrainment in an already given culture and socially shared form of life (which nonetheless is still in the making). The space of meanings, generally assumed to be fixed and universal, can consequently be seen as having a natural history. This space remains open to revision and change, even acquiring relative autonomy, yet never becomes independent of the interchanges by which meanings are shaped, negotiated, and revised. It could be observed that this transition to a generalized "other" is a consequence of changes in the social context in which living beings are embedded. As already noted, Alison Wray stressed the importance of the shift from small groups of intimates to large communities of strangers as decisive for the transition from holistic, formulaic speech to analytic, syntactically complex language from a phylogenetic point of view (1998; 2002). A similar interpretative perspective could be applied to the ontogenetic approach: mainly holistic, affective-based proto-conversations are deeply connected with the intimate bonds between a baby and it caregiver, but require a gradual stabilization of responses and references as the child's community expands and adults' lives develop.

The primarily affectively based, qualitative functioning of language, however, does not disappear but is profoundly reshaped by the advent of a complex web of symbolic connections—as the very existence of poetry and literature shows.[22]

10. Conclusion

To conclude with a brief balance, my main purpose in these two last chapters has been to resume the Pragmatists' effort to go beyond the artificial opposition between experience and language in the human world, and to support a view of human experience as enlanguaged. This conception emphasizes the insight that language is irreversibly part of each human being's experience and that human experience is always embedded in linguistic contexts and practices, although this feature has emerged contingently, because of natural and fortuitous circumstances in human development. Far from considering language a quasi–a priori enabling condition of human experience, I have opted for a naturalistic yet not reductive approach to linguistic utterances as deriving from previously existing organic and environmental resources, but also as having important feedback actions on them and causing a profound reorganization of animal sensibility, action, and cognition.

My choice to focus on human experience as enlanguaged, rather than on language and its structures in isolation, stems from an acknowledgment of the fact that humans do not primarily experience language as a separate domain. This is evident if one approaches language starting from ordinary human exchanges, which are embedded in the sociocultural institutions in which everyday life unfolds, rather than from the grammatical or logical structure of language, regarded as an allegedly independent realm. Language has been envisaged as a constitutive part of human behavior that mixes, overlaps, and intertwines with other gestural forms of communication, as well as with other practices and ways of doing or enduring things. Usually, humans have no primarily isolated or exclusive experience of words, but are embedded in a form of life; and it is through this mixed or mongrel (Margolis 2017) character that they operate most of the time.

In accordance with the view of enlanguaged experience I have suggested, I have identified, gathered, and radicalized resources derived from the Pragmatists, and compared them to theoretical perspectives within contemporary debates. This approach has enabled me to emphasize that Dewey, Mead, and Lorimer, but also James to some extent, envisaged language as a mode of behavior that plays a crucial role in the shaping of peculiarly human forms of life. They abandoned the idea of language as merely the external cloth of thinking, understood as an essentially mental event. They radically rejected individualism as the standard methodological approach, by regarding shared contexts and participatory situations (be they peaceful or aggressive) as the natural human condition, rooted in the strong mutual dependence characterizing human communities from their organic constitution.

By contrast to a one-sided epistemological focus on language—considered exclusively as an extremely powerful tool for making references and inferences—these thinkers assumed language to be a very rich, multilayered, and multifunctional phenomenon that supports social ties on mainly qualitative-affective grounds, makes things and events common, mutually coordinates social behavior on different scales, and operates both analytically and holistically. They highlighted not only that language is the main means to scaffold reflection and inference, but also that it enters human experience as immediate enjoyment or suffering in relation to circumstances that are either favorable or adverse to human life. In other words, the Pragmatists' work supports the claim that language and sensibility are not two separate and hierarchically ordered levels of cognition, but are intimately intertwined in human experience.

Dewey, Mead, and Lorimer developed an idea of human experience as continuous with other nonhuman forms of experience and, at the same time, as profoundly reorganized by the advent of verbal communication. Language emerged through the interaction of previous organic forms of intelligence with animal natural environments that were already social to a greater or lesser extent. However, its advent caused a deep loop-effect and reorganization of previous forms of animal sensibility, cognition, and sociality, giving rise to peculiarly cultural natural living beings: humans.

From this perspective, the position on human nature I derive from the Pragmatists largely converges with Ian Tattersall's approach (2017). Tattersall's claim is rooted in the hypothesis that the biological features underlying linguistic development and human cognition first emerged 200,000 years ago, but remained for the most part inactive until 100,000 years ago. Language worked as a behavioral stimulus, eliciting a change from both the point of view of speed and quality. Tattersall argues that human language, which was initially grounded in a computational mental process, exercised a feedback action on symbolic and cognitive processes. According to him, thanks to the advent of language, the biological structures that gave rise to Homo sapiens 200,000 years ago underwent an exaptive rather than adaptive change because of innovations occurring on the behavioral level. In other words, through the advent of language, preexisting resources were co-opted for a new function, based on dynamics of exaptation and emergence.[23]

The Pragmatists arrived at a similar account of human nature but, as should be clear by now, their narrative has the merit of immediately rejecting any mentalistic framework for understanding human cognition and language.

Moreover, according to the antidogmatic perspective I have suggested in the Introduction, I think that language should not in turn be isolated as the only decisive factor in the emergence of an allegedly linear process, although language played—and continues to play—a decisive role in the shaping of human nature. The shaping of a human form of life appears to be a dynamic process that is still open and depends on many factors—language, sociality, sensibility, physiology, technology, and cultural heritage—that are interconnected by loop effects, a circular causality, and mutually constitutive relations. Searching for the ultimate truth or cause would mean losing sight of human experience itself through the old metaphysical habit of trying to go beyond it.

Conclusion

A Pragmatic/Pragmatist Balance

Having reached the end of this book, I do not wish to bore my patient reader by offering a summary of the topics I have been dealing with. Instead, I will make the most of these last pages to consider a question that possibly constitutes an objection to my whole project. The issue at stake has already been stated in the *Introduction* (in section 3) and is easy enough to define: it regards the choice to characterize the (provisional and nonexhaustive) picture of human nature suggested here—a contingent nature open to change—as "pragmatist."

The objection coming from the pragmatist field could sound like this:

> You have made a broad—maybe too broad, readers with different philosophical attitudes might say—use of arguments, theories, and terms drawn from James, Dewey, and Mead. You have also recovered Frank Lorimer's contribution from oblivion. Your anthropology clearly encompasses some of the pivotal tenets of Pragmatism: a strong cultural naturalism, a clear adhesion to contingentism, the renouncing of any apriorism and any extra-empirical matrix for explaining human experiences, a penchant for pluralism and open-mindedness, and a nondogmatic realism, assuming that reality is neither separate from living beings nor already completely made before they start interacting with it. Your book even presents the idea that what you currently think is true represents an individual contribution to "the previous truths of which every new inquiry takes account" (James 1975, 118), so much that

this assumption shapes the way you conduct your research. However, this is not enough to qualify a proposal as "pragmatist" because Pragmatism—by definition and by its very mission—does not consist exclusively in a legacy of theories and theoretical stances. Rather, in James's words, it has to do with the "respective practical consequences" (1975, 28) of each notion. "If no practical difference whatever can be traced, then the alternatives mean practically the same thing, and all dispute is idle." (1975, 28)

Honestly, I do not believe that the notions I have worked out in this book—my account of sensibility, the conception of habits I have defined, my idea of human experience as enlanguaged—have any "melioristic" value, in the sense of directly suggesting ways for living a fuller or better life. Positive solutions to this fully legitimate aspiration, in my opinion, should be determined each time within a specific context: they cannot really be defined in a meaningful way at a general level.

Nonetheless, I would argue that the sort of philosophical anthropology I have proposed can make a difference in practice, at least in terms of the way we look at our current situation. Maybe a good strategy for testing and possibly responding to the above objection is to consider some specific cases and issues from a practical point of view.

The first issue has to do with the so-called contemporary crisis of democracy in the Western world; more specifically, my concern is with the widespread trend among vast portions of the electorate both in Europe and in the US of voting for political leaders who tend to limit or twist those guarantees and inclusive behaviors supporting democracy itself—for example, by substituting political discussions in Parliament with journalistic declarations and social media appearances—and/or who promote economic and fiscal policies that could have noxious effects precisely on the weakest part of their voting base, for example, by adopting a flat-taxation system. Can these states of affairs be understood and eventually changed by assuming the paradigm of "communicative action" and deliberative democracy, or through the "[D]enk-Mittel" (James 1975, 84), that is, instruments of thought, worked out in the universalists versus communitarians debate?

Let me share an anecdote to better explain this point, although it might seem like a digression at first. Last summer, I was in Nuremberg, visiting the Documentation Center of the Nazi Party, which was offering visitors a rich and detailed reconstruction of the terrific capacity of the Nazi system to manipulate and exploit German people's feelings through an exhibition with a very revealing title, "Fascination and Terror." The exhibition featured Leni Riefensthal's films, pictures of Hitler by his official photographer Heinrich Hoffman, Albert Speer's scenic architecture, and a series of documents testifying to the Nazi Party's huge capacity to create a sense of belonging through magnificent ceremonies and popular festivals, as well as through a skillful use of sport competitions. At a certain point, I found a poster that revealed the assumption at the root of this impressive exhibition: the title opposed *Gesellschaft* to *Gemeinschaft*, which is to say the idea of society as an enlightened group of people governed by rational, possibly universal (or at least publicly shared) norms to the model of community based on feelings common to a group of people assumed to be basically closed, and entailing a clear boundary between those who are within the community itself and those outside of it. Probably, in the immediate aftermath of the World War II, this picture responded to the need to free Germany and other young European democracies from the spread of a culture that had nourished totalitarianism in the first decades of the twentieth century (see Mosse 1964) and to favor a more critical attitude toward government authorities. However, I think the picture in question no longer fits the situation.

In order to understand the political behavior of a broad section of the electorate, we cannot abstractly oppose an alleged purely rational form of decision making to merely emotional adherence; we need a conception of moral and political choices as reasonable and responsible as possible, grounded in informed arguments, and taking actual conditions and probable consequences into account, without forgetting that they are scaffolded by habits of behavior and feeling in which each person finds him- or herself already embedded. Institutions are crystallized habits, as Dewey put it, which is to say that they spring from habits of action and thought, continue to be supported by habits, or decay, and become different. They are nourished by affective habits, for example, a sense of belonging and the need to guide or to be guided, as well as by every individual's passionate aspiration to live a good life, whatever this means, and to share it with those he or she loves. So changing one's attitude depends not only on introducing new laws and norms, but also on cultivating habits and sensibility, and becoming able to think and feel differently, to use a different vocabulary. Who are the stakeholders involved in these processes and how should they operate? Schools and universities, literature, magazines, and social media, and political and religious groups, each on its own, or all of them in a dialectical tension? These are the questions, I think, we should pose, considering that there is no space for action free of habits and sensibility in the human form of life.

A second case I submit to the reader's attention regards consumers' behavior. For a long time, economic theory accepted the notion of *homo oeconomicus* as the anthropological standard for understanding economic decision-making and actions. For twentieth-century economists, "*homo oeconomicus* indicates an instrumentally rational economic agent who has (i) a complete and consistent ordering of preferences; (ii) perfect information; (iii) full computing power" (Cremaschi 1998). What about the explanatory power of this abstraction at a time in which people buy things they do not need and they are not informed about, or, increasingly, no longer buy commodities or services but experiences—possibly extraordinary and exclusive ones? Advertisements do not inform people about the technical features and performances of a specific car, but rather encourage people to buy a sensuous, luxurious driving experience, promising it will give them a perspicuous and exclusive character and consequently social recognition. Veblen's idea of perspicuous consumption and Bourdieu's conception of aesthetically based social distinction have been largely confirmed, adopted, and exploited by marketing strategists (Pine-Gilmore 1999; Ferraresi-Schmitt 2006), who have understood and driven the change in consumers' behavior more quickly than economists. They have rapidly adopted a much more embodied and emotionally guided anthropological paradigm—one might speak of *homo aestheticus* or *sentimentalis*—to explain and manipulate consumers' decision-making within a deeply laissez-faire capitalistic framework. One problem now is: how can people be directed toward more critical forms of consumption— for example, toward buying a car because it uses less fossil fuel and is more environmental-friendly? Certainly, material conditions should be changed—the cost of electric and hybrid vehicles should be reduced and the network of electric refueling stations should become widespread. But can a claim to a rational and austere form of decision-making, deprived of any aesthetic, emotional implications, resist this pervasive trend in postindustrial societies? I think it is not enough: not because of the alleged omnipotence of the capitalist system—without any doubt, economic and political institutions are hugely powerful, but I resist the idea they form a unitary system surreptitiously driving everyone's behavior. Rather, I think that the need to find satisfaction in the actions we are performing, as well as to find our own proper place within the web of social relations, is not produced by the "cultural industry," even if the kind of commercial supplies we are exposed to contribute to forging our needs and demands. From the point of view I have tried to develop in this book, the focus should consequently be on shaping alternative aesthetic habits and exposing people to different kinds of sensibility and alternative habits of consumption—many of which might have a disruptive effect and cause a crisis in previous habitual practices and actions.

A third, last case where my idea of enlanguaged experience might make a significant difference is the current evolution of political discourse. A lot of time and many words have been spent in journalistic, popular, and expert debates about so-called fake news. Evidently, it is very important to distinguish between true and false information, but I do not wish to focus on this aspect. My interest is in the strong increase within political communication of the use of insults, delegitimization, and provocation, which are becoming more and more widespread as linguistic habits capable of having an immediate impact on people's sensibility—also thanks to a skillful and pervasive use of social media. They are rapidly becoming code words, a formulaic language that is able to influence people's feelings, that is, dispositions to act. One revealing field in Italy is that of migration: expressions like "Go back home," "Stop the invasion," and "The fun is over for migrants" have impacted public opinion, contributing to justifying a new explicit form of closure and intolerance, on the one hand, and causing disdain on the other. Although pragmatics has developed a vast range of tools for dealing with these phenomena, one still ambiguous point pertains to its position with reference to syntax and semantics. One can consider a range of linguistic acts—perlocutory and illocutory acts, beyond locutory acts—as well as conversational implicatures to be very significant for understanding meaning. However, if the logical form of language is still regarded as the ground for the use of language and if semantics is taken to represent the standard mode of contact between language and the word, it is difficult to understand how political injuries can have an impact on people's actions, feelings, and thought. By contrast, the idea of human experience as enlanguaged points to a wide range of linguistic practices, where it is difficult to draw sharp boundaries between properly linguistic and behavioral aspects, that is, where words and utterances are an integral part of an interchange. What I have in mind here are very common situations like greeting, fighting, offending, supporting, inviting, and so on. These are all complex behaviors: for example, in offending someone, the insult or the injury is not separate from the tone of the voice or the bodily posture of the speaker and her/his occupying an interlocutor's peri-personal space. I wonder what the best approach might be to understand these behaviors. Is it better to assume that they result from the association of self-subsistent linguistic features whose mutual relationships and connections with an existential context must be investigated—along with their use within a verbal interchange—or to assume that these distinctions derive from a primarily integral enlanguaged experience and do not offer a description of the ultimate components of reality? Clearly, my preference is for the latter strategy, which considers the close intertwining and mutual scaffolding between linguistic practices and experience in the human world as already given and tries to draw functional distinctions within this continuum in order to solve specific problems when they arise.

Of course, these are just a few cases, which would actually deserve a much more detailed working out than the rough sketches I have drawn here. Nonetheless, it seems to me that this agrees with what James wrote about the pragmatic method, namely, that "[i]t appears less as a solution [. . .] than a program for more work" (1975, 32)—a work, I would add, that, evidently, cannot be done by philosophers alone (including Pragmatists), but must be carried out together with other experts, scientists, politicians, and common people who are involved in specific problems and can contribute to it through their own vocabulary, habits, and sensibility. Pluralism is a necessity and it is definitely time to abandon Descartes's prejudice: "there is seldom so much perfection in works composed of many separate parts, upon which different hands have been employed, as in those completed by a single master" (1850, 54).

Notes

Notes to Chapter 1

1. Tim Ingold's frequently used expression is "Anthropology is philosophy with the people in," as in Ingold 2014. See also Ingold 2008 and Ingold 1992.

2. As far as James is concerned, my preference is for a naturalistic interpretation of his contribution to philosophy, in a nonreductive and continuistic sense, as supported by Dewey's reading of his work. This position is far from Gale's and closer to how James's philosophy was understood by Dewey (Gale 1999, 335 and ff.).

3. See Ellen Dissanayake (in Dissanayake & Malotki 2018, 118), who claims that "It is also useful for members of highly literate societies to understand that speech, one of humankind's most remarkable endowments, has prosodic (or expressive) as well as symbolic, syntactical, and semantic components. When we talk, we do not merely exchange information or ideas—what linguists call 'propositions' (or 'complex propositions'). As neuroscientist Jaak Panksepp says, 'The brain mechanisms for language were designed for social interactions, not for the conduct of science.' After living for years with nonliterate Trobriand Islanders a century ago, British anthropologist Bronislaw Malinowski suggested that language serves not to imitate thought but to move another to act."

4. In this section, I am freely drawing on Dreon 2017.

5. See Dewey's letter to Robert V. Daniels in 1947, where he declares the following:

> I believe anthropology, especially that of such men as Boas (*Mind of Primitive Man*), Malinowski's various writings, Thurnwalds, etc., is much the most advanced as far as effective indication of method is concerned. Psychology on the other hand is on the whole, in my opinion, the most inept and backwards a tool and organ of study and report as there is. It is much of it actually harmful because of wrong basic postulates—maybe not all was stated, but actually there

when one judges from what they do—the kind of problems attacked and the way they attack them. So I was glad to hear that you were inclining to that approach. Some of the social psychologists are doing much better than the experimentalists etc., but I doubt if they use anthropological material as much as they might. (1999, vol. 3)

A note explains that what Dewey meant by "that approach" was cultural anthropology.

6. As is widely known, Peirce declared that he had borrowed the term *Pragmatism* from Kant in his essay, "What Is Pragmatism," published in *The Monist* in 1905. However, it is not clear which Kantian textual source could be at the origin of this choice: there is no explicit reference to Kant's *Anthropology from a Pragmatic Point of View*, while Peirce stated having being inspired by the *Critique of Pure Reason* in his formulation of the pragmatic maxim. The whole issue has been clearly reconstructed by Riccardo Martinelli in Martinelli 2015. More specifically, as far as I know, Peirce made no reference—even though he could have—to Kant's distinction between physiological or natural anthropology, conceived as descriptive knowledge, and pragmatic anthropology. According to Kant, the latter anthropology implies a practical engagement with the world which directly involves the subject (2006, *Preface*).

7. Peirce, James, and Mead went so far as to suggest a fully fledged conception of continuity, extending it even to inanimate nature and the entire cosmos.

8. I am grateful to Gian Luigi Paltrinieri for this revealing Kantian quotation.

9. I am grateful to Kenneth Stikkers for his remarks on this important point.

10. Michael Quante's "pragmatistic anthropology" is an interesting project, sharing some important points of contact with the current proposal: "the fact of the finiteness of our existence, the finiteness of the controllability of our actions, the fallibility of all our decisions and convictions" (2018, 19), as well as a lucid awareness of the fragility of social institutions, which are nonetheless assumed to be prior to individual autonomy. However, in spite of its title, Quante's book does not draw on concepts and arguments derived from the Classical Pragmatists, but rather turns to "classical German Philosophy, whilst counting Wittgenstein as part of this tradition" (2018, 13). His characterization of anthropology as pragmatistic—that is, grounded in the "conviction that human concepts are tools for coping with tasks we are met with in life" (2018, 20)—has its roots in Kant's *Anthropology from a Pragmatic Point of View*.

11. See Tattersall, who distinguishes between human sociality and that of other animals: in our case (for example, in highly urbanized contexts), the social environment covers almost the totality of our environment (1998, speaking about "Intelligence and Society" in chapter 2.3.).

12. See Tattersall's interesting distinction between human hunting and hunting among primates as two forms of socially organized enterprises, the former involving a collective distribution of the pray according to rules and the latter one simply based on strength relations (1998, speaking about "Behavior and Intelligence," in chapter 2.2.).

13. See Nietzsche, *Beyond Truth and Evil*, beginning of part I, *On the Prejudices of Philosophers* (2014).

14. On the different conceptions of naturalism within American thought, see Shook 2011.

15. This position entails an important break with Samuel Alexander's conception of emergentism, which admits the possibility of God within the natural world, although his conception was important for Mead through Morgan's appropriation of some of Alexander's views (El-Hani and Pihlström 2002).

16. In his *Emergent Evolution* (1923), Morgan suggested that an emergent novelty should be understood in terms of a new form of relatedness among already existing elements and factors (1923, 15–16).

17. The first example to illustrate the word *emergence* occurs in Lewes's *Problems of Life and Minds*, but an earlier use of the concept is implicitly found in John Stuart Mill's *System of Logic*.

18. Lawrence Cahoone reports: Lloyd Morgan formulated his view in 1912–15 and presented it publicly just before Samuel Alexander gave his own Gifford lectures of 1916–18, although Alexander's book was published before Morgan's (1923). They had been corresponding since the 1880s, and Alexander mentioned Conwy Lloyd Morgan as his source for the term 'emergent'" (2013, 321).

19. On Mead's conception of emergence see Cahoone (2019).

20. For a detailed account of convergences between Mead and Morgan on emergence see Baggio (2019).

21. Of course, he could not be acquainted with the technical distinctions between emergence and supervenience born out of the debate on dualism, physicalism, and Donald Davidson's so-called anomalous monism (1970; Kim 1993).

22. See Cahoone (2013, 321).

23. On this point, there are important convergences with Chauncey Wright's criticism of the conception of evolution as an "aprioristic" process and his understanding of novelty as an unexpected event, rather than as the product of a "pre-formational process of 'evolution'" (Parravicini 2019, §§ 3.1 and 3.2).

24. Cf. "Darwin opened our minds to the power of chance-happenings to bring forth 'fit' results if only they have time to add themselves together" (James 1975, 57).

25. Consider that Dewey's antitheologism differs from the idea of chance theorized by Terrence Deacon in order to argue that specific teleodynamic processes occur within self-organizing systems producing new forms of order (Deacon 2006).

26. I owe this reflection to a conversation I had with Jean-Pierre Cometti at the time he was giving a lecture on Dewey's *Influence of Darwin on Philosophy* as visiting professor in Venice.

Notes to Chapter 2

1. Engaging with Reichenbach's argument, Dewey says that "It is of course an inherent part of the naturalistic view of experience that affective qualities are products of the doings of nature—of the interaction of an organism and environmental conditions. It also follows that as direct qualities their reference is primarily to the carrying on of life processes—I hardly need do more than allude to the qualities of things as loved and feared" (1991b, 28).

2. Dewey's criticism of empirical atomism (as in 1980) was evidently indebted to his reading of James's *Essays on Radical Empiricism* (1976).

3. I take the word *mongrel* from Margolis 2017, who uses it to characterize the majority of human linguistic practices. I suggest applying it to human sensibility in ordinary life circumstances.

4. See Shusterman 2014, 26: "The familiar American simplification of 'aesthetics' to 'esthetics' is a characteristic Deweyan usage that is shared by Peirce and some other pragmatists, but William James eschewed it, preferring to use the 'ae' orthography which remains the prevailing American usage and the only standard British form."

5. Cf. Mead's words: "primitive consciousness even of the physical world is social, and only becomes physical consciousness with the growing power of reflections" (2011, 3).

6. See also James, "What Pragmatism Means" (in 1978).

7. This point represents an important divergence from Wittgenstein's philosophy, particularly when compared to the so-called "resolute reading" and/or "therapeutic reading" of his thought (see Crary & Read 2000; Bronzi 2012).

8. Calcaterra strongly stresses the Classical Pragmatists' attention toward feelings and their role with respect to cognition (2003, 78). She coherently develops this interpretative line also with reference to the Neo-pragmatists, particularly Rorty, identifying an ethical use of aesthetic-affective resources, such as solidarity in the face of cruelty and suffering (2019, 81).

9. By contrast, it is clear that Russell exclusively conceives of knowledge by acquaintance as a specific cognitive relation, consisting in the direct presentation of the object: "I say that I am acquainted with an object when I have a direct cognitive relation to that object, i.e., when I am directly aware of the object itself. When I speak of a cognitive relation here, I do not mean the sort of relation which constitutes judgment, but the sort which constitutes presentation" (Russell 1910/11, 108). One page after this claim, Russell specifies that "sense data" are the most obvious example of the kind of objects one is

acquainted with (1910/11, 109). He later adds that universals—such as being yellow and being before something else—are objects of acquaintance of a second kind, of whose presence one can become aware (1910/11, 111).

10. In Russell's essay on neutral monism (1914), he seems to be aware that James's idea of acquaintance contains further features, such as feelings, emotion, and volition, but he discards them as "non-cognitive," which is to say as not relevant at all with respect to epistemic issues, according to his approach. He also accuses James of providing too vague an account of them.

11. See Dewey (1980). These doubts about James's view of experience are well founded with reference to the *Principles*; nevertheless, I would argue that Russell was wrong to attribute a still subjective view of experience to the *Essays in Radical Empiricism* (1914, 168–69). His disappointment about the use of a biologically oriented notion of experience and the mind is also evident in his negative remark on Perry's comment (1914, 183–84).

12. According to a suggestion provided by Francesca Bordogna at a conference, this kind of use of the word aesthetic/esthetic" may partly have been derived from Alexander Bain.

13. Here I am freely reworking some parts of a paper I have published in *Synthese* (Dreon 2019a).

14. On the meaning of "interest" from a pragmatist point of view, see Santarelli 2019, who supports his analysis also through a reconstruction of the history of the concept and its relatively late restriction to a primarily economic field.

15. Incidentally, I should point out that this limited conception of knowledge compared to a broader conception of experience as basically consisting in organic-environmental interactions marks a divergence between Pragmatism and Enactivism, to which I will return later. For a discussion of this point see Dreon (2019a).

16. See also Steiner (2019, 200 ff.), who makes use of a strategy à la Wittgenstein (and à la Rorty) to face the issue of subjective qualities, by focusing on differences among vocabularies.

17. See Inukai (2010) for a different interpretation of Hume with reference to relations and closer to James's own position.

18. According to Claudine Tiercelin (2019), a convergent line of thought can be found in Peirce supporting a conception of entities as specific bundles of relations rather than as substances. See also John Ryder's argument for a relational ontology, grounded in the work of Justus Buchler and following a similar approach (2020).

19. See Margolis (1974) on works of art as "culturally emergent" entities.

20. Dewey adopted an adverbialist conception of the mind itself as argued by Steiner (2008) and by Dreon (2012, 66 ff.).

21. Most parts of this section and the two following ones have been published as Dreon 2021.

22. Pierre Steiner has pointed out to me that the enactive tradition (Varela, Thompson, & Di Paolo) has also come to embrace a similar view by drawing on Hans Jonas. On the contrary, Nussbaum supports an alternative view (2001). I have discussed that position in Dreon 2012, 85 ff.

23. I have found a convergent view in Colombetti (2007). For a discussion of the different uses and meanings of the word "valence" in affective sciences, see also Colombetti (2005).

24. On the intertwining of perception and affectivity characterizing the aesthetic component in human experience, see Matteucci (2019).

25. Cf. the work of Plessner and Gehlen, as well as that of Marjorie Grene, who derived philosophical consequences from arguments developed by von Uexküll and Portmann. Within evolutionary biology, the work of Stephen Jay Gould can be seen to provide further convergent contributions to this kind of approach.

26. In discussing the so-called objection of Causal-Constitutive Fallacy moved against Clark and Chalmers, Gallagher reaches the conclusion that "the confusion about causality and constitution, rather than a problem for the EMH [Extended Mind Hypothesis] is actually a problem for those who want to maintain a strict distinction" (2018b, 430).

27. This kind of antinaturalistic prejudice becomes particularly strong when characterizing human death as ontologically different from other animals' end.

28. This point suggests a possible convergence with nonrepresentational views of cognition derived from Gibson's ecological approach and emphasizing a broad conception of affordance (see Rietveld & Kiverstein 2014). In a Deweyan perspective, a richer "landscape of affordance" should explicitly include affective affordances.

29. To be honest, McDowell's position seems to be more nuanced in certain of his papers (2013). The problem, for me, is that the debate has tended to polarize and oversimplify the two positions, leading to negative consequences that I would like to avoid.

30. Hutto and Myin assume a distinction between basic cognition, which is supposed to be contentless, and content-involving cognition, which requires public linguistic practices, shared cultural symbols and norms. In Hutto and Myin (2017), their aim is to explain the relations between the two forms of cognition.

31. Nonetheless, in Johnson's book there also seems to be room for a different conception of the relationships between qualitative, embodied experience and language: for he quotes Eugène Gendlin, who "cautions us against the mistake of thinking that there are two distinct and autonomous sides of any experience—the felt sense (the implicit) and the formal expression (the explicit)" (2007, 82). Moreover, I agree with Johnson when, in speaking about neural processes, he states that "cognitive processing does not occur in a linear direction from core to shell structures. There are reentrant connections, so that what occurs at 'higher,' or more differentiated, levels can influence what happens

in limbic areas; these areas then affect shell regions, in a never-ending dance of changing experience" (2007, 101).

32. Cf. the work of Dean Falk (2004; 2009) and Ellen Dissanayake (2000; 2001; 2011) for a specific focus on mother-infant interaction as a basis, respectively, for the development of language in humans and for "aesthetics incunabula."

33. On the concept of language as a biocultural niche see Sinha (2009; 2015).

34. I would argue that this is how some artistic practices are rooted in human anthropology, as well as how they have contributed to forging the human condition. See Margolis (2009).

Notes to Chapter 3

1. At present, things are changing, as can be seen from a couple of volumes in Italian (Caruana & Viola 2018; Baggio et al. 2020).

2. The following treatment will essentially be based on a couple of previous papers I have published on the subject, Dreon (2015; 2019b).

3. Both italics and capitals are James's.

4. On the difference between Pragmatism and Behaviorism see Mead (1934/2015).

5. On this point see Dewey (1988b).

6. For a detailed criticism of intentionality even in its embodied version, see Pierre Steiner, *Décliner l'intentionalité* (unpublished manuscript, 3 and 293 ff.).

7. Jim Garrison suggests the idea that Dewey admired James's functionalistic account of the psychic and quotes Dewey by pointing out that James's idea of the organism was not a static one; on the contrary, he tended to "think life in terms of life in action" (2003, 405).

8. Concerning this aspect, see in particular the chapter which James devoted to habits in his book (1981). There he speaks about the development of neural paths through use and environmental exposure.

9. On this conception of the feeling body see Goldie (2002, 236). This point is further confirmed by James's *The Physical Basis of Emotion* (1894), where he argues that an emotion is a kind of secondary feeling indirectly aroused by an object, that is, a feeling of one's own body being affected by an external object. Besides, in the 1891 paper, James speaks about the possibility both of afferent currents in the nervous system going from the objects to the body and of other kinds of affective currents, going from the center to the periphery.

10. Mead focuses on this point specifically in an abstract titled *A Theory of Emotions from the Physiological Standpoint*.

11. Mead's intuition about a primarily social configuration of affectivity in humans could push the idea of participatory sense-making further (De Jaegher & Di Paolo 2007), making its affective characterization more explicit (see

Gallagher 2013; Krueger 2013). In his last book, *Action and Interaction*, Shaun Gallagher supports a conception of interaction as the background of individual action. He also devotes some pages to the issue of perceiving intentions and emotions (2020, 122 ff.). However, the idea I am deriving here from Mead further involves the claim that intersubjectivity is primarily configured as an affectively based conversation or interaction.

12. Dewey quotes not only from the *Principles*, but also from James's paper *The Physical Basis of Emotion*.

13. Concerning Dewey, it must be remembered that this subject will remain a key one for the development of his thought: important reflections are presented both in *Experience and Nature* and in *Art as Experience*. On this subject see Dreon (2012, chaps. 2 and 3). See also Quéré (2013), who points out that Dewey's early conception of emotions should be integrated with the idea he developed more explicitly in the 1920s and 1930s (in particular, in Dewey 1988a; 1989).

14. The psychologist's fallacy argument, in my opinion, misses one important point, later taken up by Mead: human actions are always social in principle, in the sense that they are subject to be seen by other people, and individuals are almost always partially aware of this (as James noted in his seminal paper, although he did not further expound on the idea elsewhere). I will return to this aspect later on, when discussing Mead's contributions to the pragmatist conception of emotions.

15. This Deweyan position is partially convergent with the idea—coming from Wittgenstein's reflections on the philosophy of psychology—that the whole issue derives from the failure to distinguish between different linguistic games or vocabularies. For a treatment of "the problem of the inner and the outer" along these lines, see Steiner (2019, 133 ff.).

16. The intertwining of emotions and cognition represents the core of Laura Candiotto's research, as it can be seen in Candiotto (2016; 2019).

17. "Intentional structure" here does not involve an alleged content in one's own mind; on the contrary, it involves the quality of being referred to something or about something, in opposition to a conception of emotion as fundamentally private states of mind. I suggest using this term here in a nondogmatic sense, because—as the following lines show—the possibility of characterizing this structure as intentional does not involve the idea of intentionality as any peculiar quality characterizing the mental and emotions, more specifically, apart from and prior to any form of linguistic practice, shared culture, and norms. For an exhaustive treatment of intentionality with reference to Pragmatism see Pierre Steiner's "Manuscript inédit," where he argues that this theory was foreign to the Classical Pragmatists, who had no need for it, given their strong adherence to the idea of a natural continuity between the mind and the world, the physical and the mental, nature and culture (unpublished manuscript, 331 ff.).

18. The first text to be considered is the abstract for A *Theory of Emotion from the Physiological Standpoint* (Mead 1895), a paper Mead presented to the American Psychological Association in 1894 (that is, the very year in which Dewey published his essay "Emotional Attitude"). The second text is "Emotion and Instinct" (2011, 27–29), an unpublished essay, probably written sometime between the previous paper and another crucial text, "The Social Character of Instinct" (2011, 3–8). This is another unpublished paper, which was certainly written after 1905, because it contains a reference to James Rowland Angell's book *Psychology*, which appeared in a first edition in 1904. There are also other essays by Mead to be taken into account in the background, that is, "Social Psychology as Counterpart to Physiological Psychology" (2011, 9–17), published in 1909, "What Social Objects Must Psychology Presuppose?" (2011, 19–25), publicly read in the same year and published in 1910, and an unpublished essay titled "A Psychological Study of the Use of Stimulants" (2011, 73–82).

19. He will return to aesthetic stimuli of this kind in his later essay, "A Psychological Account of the Use of Stimulants," with interesting suggestions on the origin of the arts (Mead 2011, 35).

20. At this stage of his thought, Mead probably referred to Wundt's conception of symbolic stimulus. Symbolic gestures are ones that mean indirectly, namely, by means of a new application of an already existent sign, which is associated with the concept it represents through one or more ideas. Consequently, a symbolic gesture differs from demonstrative or imitative gestures because the latter kinds of signs are directly connected to what they signify. On this, see Wundt (1973).

21. On the importance of McDougall's thought for Mead see Hans Joas (1997, 91 ff.).

22. As noted by Cook (1993), Mead had a strong interest in developmental psychology from both a theoretical and experimental perspective. Furthermore, he intertwined this kind of interest with his studies in animal and comparative psychology, as well as with a strong attention to their evolutionary implications. This peculiar mix of interests contributed to configuring Mead's philosophical approach in a way that seems close to more recent and promising research trends at the intersection between philosophy of mind, cognitive and affective neuroscience, and developmental and evolutionary psychology.

23. Similar reflections can be found in the first chapter of Dewey's *Human Nature and Conduct* (1983).

24. In his latest book, Shaun Gallagher explicitly claims that he endorses "a liberal enactivist version of the extended mind idea" (2020, 212). A detailed discussion of the idea of the Extended Mind Hypothesis is worked out in Gallagher (2018b).

25. Consequently, Mead seems to be more radical than Giovanna Colombetti in the way he conceives of the connections between affectivity and

sociality, even though his account lacks certain details. In her book Colombetti (2014) approaches this issue from the perspective of the "feeling others" problem: in other words, sociality is not explicitly seen as a basic factor in configuring human affectivity. Her essays "Enactive Affectivity, Extended" (2017) seems to be more promising, even if the point in question is not fully developed.

26. Very briefly, Mead's position is clearly far from the so-called Theory-Theory or Mind-Reading account of empathy (Stueber 2006). Maybe more interestingly, his view cannot be considered a form of simulation theory, if this account is understood as based on an analogy between one's own private, introspective experience and the allegedly doubtful experience of an individual different from and external to the one who would establish the analogy.

27. On this topic see Dreon (2018), from which I derive these conclusive remarks.

Notes to Chapter 4

1. Clare Carlisle suggests that another main trend in the thinking about habit within the history of philosophy is its conception as "an obstacle to reflection and threat to freedom" (2014, 3).

2. In this chapter, I have partially redeveloped parts of some past essays of mine, namely, Dreon 2010, and 2016c.

3. On the differences between the current trend toward naturalization in philosophy and the kind of naturalism characterizing the Classical Pragmatists, see Margolis (2002, 6–7). See also Dreon (2019e).

4. For a convergent view, see Steven Mithen and Lawrence Parsons (2008), who consider the human brain not simply a biological entity, completely determined before cultural evolution, but one that is also shaped—both anatomically and functionally—through the influence of a cultural environment. A similar idea can already be found in Clifford Geertz's *The Interpretation of Cultures* (1973).

5. Egbert and Barandarian (2014) focuses on the use of the so-called Hebb's rule in dominant scientific formulations of habit as a self-reinforcing repetitive pattern of behavior and as primarily associated with neural properties. They argue that "from their early conception, these theories found a material basis for habit on the plasticity of nervous 'vibrations' or pathways, to be much later developed into a scientifically mature hypothesis about synaptic plasticity on what is now widely known as 'Hebb's rule.' But this neuronal principle soon became almost exclusively applied within an informational or representational framework in cognitive neuroscience, and the sensorimotor and embodied development of this principles still remains relatively underexplored" (2014, 2). Nonetheless, I think that this is not the case with James. In the chapter on habits, we find the idea of neural plasticity as the origin of neuronal group formation, with the

simultaneous activation of several neurons and consequently producing stable neural paths. James also foreshadowed the idea of a loop effect or retroaction of behavior on brain physiology, chemistry, and physics; he realized that neural structures are not to be understood as constituted by an already complete set of innate neural programs, but rather as part of an open process of mutual between organic and behavioral factors.

6. In a later essay titled "The Vanishing Subject in the Psychology of James," Dewey (1988c) emphasizes the double tendency characterizing James's *Principles of Psychology*. While explicitly adopting a dualistic epistemology, based on the distinction between the psychic and the physical, James allowed the subject to be dissolved into an organism whose behavior was not seen to spring from within the organism itself, but rather was conceived as a function of the environment.

7. See also Calcaterra (2016), who strongly emphasizes James's continuistic stance across the fields of philosophy, psychology, and biology and its connection to his deeply undeterministic attitude in ethical and political matters. Instead, I disagree with Richard Gale's dichotomic reading of James, and particularly with his criticism of Dewey's naturalistic interpretation of Jamesian thought in his volume *Appendix* (1999).

8. I will devote some attention to Frank Lorimer's inquiry into the role of language in the shaping of human reason in the next chapter.

9. In one of his letters to William Rainey Harper dating back to 1903, Dewey mentioned Morgan as one of several scholars who could profitably be invited to the University of Chicago. Mead was also interested in his work and wrote a review of Morgan's book *An Introduction to Comparative Psychology*. On Morgan's conception of "emergent evolution" and Dewey's position, see the introductory chapter, section 5 (with a discussion of the whole issue).

10. By "structural" I mean constitutive, insomuch as, on the one hand, the organism can live and forge itself only through interactions with its environment, and, on the other hand, these same interactions contribute to continuously changing the environment, considered as an open and dynamic context of life inhabited by living beings.

11. Another interesting case of this kind is the one suggested by Ellen Dissanayake, who argues that the term *predisposition* is a useful way out from the dichotomy between innate and acquired behaviors. Hunter-gatherer children, she told me, probably would not show signs of Attention Deficit Hyperactivity Disorder (ADHD), because they are not expected to sit for a long time in school or otherwise be regimented into a schedule. Being hyperactive might be an advantage (not a disorder) in premodern individuals.

12. Although he considered the social space to be the primary setting for the enactment of a habitus, Bourdieu did not focus on the process of the individual appropriation of a social habit. Rather, he was interested in the

reproduction of a social habitus from one field of action to another in relation to the same agent, giving rise to a whole lifestyle. He introduced the concepts of transfer, metaphorical conveyance, and osmotic transition (1977; 1984; 1992). However, I have some doubts as to the efficacy of the use of these concepts for understanding the individual acquisition of a habit already existing within the social group one belongs to.

13. Among the kinds of habits he considered, it is also worth mentioning swimming, birth-giving, and crouching.

14. See Dreon (2012b).

15. However, Hutto and Myin's position seems to have evolved in their 2017 book, where they insist on the continuity (and not dichotomy) between basic and nonbasic cognition (ch. 7).

16. See Dreon (2020b).

17. See Edel's systematic analysis of the connection between Dewey's ethics and his anthropology of habits (2001).

18. From this point of view, Dewey seems clearly to move away from Kant's aprioristic and formal account of morality, while at the same time moving closer to Aristotle, insofar as he distinguishes between two occurrences of habits—as mastery and as virtuous dispositions (Δ, 20, 1022b, 4–14). However, in Dewey's deflationary and genuinely pluralistic view of ethics, the distinction remains functional and open, as no disposition can be assumed to be virtuous once and for all, but each can and must be carefully determined.

19. For a general comparison between Helmuth Plessner—one of the leading figures in German philosophical anthropology (together with Max Scheler and Arnold Gehlen)—and Classical Pragmatism, see Krüger (2009).

20. Part of this section is drawn from Dreon (2016c).

21. As summed up by Thompson, Krovitz, and Nelson (2003, 174), precocial mammals usually have a long gestation period and their young are born at a more advanced state of development; by contrast, altricial mammals have short gestation periods and produce strongly immature, helpless young. Humans are unusual because they have a long gestation period, like precocial mammals, but their babies are helpless and dependent on the adult group for a long period, like altricial mammals.

22. Dissanayake and Falk focused on the consequence of this dependence on the development, respectively, of proto-aesthetic behaviors and verbal communication in Dissanayake (2000) and Falk (2009).

23. On this issue see Shusterman (2008).

24. Bourdieu declared to have originally derived the concept of habit from Erwin Panofsky, whose work *Gothic Architecture and Scholasticism* (1951) he was translating into French (Krais & Gebauer 2002, ch. 2). His first formulations of the concept are in Bourdieu 1977.

25. Interesting (and more or less extensive) comparisons between the two authors regarding the issue under investigation have been developed by different scholars in the last few years. See Colapietro (2004b), Dreon (2010), Crossley (2013), and Quéré (2016).

26. To be more precise, the Latin word *habitus* is a fourth-declension noun and, consequently, there is a little difference between its singular and plural nominative forms, apart from the length of the last vowel (*habitŭs* in the singular and *habitūs* in the plural). This distinction in terms of vowel length is not maintained in contemporary occurrences of the term. However, it is clear from the contexts of use that Bourdieu employs the noun in its singular form. As stated within the text, when the term appears as a plural noun, each single agent is characterized by a single habitus (see Bourdieu 1992, 52, ff.).

27. This idea presents certain similarities with Wittgenstein's notion of seeing differently, but its roots could be traced back to the aesthetic tradition of Schiller's *Letters on Human Education*.

28. See Bourdieu (2000). Both Loïc Wacquant (1998) and Krais and Gebauer (2002) insist on a more flexible understanding of *habitus*.

29. For an interesting analysis of different meanings of power, see John Ryder (2020).

Notes to Chapter 5

1. On the differences between Neo-Pragmatism and the Classical Pragmatists, see also Cometti (2010).

2. On this point see Adam Kendon (2009; 2011), who sees "languaging" as a "poly-modalic activity," by problematizing the criteria for deciding "what is 'in' the language and what is 'outside' it" (2011, 103), namely, for a sharp separation between the paralinguistic and the properly linguistic features of language.

3. I am grateful to Giovanna Colombetti, who informed me about this group of scholars after I had already formulated my idea of enlanguaged experience.

4. The present and the following sections partially rework some materials from a series of previous texts of mine (Dreon 2007, 165 ff.; 2014; 2019d).

5. Cf. Wittgenstein 1953, 25: "Commanding, questioning, recounting, chatting, are as much a part of our natural history as walking, eating, drinking, playing."

6. Probably, Dewey matured these ideas through his readings of Darwin, maybe by indirectly relying on Chauncey Wright's understanding of human evolution through James's and Peirce's mediation. However, as emphasized by Kenneth Stikkers (personal communication), Dewey mentions Wright only once in his entire corpus, and not in his famous essay on Darwin's influence, but only

briefly in his eulogy to James. Dewey was not a member of the Metaphysical Club, as Peirce and James were, and probably never realized or understood Wright's profound influence on them. In contrast, James praised Wright's work highly in James 1875 (now in James 1987, 15–18).

7. However, Dewey's answer is different from the still mentalistically oriented solution provided by Tomasello, as I will be arguing later on in relation to Mead. See section 10 of this chapter.

8. The case dealt with is astonishingly similar to the famous *"gavagai"* story told by Quine in his essay on *Ontological Relativity* (Quine 1969). Is *gavagai* the word for rabbit, for some part of the rabbit's body, or for an action performed by the animal? Although Quine's reflections are different from Dewey's, it is interesting to note that the content of that paper derives from a couple of lectures that Quine delivered at Columbia University in 1968, and which constitute the first edition of the John Dewey Lectures. Quine begins his paper by recalling that he attended Dewey's lesson on art as experience in 1931, after obtaining his master's degree.

9. Here I am making free use of parts of a paper I have published on mind and cognition in Dewey (Dreon 2019a).

10. For a treatment of rhythm as key feature in human experience, see Vara Sanchez (2020).

11. With regard to this point, a substantial degree of convergence is to be found with Varela, Thompson, and Rosch's position on evolutionism (1991, 185 ff.). These researchers strongly criticized the neo-Darwinian view of evolution centered on adaptation, considered as a *telos* (a "Mount Fittness," 1991, 193) to be pursued by genes in a predetermined environment, by adapting to the latter's allegedly already fixed constraints. On the contrary, they endorsed an idea of evolution as a "natural drift" (1991, 201), while also emphasizing Richard Lewontin's refusal to regard the environment as separate from what organisms are and from what they do in it (1991, 198).

12. For an extensive interpretation of Dewey's adverbialist approach to the mental, see Pierre Steiner's book, *Desaturer l'esprit* (2019). Steiner also provides reasons in support of the claim that Dewey's characterization of human interactions as mental does not involve intentionality, understood as a special intrinsic property of the mind connecting it with objects in the world, independently of any linguistic practice, shared norm, or common form of life (see *Manuscript Inédit*). Rather, thinking for Dewey is a fully embodied and fully extended mode of interaction with the environment through which human organisms are able to do things in common (2004, 9).

13. See the 1908 essay *The Logical Character of Ideas*, reprinted in *Essays in Experimental Logic* in 1916 (Dewey 2004).

14. "One the one hand, the biological characteristics of the human species display no dramatic discontinuities with those of other species; yet, on the other,

human cognitive capacities, and human cultural constructions, appear from our current vantage point to be as exceptional in the living world as they did to Descartes" (Sinha 2009, 4).

15. On this topic see Dreon (2018).

16. Previously, he had received a master's degree from the University of Chicago in 1921.

17. His book *Culture and Human Fertility*, edited by Lorimer and published in 1954, received considerable attention.

18. In the *Preface* Lorimer explicitly declares that his book was inspired by Dewey's work and that he enjoyed "his counsel in its preparation" (1929, V). A copy of the book with some handwritten annotations by John Dewey himself is preserved at the Special Collection Center of Morris Library in Carbondale. *The Correspondence of John Dewey* (1999) also includes some letters he exchanged with Lorimer, showing that the latter sent a copy of his work to Dewey, who after a while wrote back to say that he had read and appreciated the book.

19. Significantly, this passage is underlined in Dewey's own copy of the book.

20. The paper was originally published in the *Philosophical Review I* (1982): 613–24; it has now been collected in *Volume 13: Essays in Psychology*, 278–91, of the works of William James.

21. But see Tecumseh Fitch's reservations on the hypothesis that anatomical vocal tracts can prove decisive for the emergence of language (2010, ch. 9).

Notes to Chapter 6

1. In his early essay, Dewey emphasized the predominance of verbs in early infants' language and also reinterpreted the use of some nouns (such as "ball" or "door") as involving a reference to acts ("throw the ball at me" or "close the door"). His source was a study on "The Language of Childhood" by F. Tracy, published in the *American Journal of Psychology* in 1893.

2. Lorimer mentions Donovan, *The Festal Origin of Human Speech* (1891).

3. This section derives from Dreon (2020a).

4. Henry Jackman claims that James did not support a private view of language, as I do, although on the basis of different arguments. He also contends that "there is reason to doubt that Wittgenstein even *attributed* such a theory to James" (2017, 177). Considering that James's claim focuses on the existence of relations, rather than on their having a role in the fixation of meanings, it is possible to conclude that Wittgenstein worked with James (rather than criticizing him), because James's argument in favor of the reality of relations helped him oppose the empiricist atomistic conception of language (2017, 182).

5. On the conception of conscious life as a continuum, see Gurwitsch (1943, 449, ff).

6. In any case, William Gavin has the crucial merit of having showed that James's remarks are insights into the possibilities and limits of language—a perspective that has generally been overlooked in favor of other interpretations of James's stream of consciousness (from Gurwitsch 1943 to more recent inquiries such as Bailey 2000).

7. This hypothesis that James was inviting the reader to focus on language as it occurs, notwithstanding our strong tendencies to misunderstand it, could be convergent with Wittgenstein's claim in favor of a philosophical focus on language as it ordinarily works. See Luigi Perissinotto (2018, 63), who strongly supports this view of Wittgenstein's approach to language even in relation to the *Tractatus* and in continuity with the Austrian philosopher's later work. Consequently, this tendency to look at language, and not beyond or outside it, might be regarded as an interesting aspect of Wittgenstein's reading of *The Principles*.

8. I do not wish to completely deny that there are some ambiguous fluctuations in James's pages, as when he claims that there is "an altogether specific affection of our mind" (1981, 245). Nonetheless, my point is that the text also supports my interpretation, which is more coherent with James's main aim in this chapter—namely, to oppose an atomistic conception of thought.

9. Interestingly, James also conceived brain processes as never occurring in isolation, but always framed within a network of other mutually conditioning neural processes. He spoke of a "fringe," "psychic overtone," or "suffusion" to characterize even brain activity, precisely after his remarks on harmonic sounds in music (1981, 249). In keeping with his emphasis on brain plasticity, his view of neural functioning is long-sighted and far from being a modular conception of brain activity, based on preestablished neural programs.

10. This claim is consistent with James's assumption that feeling and knowing are only apparently opposed, because "[f]eelings are the seed and starting point of cognition, thoughts the developed tree" (1981, 218). See my suggestion to view "knowledge by acquaintance" and "knowledge about" in James as continuous in the chapter 2, section 2.

11. As I have argued in Dreon (2014), I endorse a nondualistic view of the relationships between experience and language, based on Classical Pragmatism. For a similar interpretative approach, see Faerna (2018).

12. In this section and the following one I have partly reworked some reflections first put forward in Dreon (2019d).

13. For a similar hypothesis see Caruana (2017).

14. Mead was interested in both comparative and infant psychology—which he practiced through laboratory experiments and within educational contexts—from his first research period in Germany to his work in Michigan and Chicago (cf. Huebner 2014, ch. 2).

15. On the overcoming of the opposition between emotion and cognition among the Classical Pragmatists, see Calcaterra (2003). On the same topic within the current debate in the cognitive sciences, see Candiotto (2019).

16. For an extensive investigation into the Classical Pragmatists' (and especially Dewey's) treatment of interest, see Santarelli (2019).

17. See Candiotto and Piredda (2019) for an interesting proposal on the self within the framework of situated affectivity.

18. See also the promising category of conversational proto-habitus—as important elements in a first narrative of belonging—introduced by Maya Gratier and Colwyn Trevarthen (2008, 135).

19. On language as the human environmental niche see also Sinha, previously referred to in section 2. Andy Clark (2006 and 2008) supports the claim that language represents a new cognitive niche for humans.

20. With regard to this point, I wish to thank Vincent Colapietro, who, when discussing a first draft of the present chapter with me, noted that this perspective might be a good starting point to meet the requirement of finding acceptable ways of envisaging inner experiences, once we have rejected the dualism between internal and external, and the idea of an essentially private and interior primary experience, in the footsteps of the Pragmatists and Wittgenstein.

21. Obviously, a further very important pragmatist strategy for considering symbolism, reference, and the cognitive and logical aspects of language could be developed through Peirce's work. This enterprise, however, exceeds my competencies and energies, so I will leave it to experts on Peirce's philosophy who could develop an approach to language as an integral part of human experience.

22. See Teresa Bejarano (2014) for an interesting hypothesis on the transition from holophrastic language to syntactic combination—matching the transition from more gesture-based conversation to eminently vocal communication—that is conceived of as taking place within interpersonally embodied contexts.

23. For a similar claim in favor of an emergentist approach for explaining the complex evolution of human behavior, see Tattersall (2001; 2016).

References

Alexander, T. M. (1987). *John Dewey's Theory of Art, Experience, and Nature: The Horizons of Feelings.* Albany: State University of New York Press.
Apel, K. O. (1972). The a priori of communication and the foundation of humanities. *Man and World,* 5, 3–37.
Bailey, A. R. (2000). Beyond the fringe: William James on the transitional parts of the stream of consciousness. In Varela, F. and Shear, J. (eds.), *The View from Within: First-person Approaches to the Study of Consciousness.* Thorverton, UK and Bowling Green, OK: Imprint Academic, 141–53.
Baggio, G. (2015). *La mente bio-sociale: Filosofia e psicologia in G. H. Mead.* Pisa. Italy: ETS.
———. (2017). Il comportamento come dispositivo logico-semiotico: Tra teoria dell'emozione e giudizio di pratica. In Bertollini, A. and Finelli, R. (eds.), *Soglie del linguaggio: Corpo, mondi, società.* Rome: Roma Tre Press, 115–31.
Baggio, G., Caruana, F., Parravicini, A., Viola, M. (2020). *Emozioni. Da Darwin al pragmatismo.* Turin, Italy: Rosenberg & Sellier.
Barandiaran, X. E., Di Paolo, A. E. (2014). A genealogical map of the concept of habit. *Frontiers in Human Neuroscience,* 9, 1–7.
Beebe, B., Sorter, D., Rustin, J., Kblauch, S. (2003). A comparison of Meltzoff, Trevarthen, and Stern. *Psychoanalytic Dialogues,* 13(6), 777–804.
Bejarano, T. (2014). From holophrase to syntax: Intonation and the victory of voice over gesture. *Humana.Mente: Journal of Philosophical Studies,* 27, 21–37.
Benedict, R. (1934). *Patterns of Culture.* New York: Houghton Mifflin.
Bernardi Della Rosa, S. (2017). *L'abito in Peirce: Natura ed evoluzione di un concetto.* MA thesis, Bologna, Italy, Alma Mater University.
Black M., (1962), Dewey's philosophy of language. *Journal of Philosophy,* 59(19), 505–23.
Blumenthal, L. A. (1973). Introduction. In W. Wundt, *The Language of Gestures.* The Hague, the Netherlands and Paris: De Gruyter, 1–19.
Bolk, L. (1926). *Das Problem der Menschwerdung.* Jena, Germany: Fischer.

Boncompagni, A. (2012). Streams and river-beds: James's stream of thought in Wittgenstein's manuscripts 165 and 129. *European Journal of Pragmatism and American Philosophy*, IV(2).
Bourdieu, P. (1977). *Outline of a Theory of Practice*. Cambridge, UK: Cambridge University Press.
Bourdieu, P. (1984). *Distinction*. London: Routledge and Kegan Paul.
———. (1989). Social space and symbolic power. *Sociological Theory*, 7(1), 14–25.
———. (1992). *The Logic of Practice*. Cambridge, UK: Polity.
———. (2000). *Pascalian Meditations*. Cambridge, UK: Polity.
Brandom, R. (1994). *Making It Explicit: Reasoning, Representing, and Discursive Commitment*. Cambridge, MA: Harvard University Press.
———. (2000). *Articulating Reasons: An Introduction to Inferentialism*. Cambridge, MA: Harvard University Press.
Bronzo, S. (2012) The resolute reading and its critics: An introduction to the literature. *Wittgenstein-Studien*, 3, 45–80.
Brown, S. (2000). The "musilanguage" model of music evolution. In Lennart Wallin, N. Merker, B., Brown, S. (eds.), *The Origins of Music*. Cambridge-London: MIT Press, 271–300.
———. (2017). A joint prosodic origin of language and music. *Frontiers in Psychology*, 8, 1894.
Cahoone, L. (2013). Mead, joint attention and the human difference. *The Pluralist*, 8(2), 1–25.
———. (2019). Mead and the emergence of the joint intentional self. *European Journal of Pragmatism and American Philosophy*, XI(2).
Calcaterra, R. M. (2003). *Pragmatismo: I valori dell'esperienza. Letture di Peirce, James e Mead*. Rome: Carocci.
———. (2011). Varieties of synechism: Peirce and James on mind-world continuity. *Journal of Speculative Philosophy*, 25(4), 412–24.
———. (2016). Constructing on contingency: William James from biology to ethics and politics. *Cognitio*, 13(1), 219–31.
———. (2019). *Contingency and normativity: The challenges of Richard Rorty*. Leiden, the Netherlands and Boston, MA: Brill Rodopi.
Camic, C. (1986). The matter of habit. *American Journal of Sociology*, 91, 1039–87.
Candiotto, L. (2016). Extended affectivity as the cognition of primary intersubjectivity. *Phenomenology and Mind*, 11, 233–41.
———. (2019). From philosophy of emotions to epistemology: Some questions about the epistemic relevance of emotions. In Candiotto, L. (ed.), *The Value of Emotions for Knowledge*. London: Palgrave MacMillan, 3–24.
Candiotto, L., Dreon, R. (2021). Affective scaffoldings as habits: A pragmatist approach. *Frontiers in Psychology*, 12, 1–14.
Candiotto, L., Piredda, G. (2019). The affectively extended self: A pragmatist approach. *Humana.Mente: Journal of Philosophical Studies*, 12(36), 121–45.

Carlisle, C. (2014). *On Habit: Thinking in Action*. London and New York: Routledge.

Caruana, F. (2017). What is missing in the "basic emotions vs. constructionism" debate? Pragmatist insights into the radical translation from the emotional brain. *Pragmatism Today*, 8(1), 87–103.

Caruana, F., Viola, M. (2018). *Come funzionano le emozioni*. Bologna, Italy: Il Mulino.

Chauviré, C., (2002), Dispositions ou capacités? La philosophie sociale de Wittgenstein. In Chauviré, C. and Ogien, A. (eds.), *La régularité. Habitude, disposition et savoir-faire dans l'explication de l'action*. Paris, Éditions de l'EHESS, 25–48.

Chemero, A. (2009). *Radical Embodied Cognitive Science*. Cambridge, MA and London: MIT Press.

Chevalier, J.-M. (2015). The role of emotional interpretants in Peirce's theory of belief and doubt. *Sign Systems Studies*, 43(4), 483–500.

Clark, A. (2006). Language, embodiment, and the cognitive niche. *Trends in Cognitive Neurosciences*, 10(8), 370–74.

———. (2008). *Supersizing the Mind: Embodiment, Action, and Cognitive Extension*. Oxford, UK: Oxford University Press.

Clark, A., Chalmers, D. (1998). The Extended Mind. *Analysis*, 58(1), 7–19.

Colapietro, V. (2004a). The routes of significance: Reflections on Peirce's theory of interpretants. *Cognitio*, 5(1), 11–27.

———. (2004b). Doing—and undoing—the done thing: Dewey and Bourdieu on habituation, agency, and transformation. *Contemporary Pragmatism*, 2, 65–93.

Colombetti, G. (2005). Appraising valence. *Journal of Consciousness Studies*, 12(8–10), 103–26.

———. (2007). Enactive appraisal. *Phenomenology and the Cognitive Sciences*, 6, 527–46.

———. (2009). What language does to feeling. *Journal of Consciousness Studies*, 16, 4–26.

———. (2014). *The Feeling Body: Affective Science Meets the Enactive Mind*. Cambridge, MA and London: MIT Press.

———. (2017). Enacted Affectivity, Extended. *Topoi*, 36, 445–55.

Cometti, J.-P. (2010). *Qu'est-ce que le pragmatisme?* Paris: Gallimard.

———. (2016). *La démocratie radicale: Lire John Dewey*. Paris: Gallimard.

———. Le naturalism pragmatiste: Experience, langage et action sociale. Unpublished manuscript.

Cook, G. A. (1993). *George Herbert Mead: The Making of a Social Pragmatist*. Urbana and Chicago: University of Illinois Press.

Corballis, M. C. (2002). *From Hand to Mouth*. Princeton, NJ: Princeton University Press.

Crary, A., Read, R. (2000). *The New Wittgenstein*. London and New York: Routledge.

Cremaschi, S. (1998). Homo oeconomicus. In Kurz, H. D. and Salvadori, N. (eds.), *The Elgar Companion to Classical Economics*. Cheltenham, Camberley, and Northampton, UK: Edward Elgar, 377–81.

Crossley, N. (2013a). Pierre Bourdieu's habitus. In T. Sparrow, T. and Hutchinson, A. (eds.), *A History of Habit: From Aristotle to Bourdieu*. Lanham, MD: Lexington Books, 291–307.

———. (2013b). Habit and habitus. *Body and Society*, 19, 136–61.

———. (2016). The concept of habit and the regularities of social structure. *Phenomenology and Mind*, 6, 178–92.

Cunningham, S. (1995). Dewey on emotions: Recent experimental evidence. *Transactions of the Charles S. Peirce Society*, 31(4), 865–74.

Davidson, D. (1980). Mental Events. In *Essays on Actions and Events*. Oxford, UK: Clarendon Press, 207–25.

Deacon, T. (1998). *The Symbolic Species: The Co-Evolution of Language and the Brain*. New York: Norton.

———. (2006). Emergence: The hole at the wheel's hub. In Clayton, P. and Davies, P. (eds.), *The Re-emergence of Emergence: The Emergentist Hypothesis from Science to Religion*. Oxford, UK: Oxford University Press, 111–50.

De Jaegher, H., Di Paolo, E. (2007). Participatory sense-making: An enactive approach to social cognition. *Phenomenology and the Cognitive Sciences* 6, 485–507.

Dennett, D. C. (1988). Quining Qualia. In Marcel, A. and Bisiach, E. (eds.), *Consciousness in Modern Science*. Oxford, UK: Oxford University Press.

Descartes, R. (1850). *Discourse on the Method of Rightly Conducting the Reason, and Seeking Truth: Dinburg*. Sutherland and Knox, Edinburgh and London: Simpkin, Marshall.

Dewey, J. (1971a). The theory of emotion. In *The Early Works, Volume 4*. Carbondale and Edwardsville: Southern Illinois University Press, 66–69.

———. (1971b). The psychology of infant language. In *The Early Works, Volume 4*. Carbondale and Edwardsville: Southern Illinois University Press, 152–88.

———. (1972). The reflex-arc concept in psychology. In *The Early Works, Volume 5*. Carbondale and Edwardsville: Southern Illinois University Press, 96–110.

———. (1978). *Ethics. The Middle Works, Volume 5*. Carbondale and Edwardsville: Southern Illinois University Press.

———. (1980). The need for a recovery of philosophy. In *The Middle Works, Volume 10*, Carbondale and Edwardsville: Southern Illinois University Press, 3–48.

———. (1981). *Experience and Nature. The Later Works, Volume 1*. Carbondale and Edwardsville: Southern Illinois University Press.

———. (1984a). The public and its problems. In *The Later Works, Volume 2*. Carbondale and Edwardsville: Southern Illinois University Press.

———. (1984b). Body and mind. In *The Later Works, Volume 2*. Carbondale and Edwardsville: Southern Illinois University Press.

———. (1984c). Three independent factors in morals. In *The Later Works, Volume 5*. Carbondale and Edwardsville: Southern Illinois University Press.

———. (1984d). A naturalistic theory of sense-perception. In *The Later Works, Volume 2*. Carbondale and Edwardsville: Southern Illinois University Press, 44–54.

———. (1984e). Substance, power and quality in Locke. In *The Later Works, Volume 2*. Carbondale and Edwardsville: Southern Illinois University Press, 141–57.

———. (1984f). Affective thought. In *The Later Works, Volume 2*. Carbondale and Edwardsville: Southern Illinois University Press.

———. (1984g). *The Quest for Certainty: A Study of the Relation of Knowledge and Action. The Later Works, Volume 4*. Carbondale and Edwardsville: Southern Illinois University Press.

———. (1985a). *Ethics. The Later Works, Volume 7*. Carbondale and Edwardsville: Southern Illinois University Press.

———. (1985b). *Essays, Reviews, and Miscellany. The Later Works, Volume 6*. Carbondale and Edwardsville: Southern Illinois University Press.

———. (1988a). *Human Nature and Conduct. The Middle Works, Volume 14*. Carbondale and Edwardsville: Southern Illinois University Press.

———. (1988b). Qualitative thought. In *The Later Works, Volume 5*. Carbondale and Edwardsville: Southern Illinois University Press, 243–62.

———. (1988c). The vanishing subject in the psychology of James. In *The Later Works, Volume 14*. Carbondale and Edwardsville: Southern Illinois University Press, 155–67.

———. (1989). *Art as Experience. The Later Works, Volume 10*. Carbondale and Edwardsville: Southern Illinois University Press.

———. (1991a). *Logic: The Theory of Inquiry. The Later Works, Volume 12*. Carbondale and Edwardsville: Southern Illinois University Press.

———. (1991b). Experience, knowledge and value: A rejoinder. In *The Later Works, Volume 14*. Carbondale and Edwardsville: Southern Illinois University Press.

———. (1999). *The Correspondence of John Dewey*. Arlington Heights, IL: InteLex Corporation—electronic edition.

———. (2004). *Essays in Experimental Logic*. Mineola, New York: Dover.

———. (2007). The influence of Darwin on philosophy. In Dewey, J. *The Influence of Darwin on Philosophy and Other Essays on Contemporary Thought*. Carbondale: Southern Illinois University Press, 3–12.

Dings, R. (2018). Understanding phenomenological differences in how affordances solicit action. An exploration: *Phenomenology and the Cognitive Sciences, 17*, 681–99.

Di Paolo, E., Thompson, E. (2014). The enactive approach. In Shapiro, L. (ed.), *The Routledge Handbook of Embodied Cognition*. London: Routledge, 68–78.

Di Paolo, E., Cuffari, E. C., De Jaegher, H. (2018). *Linguistic Bodies: The Continuity between Life and Language*. Cambridge, MA and London: MIT Press.

Dissanayake, E. (2000). *Art and Intimacy: How the Arts Began*. Seattle: University of Washington Press.

———. (2001). Aesthetic Incunabula. *Philosophy and Literature*, 25(2), 335–46.

———. (2011). Prelinguistic and preliterate substrates of poetic narrative. *Poetics Today*, 32(1), 55–79.

Dissanayake E., Malotki E. (2018), *Early Rock Art of the American West*. Seattle: University of Washington Press.

Donovan, J. (1891). The festal origin of human speech. *Mind*, 3, 498–506.

Dreon, R. (2007). *Il sentire e la parola: Linguaggio e sensibilità tra filosofie ed estetiche del novecento*. Milan, Italy: Mimesis.

———. (2010). John Dewey: L'abito fa il naturalismo culturale. *Bollettino filosofico*, XXVI: 169–82.

———. (2012a). *Fuori dalla torre d'avorio: L'estetica inclusiva di John Dewey oggi*. Genova: Marietti. French translation by Orsoni J. (2017) *Sortir de la tour d'ivoire. L'esthétique inclusive de John Dewey aujourdu'hui*. Paris: Questions théoriques.

———. (2012b). Abiti, tecniche corporee e stili di vita. In Dreon, R., Goldoni, D., and Shusterman, R. (eds.), *Stili di vita: Qualche istruzione per l'uso*. Milan and Udine, Italy: Mimesis, 41–58.

———. (2014). Dewey on language: Elements for a non-dualistic approach. *European Journal of Pragmatism and American Philosophy*, VI(2), 109–24.

———. (2015). Emozioni pragmatiste. In Striano, M., Olivero, S., and Santarelli, M. (eds.), *Nuovi usi di vecchi concetti: Il metodo pragmatista oggi*. Milan and Udine, Italy: Mimesis, 151–64.

———. (2016a). Merleau-Ponty from perception to language: New elements of interpretation. *Lebenswelt*, 9, 48–76.

———.(2016b). La sensibilità nel linguaggio: Una prospettiva pragmatista sulla lettura. *Ermeneutica letteraria*, XII, 139–50.

———. (2016c). Understanding rules as habits: Developing a pragmatist anthropological approach. *Paradigmi*, XXXIV, 103–17.

———. (2017). On Joseph Margolis' philosophy: An introduction. In Margolis. J., *Three Paradoxes of Personhood: The Venetian Lectures*, vol. 21. Milan and Udine, Italy: Mimesis, 9–30.

———. (2018). Is there any room for immediate experience? Looking for an answer in Dewey (and Wittgenstein) via Peirce and James. *Pragmatism Today*, 9, 59–63.

———. (2019a). Framing cognition: Dewey's potential contributions to some enactivist issues. *Synthese, Radical Views on Cognition*, 1–22.

———. (2019b). A pragmatist view of emotions: Tracing its significance for the current debate. In Candiotto, L. (ed.), *The Value of Emotions for Knowledge*. London: Palgrave Macmillan, 73–99.

———. (2019c). On a certain vagueness in the definition of art: Margolis' aesthetics and Wittgenstein's legacy. In Mantoan, D. and Perissinotto, L. (eds.), *Paolozzi and Wittgenstein: The Artist and the Philosopher*. London: Palgrave MacMillan, 167–83.

———. (2019d). Gesti emotivi e gesti verbali: L'eredità di George Herbert Mead sulla genesi del linguaggio umano. *Sistemi intelligenti*, *1*, 115–33.

———. (2019e). Il naturalismo culturale di Dewey. In Bagnati, G., Cassan, M., and Morelli, A. (eds.), *Le varietà del naturalismo*, vol. 4. Venice, Italy: Edizioni Ca'Foscari, Digital Publishing, 154–69.

———. (2020a). James on the stream of language: With some remarks on his influence on Wittgenstein. *Cognitio*, *21*(1), 68–82.

———. (2020b). Dewey's fully embedded ethics. In Frega, R. and Levine, S. (eds.), *John Dewey's Ethical Theory: The 1932 Ethics*. London: Routledge, 181–96.

———. (2021). More than action and perception: A pragmatist view on sensibility. *Reti, saperi, linguaggi*, *1*(19), 45–72.

Dreyfus, H. (2005). The return of the myth of the mental. *Inquiry*, *50*(4), 352–65.

———. (2007). Overcoming the myth of the mental: How philosophers can profit from phenomenology of everyday expertise. *Proceedings and Addresses of the American Philosophical Association*, *2*(79), 47–65.

———. (2014). *Skillful Coping: Essays on the Phenomenology of Everyday Perception and Action*. Oxford, UK: Oxford University Press.

Dupré, J. (2001). *Human Nature and the Limits of Science*. Oxford, UK: Clarendon Press.

Eames, S. M. (2003), *Experience and Value: Essays on John Dewey and Pragmatic Naturalism*. Carbondale and Edwardsville: Southern Illinois University Press.

Edel, A. (2001). *Ethical Theory and Social Change: The Evolution of Dewey's Ethics, 1908–1932*. New Brunswick, NJ and London: Transaction Publishers.

Egbert, M. D., Barandiaran, X. E. (2014). Modelling habits as self-sustaining patterns of motor-behavior. *Frontiers in Human Neuroscience*, *8*, 1–15.

Ekman, P. (1999). Basic emotions. In Dalgleish, T., and Power, M. (eds.), *Handbook of Cognition and Emotion*. Sussex, UK: John Wiley, 45–60.

El-Hani, C. N. Pihlström, S. (2002). Emergence theories and pragmatic realism. *Essays in Philosophy*, *3*(2).

Faerna, A. M. (2018). In search of lost body: On pragmatism, experience, and language. *Pragmatism Today*, *9*(2), 107–19.

Falk, D. (2004). Prelinguistic evolution in early hominins: Whence motherese? *Behavioural and Brain Sciences*, *27*(4), 491–541.

———. (2009). *Finding our tongues: Mothers, infants, and the origins of language*. New York: Basic Books.

Feodorov, A. (2017). Habit beyond psychology: The evolution of the concept. *European Journal of Pragmatism and American Philosophy*, *IX*(1).

Ferraresi, M., Schmitt, B. (2006). *Marketing esperienziale: Come sviluppare l'esperienza di consumo.* Milan, Italy: Franco Angeli.
Fischer, J. (2009). Exploring the core identity of philosophical anthropology through the works of Max Scheler, Helmuth Plessner, and Arnold Gehlen. *Iris*, 1(1), 153–70.
Fitch, T. (2010). *The Evolution of Language.* Cambridge, UK: Cambridge University Press.
———. (2012). Evolutionary developmental biology and human language evolution: Constraints on adaptation. *Evolutionary Biology*, 39, 613–37.
Fogel, A., Nwokah, E., Jae Young, D., Messinger, Dickson, D. K. L., Matsusov, E., Holt, S. H. (1992). Social process theory of emotion: A dynamic systems approach. *Social Development*, 1(2), 122–42.
Foucault, M. (1971). *The Order of Things: An Archeology of the Human Sciences.* New York: Pantheon Books.
Freeman, L. (2015). Defending a Heideggerian account of mood. Dahlstrom, D. O., Elpidorou, A., and Hopp, W. (eds.). *Phenomenology and Philosophy of Mind*, London: Routledge.
Freud, S. (1919). *Totem and Taboo.* New York: Moffat Yard.
Fusaroli, R., Gangopadhyay, N., Tylén, K. (2014). The dialogically extended mind: Language as skillful intersubjective engagement. *Cognitive Systems Research*, 29(30), 31–39.
Gadamer, H. G. (2004). *Truth and Method*, London and New York: Continuum.
Gale, R. (1999). *The Divided Self of William James.* Cambridge, UK and New York: Cambridge University Press.
Gallagher, S. (2013). The socially extended mind. *Cognitive Systems Research* 25–26, 4–12.
———. (2017). *Enactivist Interventions.* Oxford, UK: Oxford University Press.
———. (2018a). New mechanisms and the enactive concept of constitution. In Guta, M. P. (ed.), *The Metaphysics of Consciousness*, London: Routledge, 201–20.
———. (2018b). The extended mind: State of the question. *Southern Journal of Philosophy*, 56(4), 421–47.
———. (2020). *Action and Interaction.* Oxford, UK: Oxford University Press.
Garrison, J. (2003). Dewey's theory of emotions: The unity of thought and emotion in naturalistic functional "co-ordination" of behavior. *Transactions of the Charles S. Peirce Society*, 39(3), 405–43.
———. (2009). Dewey's constructivism: From the reflex arc concept to social constructivism. In Hickman, L. A., Neubert, S., and Reich, K. (eds.), *John Dewey between Pragmatism and Constructivism.* New York: Fordham, 84–105.
Gauvain, M. (1995). Thinking in niches: Sociocultural influences on cognitive development. *Human Development*, 38, 25–45.
Gavin, W. J. (1992). *William James and the Reinstatement of the Vague.* Philadelphia, PA: Temple University Press.

Geertz, C. (1973). *The Interpretation of Cultures: Selected Essays*. New York: Basic Books.
Gehlen, A. (1988). *Man: His Nature and Place in the World*. New York: Columbia University Press.
Gibson, J. J. (1979). *The Ecological Approach to Visual Perception*. Hillsdale, NJ: Lawrence Erlbaum.
Goldie, P. (2002). Emotions, feelings and intentionality. *Phenomenology and the Cognitive Sciences*, 1, 235–54.
Goodman, R. B. (2002). *Wittgenstein and William James*. Cambridge, UK: Cambridge University Press.
Gould, S. J. (1977). *Ontogeny and Phylogeny*. Cambridge, MA: Harvard University Press.
Gould, S. J., Vrba, E. S. (1982). Exaptation: A missing term in the science of form. *Paleobiology* 8, 4–15.
Gratier, M., Trevarthen, C. (2008). Musical narrative and motives for culture in mother–infant vocal interaction. *Journal of Consciousness Studies*, 15(10–11), 122–58.
Greenough, W. T., Black, J. E., Wallace, C. S. (1987). Experience and brain development. *Child Development*, 58, 539–59.
Grene, M. G. (1974). *The Understanding of Nature: Essays in the Philosophy of Biology*, Dordrecht, the Netherlands and Boston, MA: Reidel.
Gurwitch, A. (1943). William James's theory of the "transitive parts" of the stream of consciousness. *Philosophy and Phenomenological Research*, 3(4), 449–77.
Hatzimoysis, A. (2012). Emotions in Heidegger and Sartre. In Goldie, P. (ed.), *Oxford Handbook of Philosophy of Emotions*. Oxford: Oxford University Press, 215–35.
Hebb, D. (1949). *The Organization of Behavior: A Neuropsychological Theory*. New York: Psychology Press.
Heidegger, M. (1962). *Being and Time*, Oxford, UK: Blackwell.
Hildebrand, D. (2003). *Beyond Realism and Antirealism: Dewey and the Neopragmatists*. Nashville, TN: Vanderbilt University Press.
———. (2014). Language or experience: Charting Pragmatism's course for the 21st century. *European Journal of Pragmatism and American Philosophy*, VI(2).
Hookway, C. (1997). Design and chance: The evolution of Peirce's evolutionary cosmology. *Transactions of the Charles S. Peirce's Society*, 33(1), 1–34.
Huebner, D. (2014). *Becoming Mead: The Social Process of Academic Knowledge*. Chicago, IL: Chicago University Press.
Hurley, S. (1998). *Consciousness in Action*. Cambridge, MA: Harvard University Press.
Husserl, E. (1973). *Experience and Judgment*. Evanston, IL: Northwestern University Press.
Hutto, D., Myin, E. (2013). *Radicalizing Enactivism: Basic Minds without Content*. Cambridge, MA and London: MIT Press.

———. (2017). *Evolving Enactivism: Basic Minds Meet Content*. Cambridge, MA and London: MIT Press.
Illouz, E. (2007). *Cold Intimacies: The Making of Emotional Capitalism*. Cambridge, UK and Malden, MA: Polity Press.
Ingold, T. (1992). Editorial. *Man*, 27(4), 693–96.
———. (1993). Introduction: Relations between visual-gestural and vocal-auditory modalities of communication. In Ingold, T. (ed.), *Tools, Language and Cognition in Human Evolution*. Cambridge, UK and Melbourne, Australia: Cambridge University Press, 35–42.
———. (2008). Anthropology is not ethnography. *Proceedings of the British Academy*, 154, 69–92.
———. (2014). Anthropology and philosophy or the problem of ontological symmetry. In *La Clé des Langues*. Lyon, France: ENS de LYON/DGESCO.
Innis, R. (2011). The 'quality' of philosophy: On the aesthetic matrix of John Dewey's pragmatism. In Hickman, L. A., Caleb Flamm, M., Skowroński, K. P., and Rea J. A. (eds.), *The Continuing Relevance of John Dewey*. Amsterdam and New York: Rodopi, 43–59.
———. (2014). Dewey's Peircean aesthetics. *Cuadernos de Sistemática Peirceana*, 6, 139–60.
Inukai, Y. (2010). Hume on relations: Are they real? *Canadian Journal of Philosophy*, 42(2), 185–210.
Iser, R. (1990). Fictionalizing: The anthropological dimension of literary fiction. *New Literary History*, 21(4), 939–55.
Kant, I. (1997). *Prolegomena to Any Future Metaphysics*. Cambridge, UK and New York: Cambridge University Press.
———. (2006). *Anthropology from a Pragmatic Point of View*. Cambridge, UK and New York: Cambridge University Press.
Kendon, A. (2009). Language matrix. *Gesture*, 9(3), 352–72.
———. (2011). Some modern considerations for thinking about language evolution: A discussion of *The Evolution of Speech* by Tecumseh Fitch. *Public Journal of Semiotics*, III(I), 79–108.
Kent, P. (1996). Misconceived configurations of Ruth Benedict. *Japan Review*, 7, 33–60.
Kestenbaum, V. (1992). "Meaning and the model of truth." Dewey and Gadamer on habit and *Vorurteil*. *Journal of Speculative Philosophy*, 6(1), 25–66.
Kim, J. (1993). Concepts of supervenience. In *Supervenience and Mind*. Cambridge, UK: Cambridge University Press, 53–78.
Kirchhoff, M. (2015) Extended cognition and the causal-constitutive fallacy: In search for a diachronic and dynamical conception of constitution. *Philosophy and Phenomenological Research*, 90(2), 320–60.
Köhler, W. (1925). *The Mentality of Apes*. London: Kegan Paul.
Krais, B., Gebauer, G. (2002). *Habitus*. Bielefeld, Germany: Transcript Verlag.

Kripke, S. (1980). *Naming and Necessity*. Cambridge, MA: Harvard University Press.
Krueger, J. (2013). Ontogenesis of the socially extended mind. *Cognitive Systems Research*, 25, 40–46.
Krüger, H. P. (2009). The public nature of human beings: Parallels between classical pragmatisms and Helmuth Plessner's philosophical anthropology. *Iris*, I, 195–204.
Jackman, H. (2006). Wittgenstein & James's "Stream of Thought." Available on http://www.yorku.ca/hjackman/papers/WittJames.pdf.
———. (2017). William James on conceptions and private language. *Belgrade Philosophical Annual*, 30, 175–94.
Jackson, M. (1989). *Paths Toward a Clearing: Radical Empiricism and Ethnographic Inquiry*. Bloomington and Indianapolis: Indiana University Press.
———. (1996). Introduction: Phenomenology, radical Empiricism, and anthropological critique. In Jackson, M. (ed.), *Things as They Are: New Directions in Phenomenological Anthropology*. Bloomington and Indianapolis: Indiana University Press, 1–50.
Jakobson, R. (1960). Linguistic and poetics. In Sebeok, T. (ed.), *Style in Language*. New York and London: MIT Press & John Wiley and Sons, 350–77.
James, W. (1875). Chauncey Wright. *Nation*, 21, 194.
———. (1884). What is an emotion? *Mind*, 9(34), 188–205.
———. (1894). The physical basis of emotion. *Psychological Review*, 1, 516–29.
———. (1975). *Pragmatism*. Cambridge, MA: Harvard University Press.
———. (1976). *Essays in Radical Empiricism*. Cambridge, MA: Harvard University Press.
———. (1981). *The Principles of Psychology*. Cambridge, MA: Harvard University Press.
———. (1983a). *Talk to Teachers*. Cambridge, MA: Harvard University Press.
———. (1983b). Thought before language: A deaf-mute's recollection. In *Essays in Psychology*. Cambridge, MA: Harvard University Press, 278–91.
———. (1987). *Essays, Comments, and Reviews*. Cambridge, MA: Harvard University Press.
Jensen, T. W. (2014). Emotion in languaging: Languaging as affective, adaptive, and flexible behavior in social interaction. *Frontiers in Psychology*, 5, 720.
Jespersen, O. (1922). *Language, Its Nature, Development and Origin*. London and New York: Library of Alexandria.
Joas, H. (1997). *G. H. Mead: A Contemporary Re-examination of His Thought*. Cambridge, MA: MIT Press.
Johnson, M. (2007). *The Meaning of the Body: Aesthetics of Human Understanding*. Chicago, IL and London: Chicago University Press.

Laland, K. N., Odling-Smee, J. O., Feldman, M.-W. (2000). Niche construction, biological evolution, and cultural change. *Behavioural and Brain-Sciences*, 23, 131–75.

Lambie, J. A., Marcel, A. (2002). Consciousness and the varieties of emotion experience: A theoretical framework. *Psychological Review*, 109, 219–59.

Lanfredini, R. (2017). Anti-psychologism and neutrality: The radical empiricism of Husserl and James. *European Journal of Pragmatism and American Philosophy*, IX(1).

———. (2018). Categories and dispositions: A new look at the distinction between primary and secondary properties. *Philosophies*, 3(43).

Lazarus, R. S. (1966). *Psychological Stress and Coping Process*. New York: McGraw-Hill.

Leary, D. E. (2013). A Moralist in the age of scientific analysis and skepticism. In Sparrow, T., Hutchinson, and A., Lanham (eds.), *A History of Habit: From Aristotle to Bourdieu*. Lanham, MD: Lexington Books, 177–208.

Leroi-Gourhan, A. (1993). *Gesture and Speech*. Cambridge, MA and London: MIT Press.

Lorimer, F. (1929). *The Growth of Reason: A Study of the Role of Verbal Activity in the Growth of the Structure of the Human Mind*. London and New York: Routledge.

——— (ed.). (1958). *Culture and Human Fertility*. Paris: UNESCO.

MacMullan, T. (2013). The fly wheel of society: Habits and social meliorism in the pragmatic tradition. In Sparrow, T., Hutchinson and A., Lanham (eds.), *A History of Habit: From Aristotle to Bourdieu*. Lanham, MD: Lexington Books, 229–53.

Maddalena, G. (2003). *Istinto razionale: Studi sulla semiotica dell'ultimo Peirce*. Turin, Italy: Trauben.

———. (2011). Wittgenstein, Dewey and Peirce on ethics. In Calcaterra, R. M. (ed.), *New Perspectives on Pragmatism and Analytic Philosophy*. Amsterdam and New York: Rodopi, 83–100.

———. (2015). *The Philosophy of Gesture: Completing Pragmatists' Incomplete Revolution*. Montreal, Quebec: McGill-Queen's University Press.

Madzia, R. (2016). Presentation and re-presentation: Language, content, and the reconstruction of experience. In Joas, H. and Huebner, D. R. (eds.), *The Timeliness of George Herbert Mead*. Chicago, IL: Chicago University Press, 296–314.

Malinowski, B. (1923). The problem of meaning in primitive languages. In Ogden, C. K. and Richards, I. A. (eds.), *The Meaning of Meaning*. New York: Brace, 296–355.

Marcuse H. (1955). *Eros and Civilization*. Boston, MA: Beacon Press.

Margolis, J. (1974). Works of art as physically embodied and culturally emergent entities. *British Journal of Aesthetics*, 3(14), 187–96.

———. (2002). Dewey's and Rorty's opposed pragmatisms. *Transactions of the Charles Peirce Society*, 38(1–2), 117–35.

———. (2009). *The Arts and the Definition of the Human: Toward a Philosophical Anthropology*. Stanford, CA: Stanford University Press.

———. (2016). *Toward a Metaphysic of Culture*. London and New York: Routledge.

———. (2017). *Three Paradoxes of Personhood: The Venetian Lectures*. Milan, Italy: Mimesis.

Martinelli, R. (2015). Kant sul "pragmatico" e le origini del pragmatismo in Ch. S. Peirce. *Esercizi Filosofici*, 10, 202–15.

Matteucci, G. (2019). *Estetica e natura umana. La mente estesa tra percezione, emozione ed espressione*. Rome: Carocci.

Mauss, M. (1936). Le techniques du corps. *Journal de Psychologie*, XXXII(3–4).

McDowell, J. (1996). *Mind and World*. Cambridge, MA: Harvard University Press.

———. (2007). What myth? *Inquiry*, 50(4), 338–51.

———. (2013). The myth of the mind as detached. In Schear J. K. (ed.), *Mind, Reason, and Being-in-the-World: The McDowell-Dreyfus Debate*. London and New York: Routledge, 41–58.

Mead, G. H. (1895). A theory of emotion from the physiological standpoint. *Psychological Review*, 2, 399–402.

———. (1922). A behavioristic account of the significant symbol. *Journal of Philosophy*, 19, 157–63.

———. (1932). *The Philosophy of the Present*. LaSalle, IL: Open Court.

———. (2015). *Mind, Self and Society*. Chicago, IL: University of Chicago Press.

———. (1964). *Selected Writings*. Chicago, IL: Chicago University Press.

———. (1973). Wundt and the concept of gesture. In Wundt, W. *The Language of Gestures*. The Hague, the Netherlands and Paris: De Gruyter, 11–19.

———. (2011). *Essays in Social Psychology*. New Brunswick, NJ and London: Transaction.

Merleau-Ponty, M. (1963). *The Structure of Behavior*, Boston, MA: Beacon Press.

———. (2002). *Phenomenology of Perception*. London: Routledge.

———. (1968). *The Visible and the Invisible*. Evanston, IL: Northwestern University Press.

———. (2003). *Nature: Course Notes from the Collège de France*. Evanston, IL: Northwestern University Press.

Mithen, S. (2006). *The Singing Neanderthal: The Origins of Music, Language, Mind and Body*. Cambridge, UK: Cambridge University Press.

———. (2009). Holistic communication and the evolution of language and music: Resurrecting an old idea. In Botha, R. and Knight, C. (eds.), *The Prehistory of Language*. Oxford, UK: Oxford University Press, 58–76.

Mithen, S., Parsons, L. (2008). The brain as a cultural artefact. *Cambridge Archeological Journal*, 18(3), 415–22.

Morgan, Lloyd, C. (1894). *An Introduction to Comparative Psychology*. London: Routledge-Thoemmes Press.
———. (1896). *Habit and Instinct*. London: Arnold.
———. (1912). *Instinct and Experience*. New York: Macmillan.
———. (1923). *Emergent Evolution*. London: Williams and Norgate.
Mosse, G. (1964). *The Crisis of German Ideology: Intellectual Origins of the Third Reich*. New York: Grosset and Dunlap.
Nietzsche, F. (2014). *Beyond Good and Evil*. In *The Complete Works of Friedrich Nietzsche*, Vol. 8. Stanford, CA: Stanford University Press.
Nöe, A. (2004). *Action in Perception*. Cambridge, MA and London: MIT Press.
Nungesser, F. (2015). Mead meets Tomasello: Pragmatism, the cognitive sciences, and the origins of human communication and sociality. In Joas, H. and Huebner, D. R. (eds.), *The Timeliness of George Herbert Mead*. Chicago, IL: Chicago University Press, 252–75.
Nussbaum, M. (2001). *Upheavals of Thought: The Intelligence of Emotions*. Cambridge, MA and New York: Cambridge University Press.
Ogden, C. K., Richards, I. A. (eds.). (1923). *The Meaning of Meaning*. New York: Brace & Co.
Ostrow, J. M. (1990). *Social Sensitivity: A Study of Habit and Experience*. New York: State University of New York Press.
Oyama, S. (2002). The nurturing of natures. In Grunwald, A., Gutmann, M., and Neumann-Held E. M. (eds.), *On Human Nature. Anthropological, Biological and Philosophical Foundations*. New York: Springer, 163–70.
Panofsky, E. (1951). *Gothic Architecture and Scholasticism: An Inquiry into the Analogy of the Arts, Philosophy, and Religion in the Middle Ages*. New York: Meridian.
Parravicini, A. (2012). *Il pensiero in evoluzione: Chauncey Wright tra darwinismo e pragmatismo*. Pisa, Italy: ETS.
———. (2019). Pragmatism and emergentism: In Chauncey Wright's evolutionary philosophy. *European Journal of Pragmatism and American Philosophy*, XI(2).
Parravicini, A., Pievani, T. (2018). Continuity and discontinuity in human language evolution: Putting and old-fashioned debate in its historical perspective. *Topoi*, 37(2), 279–87.
Peirce, C. S. (1868). Some consequences of four incapacities. *Journal of Speculative Philosophy*, 2, 140–57.
———. (1877). The fixation of belief. *Popular Science Monthly*, 12, 1–15.
———. (1992–1998). *The Essential Peirce: Selected Philosophical Writings*. 2 vols. Bloomington: Indiana University Press.
Perissinotto, L. (2016). Concept-formation and facts of nature in Wittgenstein. *Paradigmi*, XXXIV, 11–31.
———. (2018). *Introduzione a Wittgenstein*. Bologna, Italy: il Mulino.
———. (2019a). Introduzione. In Wittgenstein, L. *Lezioni di psicologia filosofica: Dagli appunti (1946–47) di Peter T. Geach*. Milan and Udine, Italy: Mimesis.

———. (2019b). La mobilità dei significati: Divagazioni sulla lingua comune e le sue presunte imperfezioni logiche. *Ermeneutica letteraria*, XV, 13–28.
Peterson, K. R. (2010). All that we are: Philosophical anthropology and ecophilosophy. *Cosmos and History: Journal of Natural and Social Philosophy*, 6(1), 91–113.
Pihlström, S. (1998). *Pragmatism and Philosophical Anthropology: Understanding Our Human Life in a Human World*. New York: Peter Lang.
Pine, J., Gilmore, J. (1999). *The Experience Economy*. Boston, MA: Harvard Business School Press.
Plessner, H. (1980). *Anthropologie der Sinne*. Frankfurt am Main, Germany: Suhrkamp.
Portmann, A. (1941). Die Tragzeiten der Primaten und die Dauer der Schwangerschaft beim Menschen: Ein Problem der vergleichen Biologie. *Revue Swisse de Zoologie*, 48, 511–18.
———. (1945). Die Ontogenese des Menschen als Problem Evolutionsforschung: *Verhandlungen der Schweizerischen Naturforschenden Gesellschaft*, 125, 44–53.
Quante M. (2018). *Pragmatistic Anthropology*. Paderborn, Germany: Mentis.
Quéré, L. (2013). Note sur la conception pragmatist des émotions. *Occasional Paper 11*. Paris: Institut Marcel Mauss—CEMS.
———. (2016). Bourdieu et le pragmatisme américain sur la créativité de l'habitude. *Occasional Paper 37*. Paris: Institut Marcel Mauss—CEMS.
———. (2018). L'émotion comme facteur de complétude et d'unité dans l'expérience: La théorie de l'émotion de John Dewey. *Pragmata*, 1, 10–59.
Quine, W. O. (1969). *Ontological Relativity and Other Essays*. New York: Columbia University Press.
Ratner, S. (1985). Introduction. In Dewey, J., *The Later Works, Volume 6*. Carbondale and Edwardsville: Southern Illinois University Press, xi–xxiii.
Rietveld, E., Kiverstein, J. (2014). A rich landscape of affordances. *Ecological Psychology*, 26, 325–52.
Rorty, R. (1977). 'Dewey's Metaphysics.' In Cahn, S. (ed.), *New Studies in the Philosophy of John Dewey*. Hanover, NH: The University Press of New England, 45–74.
———. (1980). *Philosophy and the Mirror of Nature*. Oxford, UK: Basil Blackwell.
———. (1982). *Consequences of Pragmatism: Essays: 1972–1980*. Minneapolis: University of Minnesota Press.
———. (1998). Dewey between Hegel and Darwin. In *Philosophical Papers*, vol. 3, Cambridge, UK: Cambridge University Press.
Rothshild, L. (2006). The role of emergence in biology. In Clayton, P. and Davies, P. (eds.), *The re-emergence of emergence: The emergentist hypothesis from science to religion*. Oxford, UK: Oxford University Press, 151–65.
Ruggenini, M. (1820/2006). *Dire la verità: Noi siamo qui forse per dire*. Genoa and Milan, Italy: Marietti.
Russell, B. (1905). On denoting. *Mind*, 14(56), 479–93.

———. (1910/1911). Knowledge by acquaintance and knowledge by description. *Proceeding of the Aristotelian Society*, 11, 108–28.

———. (1914). On the nature of acquaintance. II. Neutral monism. *The Monist*, 2(24), 161–187.

Ryder, J. (2020). *Knowledge, Art and Power. An Outline of a Theory of Experience*. Leiden, the Netherlands and Boston, MA: Brill Rodopi.

Saito, N. (2005). *The Gleam of Light: Moral Perfectionism and Education in Dewey and Emerson*. New York: Fordham University Press.

Santarelli, M. (2016). Il dispositivo logico del circuito organico nel pensiero di John Dewey: Storia, teoria e prospettive contemporanee. *Politica.eu*, 1, 27–42.

———. (2019). *La vita interessata: Una proposta teorica a partire da John Dewey*. Macerata, Italy: Quodlibet.

Savage-Rumbagh, E. S., Rumbagh, D. (1993). The emergence of language. In Ingold, T. (ed.), *Tools, Language and Cognition in Human Evolution*. Cambridge, UK and Melbourne, Australia: Cambridge University Press: 86–108.

Savage Rumbaugh, E. S., Lewin, R. (1994). *Kanzi: The Ape at the Brink of the Human Mind*. Hoboken, NJ: Wiley.

Schear, J. K. (ed.). (2013). *Mind, Reason, and Being-in-the-World: The McDowell-Dreyfus Debate*. London and New York: Routledge.

Schmitt, B. (1999). *Experiential Marketing: How to Get Customers to Sense, Feel, Think, Act, Relate*. New York: Free Press.

Schiller, F. (1993). *Letters on the Aesthetic Education of Man*. New York: Continuum.

Shook, J. (ed.). (2003). *Pragmatic Naturalism and Realism*. Amherst, NY and New York: Prometheus Books.

———. (2011). Varieties of twentieth century American Naturalism. *The Pluralist*, 6(2), 1–17.

Shusterman, R. (1997). The end of aesthetic experience. *Journal of Aesthetics and Art Criticism*, 55(1), 29–41.

———. (2008). *Body Consciousness: A Philosophy of Mindfulness and Somaesthetics*. Cambridge, UK and New York: Cambridge University Press.

———. (2011). The pragmatist aesthetics of William James. *British Journal of Aesthetics*, 51(4), 347–61.

———. (2014). The invention of pragmatist aesthetics: Genealogical reflections on a notion and a name. In Małecki, W. (ed.), *Practicing Pragmatist Aesthetics. Critical Perspectives on the Arts*. Leiden, the Netherlands: Brill, 11–32.

Sinha, C. (2009). Language as a biocultural niche and social institution. In Evans, V. and Pourcel, S. (eds.), *New Directions in Cognitive Linguistics*. Amsterdam: John Benjamins, 289–309.

———. (2015). Language and other artifacts: Socio-cultural dynamics of niche construction. *Frontiers in Psychology*, 6, 1–18.

Skorburg, J. A. (2013). Beyond embodiment: John Dewey and the integrated mind. *The Pluralist*, 8(3), 66–78.

Snowdon, C. T. (1993). A comparative approach to language parallels. In Ingold, T. (ed.), *Tools, Language and Cognition in Human Evolution*. Cambridge, UK and Melbourne, Australia: Cambridge University Press, 109–28.
Spurrett, D., Cowley, S. (2010). The extended infant: Utterance-activity and distributed cognition. In R. Menary (ed.), *The Extended Mind*. Cambridge, MA and London: MIT Press, 295–323.
Steiner, P. (2008). Délocaliser les phénomènes mentaux: La philosophie de l'esprit de Dewey. *Revue Internationale de Philosophie*, 62(245), 3, 273–92.
———. (2011). Who's on first? Living situations and lived experience. *Journal of Consciousness Studies*, 18(2), 98–124.
———. (2019). *Désaturer l'esprit: Usages du pragmatism*. Paris: Questions théoriques.
———. *Déclinér l'intentionalité. Pragmatisme, phénomélogie, philosophie analitique et sciences cognitive*. Unpublished manuscript.
Stern, D. N. (1985). *The Interpersonal World of the Infant: A View from Psychoanalysis and Developmental Psychology*. New York: Basic Books.
Stern, D. N., Hofer, L., Haft, W., Dore, J. (1985). Affect attunement: The sharing of feeling states between mother and infant by means of inter-modal fluency. In Field, T. M. and Fox, N. A. (eds.), *Social Perception in Infants*, Norwood, NJ: Ablex, 249–68.
Stikkers, K. (2011). Dewey, economic democracy and the Mondragon cooperatives. *European Journal of Pragmatism and American Philosophy*, III(2).
Straus, E. W. (1952). The upright posture. *Psychiatric Quarterly*, 26, 529–61.
Stueber, K. R. (2006). *Rediscovering Empathy: Agency, Folk Psychology, and the Human Sciences*. Cambridge, MA and London: MIT Press.
Sullivan, S. (2013). Oppression in the gut: The biological dimension of Deweyan habit. In Sparrow, T. and Hutchinson, A. (eds.), *A History of Habit: From Aristotle to Bourdieu*, Lanham, MD: Lexington Books, 255–74.
Tattersall, I. (1998). *Becoming Human: Evolution and Human Uniqueness*. New York: Harcourt Brace.
———. (2001). Evolution, genes and behavior. *Zygon*, 36(4), 657–66.
———. (2016). A tentative framework for the acquisition of language and modern human cognition. *Journal of Anthropological Sciences*, 94, 157–66.
———. (2017). How can we detect when language emerged? *Psychonomic Bulletin and Revue*, 24, 64–67.
Thibault, P. J. (2011). First-order languaging dynamics and second-order language: The distributed language view. *Ecological Psychology*, 23, 210–45.
Thompson, J. L., Krovitz, G. E., Nelson, A. J. (2003) *Patterns of Growth and Development in the Genus Homo*. London, New York, and Melbourne, Australia: Cambridge University Press.
Thompson, E., Stapleton, M. (2009). Making sense of sense-making: Reflections on enactive and extended mind theories. *Topoi*, 28, 23–30.

Tiercelin, C. (2019). *Pragmatism and Vagueness. The Venetian Lectures*. Milan, Italy: Mimesis.
Tiles, J. E. (1999). The fortunes of "functionalism." In Haskins, C. and Seiple, D. I. (eds.), *Dewey Reconfigured. Essays on Deweyan Pragmatism*. New York: State University of New York Press, 39–61.
Tomasello, M. (1999). *The Cultural Origins of Human Cognition*. Cambridge, MA: Harvard University Press.
———. (2008). *Origins of Human Communication*. Cambridge, UK: Cambridge University Press.
Tracy, F. (1893). The language of childhood. *American Journal of Psychology*, 6(1), 107–38.
Trevarthen, C. (1979). Communication and cooperation in early infancy: A description of primary intersubjectivity. In Bullowa, M. (ed.), *Before Speech: The Beginning of Interpersonal Communication*. London and New York: Cambridge University Press, 321–48.
———. (1993). The function of emotions in early infant communication and development. In Nadel, J. and Camaioni, L. (eds.), *New Perspectives in Early Communicative Development*. London: Routledge, 48–81.
———. (1998), The concept and foundations of infant intersubjectivity. In Braten, S. (ed.), *Intersubjective Communication and Emotion in Early Ontogeny*. Cambridge, UK: Cambridge University Press, 15–46.
———. (2002). Making sense of infants making sense. *Intellectica*, 1(34), 161–188.
Trevarthen, C., Hubley, P. (1978), Secondary intersubjectivity: Confidence, confiding and acts of meaning in the first year. In Lock. A. (ed.), *Action, Gesture and Symbol: The Emergence of Language*. London: Academic Press, 183–229.
Tugendhat, E. (1986). *Self-consciousness and Self-determination*. Cambridge, MA and London: MIT Press.
Uexküll, J. (1926). *Theoretical Biology*, New York: Harcourt, Brace.
———. (2010). *A Foray into the Worlds of Animals and Humans: With a Theory of Meaning*. Minneapolis and London: University of Minnesota Press.
Vara Sánchez, C. (2020). Raw cognition: Rhythms as dynamic constraints. *Journal for the Philosophy of Language, Mind and the Arts*, 2.
———. (2021). Enacting the aesthetics: A model for raw cognitive dynamics. *Phenomenology and the Cognitive Sciences*. Retrieved from https://doi.org/10.1007/s11097-021-09737-y
Varela, F. J., Thompson, E., Rosch, E. (1991). *The Embodied Mind: Cognitive Science and Human Experience*. Cambridge, MA and London: MIT Press.
Veblen, T. (1899). *The Theory of Leisure Class: An Economic Study of Institutions*. New York: Macmillan Company.
Wacquant, L. (1998). Pierre Bourdieu. In Stones, R. (ed.), *Key Sociological Thinkers*. New York: New York University Press, 215–29.

White, R. (1985). Thoughts on social relationships and language in hominid evolution. *Journal of Social and Personal Relationships*, 2(1), 95–115.

Wittgenstein, L. (1953). *Philosophical Investigations*. Oxford, UK: Blackwell.

———. (1964). *The Blue and Brown Books: Preliminary Studies for the Philosophical Investigations*. Oxford, UK: Blackwell, 1964.

Wray, A. (1998). Protolanguage as holistic system for social interaction. *Language and Communication*, 18, 47–67.

———. (2002). Holistic utterances in protolanguage: The link from primates to humans. In Knight, C., Studdert-Kennedy, M, and Hurford, J. R. (eds.), *The Evolutionary Emergence of Language*. Cambridge, UK: Cambridge University Press, 285–302.

Wundt, W. (1973). *The Language of Gestures*. The Hague, the Netherlands and Paris: De Gruyter.

Zask, J. (2003). Nature, donc culture: Remarques sur les liens de parenté entre l'anthropologie culturelle et la philosophie pragmatist de John Dewey. *Genèse*, 111–25.

———. (2015). Individualité et culture, de Boàs a Dewey: À propos des liens entre pragmatism et anthropologie culturelle. *SociologieS*.

Index

aesthetic experience as qualitative and/or affective 13, 35, 38, 44–45, 48, 50, 52, 54, 63, 65–66, 69, 77, 83–84
affectivity, 32–33, 37, 54, 186
  affective neuroscience, 58, 73
  affective valence, 52, 69
  primary/primordial affectivity, 57–58, 72–73
Alexander, Samuel, 28, 221
Aristotle, 19, 25, 97 126, 230
artification 179
associationism, 14, 138
  associationist conception of mind, 182
  associationist view of behavior, 126
  associationist view of habit, 99
  associationist view of thought and language, 181, 182
attitude, 133

Bain, Alexander, 69, 97, 223
Barandarian, Xabier, 99, 103, 104, 228
behavior, 5, 14, 27, 59, 60, 67, 74, 82, 94, 99, 107, 108, 113, 121, 126, 171
  emotive behavior, 74, 84
  habitual behavior, 74, 81, 89, 109
  linguistic behavior, 145, 150, 156
  mental behavior, 64, 161, 166
  sensorimotor behavior, 59

Benedict, Ruth, 110
biological vs. cognitive approach, 34, 37
Bourdieu, Pierre, 8, 96, 125–134
Brandom, Robert, 2, 143, 188, 201

Calcaterra, Rosa, 38, 143–144, 160, 222, 229, 234
Carlisle, Clare, 97, 228
cause, 25–27
  ultimate cause, 22, 212
chance, 98, 160
Chomsky, Noam, 17
Clark, Andy, 55, 76, 86, 224, 235
cognition, 7, 36, 39, 41, 43, 167, 169
  and experience, 37–44, 55, 58, 81, 85
  lower and higher forms of cognition, 65, 66, 96
  as sense making, 57
collective/shared/joint intentionality, 155, 188, 193, 205
Colombetti, Giovanna, 57, 63, 69, 72, 73, 81, 82, 200, 224, 227–228

conceptual rationality, 64, 170, 172
consciousness, 47, 76–77, 106, 141, 146, 183
　social and physical consciousness, 78, 85, 207
constitutive dynamic coupling, 55, 224
consumer's behaviour, 216–217
consummation, 49, 157, 159, 161, 163, 165, 169, 204
contemporary crisis of democracy, 214–216
contextualistic view of names, 185
contingency, 21, 23, 26, 29–30, 59, 68, 98, 146, 210, 213
continuity
　between animal and human forms of life, 8, 12, 20, 53, 54, 77, 84, 106, 152
　between feeling/sensibility and cognition, 39–40, 81
　between instincts and habits, 106
　between life and language, 148–149
　between mind and body, 79, 125
　between nature and culture, 102
　between sensibility and language, 13, 36, 64, 165, 172, 175–212
culture
　cultural reductionism, 25
　cultural relativism, 18

Darwin, Charles, 11, 12, 21, 29, 40, 51, 78, 79, 80, 81, 98, 101, 122, 146, 152, 160, 189, 199, 221, 222, 231, 232
Deacon, Terrence, 24, 25, 26, 27, 199, 221
Dennett, Daniel, 45, 46
Descartes, René, 5, 10, 34, 45, 48, 111, 163, 218
design, 23–30

developmental system, 22, 174
Dewey, 11–17, 19–22, 25–30, 31–35, 37–38, 40–58, 60–62, 64–65, 72–77, 86–87, 89, 147–149, 151–157, 176–177, 190, 192–193, 195, 202
　on the emergence of the human mind, 153–157, 163–165
　on the emergence of meaning, 157–162
　on emotions, 78–83
　on habits, 100–141
Di Paolo, Ezequiel, 55, 57, 65, 67, 96, 99, 104, 148–149, 167, 224, 225
dispositions/dispositionalism, 75, 82, 87, 131–133
Dissanayake, Ellen, 147, 155, 178, 197, 198, 219, 225, 229, 230
Dreyfus, Hubert, 64, 66, 96, 115, 170, 188, 201
dualism
　between feeling and cognition, 81, 85, 195
　between the innate and the acquired, 12, 17–18, 23
　between perception and action, 59–63
　between the psychical and the physical, 61, 74, 79
　between subject and reality, 56, 58, 61
Dupré, John, 17
dynamic body schema, 34, 114, 115

embodiment, 37, 54, 64, 112, 119, 123
emergence, 23–30, 43, 66–68, 122, 167, 176, 179, 199, 201, 212, 221
　of meaning, 157–165
　of the mind, 153–157

emotions, 3, 48, 58, 63, 71–91, 186, 191
   as breaks in habitual behavior, 74, 81, 89
   as embodied, 75–78
   intentionality of emotions, 76, 82, 225
   as modes of behavior, dispositions to act, 78–83, 87
   as psychic events, 22, 48
   as social functions, 83–88
enactivism, 55–63, 65, 96, 104, 116, 148, 159, 167, 170
   autonomy, 55
   cognition as sense-making, 57
   operational closure, 55
evolution, 21, 232
   cultural evolution, 25, 205, 228
   emergent evolution, 28–30, 221
exaptation, 7, 146, 173, 177, 199, 212
experience
   enlanguaged experience, 143–174
   primary and reflective experience, 36, 38, 40, 43, 63–69, 88–89, 134, 140, 161

feedback/loop effects, 23–30, 35, 37, 67 68, 73, 149, 163, 199–206, 212
feeling, 2, 13, 33–44, 52, 54, 58, 75, 79, 81, 114, 152, 160, 184, 200
   and meaning, 53, 153, 157–162, 181
Fiske, John, 55, 85, 122, 146, 193
Fitch, Tecumseh, 155

Gadamer, Hans-Georg, 32
Galileo Galilei, 44–45
Gallagher, Shaun, 24, 35, 55, 60, 86, 170, 192, 224, 226, 227
Gavin, William, 183, 185, 234

Gehlen, Arnold, 6, 24, 120 123, 224
genetic determinism vs cultural reductionism, 18
gestures, 75, 86, 164, 171, 190, 196–197
   conversation of gestures, 87, 88, 171, 186, 190, 191
   emotional gestures, 81, 87–88, 189, 190
   verbal gestures, 15, 176, 186–189, 202, 207
Gibson, James, 161, 224
Goldie, Peter, 81, 225
Gould, Stephen Jay, 123, 146, 173, 199, 224
Grene, Marjorie, 9, 24, 224
growth and change, 19, 20, 23

habits, 3, 13, 93–141, 157
   habitus, 96, 125–134, 140
   linear conception of habit, 94, 95, 102, 105, 126, 180
   unconscious nature of habits, 127–128, 140, 165
Hegel, Georg Wilhelm Friedrich, 51, 104
Heidegger, Martin, 6, 21, 58
Hildebrand, David, 56, 143
homo aestheticus/sentimentalis, 216
human difference, 12
human nature, 1–30
Husserl, Edmund, 10, 36, 45, 64, 111
Hutto, Daniel, 65, 96, 116, 153, 170, 224, 230

imitation, 86, 114, 115, 179, 180, 194
immaturity of the human infant at birth, 21, 23, 24, 54, 85, 87, 95, 110, 121–123, 192, 230
impulse, 61, 118, 121, 122, 136
impulsion, 61, 62

inquiry, 39, 40, 41, 53, 57, 89, 127, 161, 165
instinct, 19, 23, 77, 85, 101, 105, 121
intellectual fallacy, 53
interest, 42, 58, 62, 63, 195, 223
intersubjectivity, 78, 111

Jackson, Michael, 10
James, William, 11, 28, 38, 39, 44, 46, 48, 65, 73, 79, 120
   on emotions, 75–78, 79
   on habits, 97–100
   on language, 180–186
Johnson, Mark, 54, 61, 123, 143, 224

Kant, Immanuel, 9, 10, 12, 97, 119, 132
Kim, Jaegwon, 18, 26
knowledge by acquaintance and knowledge about, 38–39

language, 3, 13, 53, 65 146, 150, 201
   as contingent and yet disruptive event, 66, 146, 201, 210
   as a piece of human social behavior, 186–188
   protolanguage and analytic language, 178
   and sensibility, 36, 64–69, 186, 201
languaging, 150, 151, 231
Lazarus, Richard, 82
Leary, David, 100
linear vs. circular causality, 27, 40, 43, 61, 66, 88
linguistic bodies, 7, 67, 148, 149
Locke, John, 44–46
Lorimer, Frank, 101, 121, 152, 165–174, 176–180, 202–206, 233
   preparatory and consummatory phase of experience, 159, 169

Malinowski, Bronisław, 11, 147, 155, 156, 219
Marcuse, Herbert, 33
Margolis, Joseph, 2, 8–9, 25, 66, 88, 144, 145, 188, 199, 201, 210, 222, 223, 225, 228
Mauss, Marcel, 115, 126, 128
McDowell, John, 64, 115, 188, 201
Mead, George Herbert, 11–14, 21, 25, 28, 38, 52, 55, 58, 62, 65, 68, 73–78, 109, 114, 118, 122, 128, 147, 171, 176
   on emergence of verbal gestures, 186–199
   on emotions, 83–88
   on reference, 206–210
meaning
   antimentalistic conception of meaning, 49, 53, 69, 157, 209
   conceptual-propositional theory of meaning, 65
   and feeling, 53, 160
   as rooted in language, 49, 53
   as rooted in prelinguistic bodily perception, 63–64
   of a word, 185
Merleau-Ponty, Maurice, 10, 34, 60, 61, 63, 64, 114, 115, 126, 127, 159
methodological individualism, 4, 11, 14, 19, 103, 111, 138, 180, 206, 211
mind, 7, 30, 76, 117, 153, 195
   as association of different perceptions, 163, 182
   and body, 79, 124–125
   as emerging out of language, 154, 164
   as kind of behavior, 153, 164, 166
   "mind-stuff" argument, 75–76, 163, 184

other minds, 111, 192–193
place of mind in habits, 117–119
socially extended mind, 85–86, 125
Morgan, Conwy Lloyd, 14, 19, 28, 29, 95, 101, 105–109, 138, 221, 229
Myin, Erik, 65, 116, 170, 224, 230

naturalism
  cultural naturalism, ix, 21–25, 43, 56, 67, 94, 99, 102, 149, 193, 201, 214
  naturalization, 18, 49, 132, 228
  reductive naturalism, 8, 18, 71, 99
naturally sociocultural environment, 1, 21, 24, 26, 35, 116–117, 210
nature and culture, 23, 29, 102, 109
neoteny, 55, 122, 123, 193
newborn, 66, 85, 192, 198, 203
niche, 37, 68, 120, 146, 151, 171, 198
Noë, Alva, 35, 37, 59, 61, 115
nondogmatic realism, 56, 213
nurture, 23
Nussbaum, Martha, 49, 83, 224

organism
  organic circle/circuit, 27, 61, 104, 126
  organic intelligence, 165–169
  organic precariousness, 55
organism-environment interactions, 13, 20, 22, 30, 35, 44, 47, 49, 50, 51, 56, 62, 74, 81, 101, 103, 108, 113, 127, 146, 151, 167, 168, 173
Oyama, Susan, 22–23, 25

Peirce, Charles Sanders, 12, 38, 40, 97–99, 112, 127, 220, 223, 235
perception, 33, 42, 59–60, 67, 69, 75, 117
  and action, 59–63

and affectivity, 50
preverbal perception, 67
Perissinotto, Luigi, 34, 47, 243
phenomenology, 10, 36, 170, 201
philosophical anthropology, 1–16
  German philosophical anthropology, 120
physical causal closure 26, 99
physicalism 25
Pihlström, Sami, 9–10, 26, 56
plasticity, 76, 98–99, 120, 121, 228, 234
Plessner, Helmuth, 6, 9, 33, 224, 230
pluralism, 10, 19, 136, 213, 218
political discourse, 217–218
Portmann, Adolf, 123
Pragmatism, 1, 11–16, 20, 45, 56, 78, 88, 97, 99, 111, 122, 144, 146, 149, 170, 180, 194, 195, 200, 210, 212, 213
  Classical Pragmatism and Neo-Pragmatism, 143
  Pragmatist anthropology, 1–8
praktognosia, 127
predisposition, 229
psychoanalysis, 118

qualities
  adverbial conception of qualities, 44, 49
  primary and secondary qualities, 44
  qualitative experience, 2, 13, 34–50
  subjective and objective qualities, 33–34, 44–50, 58
Quéré, Louis, 103, 104, 132, 134, 226
Quine, Willard, 158, 232

radical empiricism, 28, 46, 47, 77, 182

reality of relations, 37, 46–47, 233
reflex arc concept, 27, 60, 102, 126
representation, 31, 50, 57, 104, 116–117, 123, 162, 167, 182, 183
Rorty, Richard, 51, 143, 144, 222, 223
Rothshild, Lynn, 27
Russell, Bertrand, 39, 222

secondness, 40
self-reflectivity, 9, 35, 68, 187, 194–198
sense data, 32, 36, 39, 41, 42, 54, 222
sense-making, 57, 149, 167, 168, 225
sensibility, 13, 31–69, 88, 134, 158, 160, 162, 164
  and cognition 39, 57, 88
  and emotions 71–75, 82
  and habits 88–91, 93
  human and animal sensibility 4, 7, 25, 35–37, 63, 68, 147, 158–159, 160–162, 172, 175–175, 188, 210–211
  and language, 13, 36, 64, 165, 172, 175–212
sensitivity, 52
Shusterman, Richard, 73, 123, 143, 222
Sinnlichkeit, 33
social and cultural-linguistic niche, 35, 37, 63, 68, 147, 171, 173, 175, 198

social psychology, 11, 85, 109, 227
Steiner, Pierre, 223, 226
Sullivan, Shannon, 110
supervenience, 28
symbol, 169, 177, 179, 191
  significant symbol, 195, 207–208
  symbolic and hypo-symbolic forms of intelligence, 202–206
  symbolic stimuli, 66, 84, 197
syntax, 204–205

Tattersall, Ian, 7, 211–212, 220
teleology, 28–29
Thompson, Evan, 55, 57, 167, 224, 232
Tomasello, Michael, 7, 25, 26, 176, 196, 205, 208, 232
transaction, 104
Trevarthen, Colwin, 66, 78, 86, 147, 155, 176, 194, 197–198, 235

Umwelt, 57, 151

Vrba, Elizabeth, 146, 173, 199, 224
von Uexküll, Jacob, 6, 24, 120, 224

Wittgenstein, Ludwig, 132, 181, 231, 233
words, 203–204
Wright, Chauncey, 11, 55, 122, 146, 200, 221
Wundt, Wilhelm, 86, 189, 194, 227

www.ingramcontent.com/pod-product-compliance
Lightning Source LLC
Chambersburg PA
CBHW030532230426
43665CB00010B/859